SHIPWRECKS OF THE
GOODWIN SANDS

SHIPWRECKS
OF THE
GOODWIN SANDS

RICHARD AND BRIDGET LARN

MERESBOROUGH BOOKS
1995

To the grandchildren,
Mark, Isobell & Rosie

Published by Meresborough Books, 17 Station Road, Rainham, Gillingham, Kent.
MR8 7RS.

Meresborough Books has published over one hundred and fifty books on Kent
history. They are also the publishers of 'Bygone Kent', a monthly magazine
launched in 1979. Current list of titles and a sample copy of 'Bygone Kent' sent on
request.

First Edition published by David & Charles in 1977

ISBN 0948193 840

Printed in Great Britain by Headley Bros Ltd, Ashford, Kent.

CONTENTS

Acknowledgements.. 6

Foreword 7

Chapter One: The Ship Swallower................................... 11

Chapter Two: 'TWOO SHIPPS THONE CALLED *GOLDEN LYON*'
1298–1699 31

Chapter Three: 'The Late Terrible Tempest': 1700–1799 47

Chapter Four: A Light for All Nations: 1800–1854......................... 61

Chapter Five: Four Lifeboats for the Goodwins: 1855–1874.......... 89

Chapter Six: Steam on the Goodwins: 1875–1899 117

Chapter Seven: The Wreck of the *Mahratta:* 1900–1919 131

Chapter Eight: Victims of Peace and War: 1920–1975................. 147

Bibliography 159

Index of Shipwrecks.. 163

General Index 189

ACKNOWLEDGEMENTS

This book would not have been possible without the assistance of others, and we extend our grateful thanks and appreciation especially to the late Will Honey, of Deal, for his encouragement, friendship, co-operation, and for making available his collection of photographs and notes. He corrected the manuscript of the first edition of this book in 1976, but regrettably is no longer with us to see this revised edition. To Colin M. Dalton, the Curator of the Deal Maritime Museum, who kindly loaned additional photographs for this edition; also to A.J. Langridge, of Deal, who also loaned photographs and other wreck and local information. Alec Reynolds of the Hydrographic Department of MOD(N), Taunton, who produced the wreck charts and maps of the Goodwin Sands area. Also to J.R. Turner, of Deal, and L. Hudson, for information and the loan of photographs. John Callis, one time editor of 'Ships Monthly', for material concerning the Ramsgate tug *Aid*. Others in the Thanet area and Kent include P.C. Derbey; C.E. Busson and G. Goldsmith Carter, who loaned material and offered suggestions, also Maureen Jacobs of Sheerness, who helped with the research.

To the Superintendents, Librarians and staff of the National Maritime Museum; HM Customs and Excise and London Guildhall Libraries; PRO London, both Kew and Chancery Lane; Colindale Newspaper Library; History Manuscript Commission and the St Austell, Cornwall, Public Library. To Lloyds Register, and Barbara Jones, Senior Information Officer in particular for her assistance. To Rex Cowan; MOD (Royal Air Force); the one time editor of the 'Navy News', Peter Powell; and Skyphotos, now Fotoflite Ltd for permission to reproduce photographs. Also to John Rose of Gorleston, who made his vessel *Flying Hart* and crew available for work on the wreck of the *Admiral Gardner*; David Ellingworth and the team of Ramsgate divers with whom we worked in 1984/5, and Alan & Beryl Ellingworth, who so kindly accommodated us one summer. Finally, to Hamish Mackay Miller, the publisher, for the opportunity to have this volume in print again.

Richard & Bridget Larn   Charlestown, Cornwall, 1995

FOREWORD

The one-time importance of the stretch of water between mainland Kent and the offshore sandbanks of the Goodwin Sands, known overall as the Downs, is not obvious today, but there was a time — as little as 150 years ago — when it was the most important waterway in Europe, if not the world. This small corner of the British Isles has, in fact, played a quite remarkable role in the maritime history of the country as a whole, harbouring ships of every nation. It was also the scene of the one and only successful invasion of England prior to the Norman Conquest; the assembly point for vast fleets of ships either preventing another invasion or conducting war overseas and, of course, the scene of hundreds of years of normal sea trading. It has been visited by every British monarch since Egbert, the Saxon king, ascended the throne in 802 AD and its historical significance cannot be over-emphasised.

For more than a thousand years, merchant ships and men o'war have used the Downs as an anchorage and watering place whilst awaiting suitable weather and tidal conditions to negotiate either the sandbank-strewn estuary of the River Thames leading to London, or alternatively the long run westward down the English Channel. At the same time the Downs, and particularly the harbour of Ramsgate, which was extended and protected specially to offer a safe berth for shipping casualties, was a haven in bad weather. With the neighbouring Goodwin Sands acting as a breakwater when the wind is from certain quarters, these sandbanks have, in consequence, been both friend and foe alike, in that they have probably saved a thousand ships or more for every one they destroyed. The sheer volume of vessels which anchored daily in the two Downs, the 'Small Downs', and the 'Downs' themselves, was quite staggering. In its early days, around 1750, the bi-weekly Lloyds List not only printed wind conditions specially for the Downs, but frequently quoted the number of merchantmen and warships at anchor, giving typically figures such as 480 and 15, or 382 and 38 respectively.

The area of the Goodwin Sands bounded by the 2m depth contour is considerable, much greater than generally thought. From the extreme northern end to the most southerly point is 9 miles (14.5km), and east to west across the Kellett Gut is 5 miles (8km). This equates to an approximate area of 12 square miles (32.6sq.km) for the North Sand, and 10 square miles (29.9sq.km) for the South Sand, some 18 square miles of dry or almost dry surface at low water spring tide. Hence the problems of distance and navigation facing the coxswain and crews of the many lifeboats stationed over the years at Broadstairs, Ramsgate, Deal and

Walmer were considerable. If the Ramsgate boat, for example, was the only one capable of reaching a wreck in Trinity Bay, they were faced with sailing and rowing at least 8 miles (12.8km) to reach the area, after which great care was necessary to avoid going on the sands themselves. This part of the Goodwins is 4 miles (6.4km) offshore, and with the coastline very flat making it near impossible to make out fisherman's land marks in anything but clear, dry conditions, one wonders how the coxswains ever knew where they were. Fortunately, in later years the Ramsgate lifeboat had the support of the early steam paddle tug *Aid*, which towed it as close as possible to a wreck, then stood by during some rescues, but the other lifeboats enjoyed no such assistance. I personally recall an incident on the South Sand in 1985 when a fine, sunny day suddenly turned to dense fog in a matter of minutes. Unable to see more than 10 yards (9m) we decided to return to Ramsgate, and in a modern 30 feet (9m), twin diesel engined craft with radio, echo sounder and compass, envisaged no difficulty, except that the compass proved to be totally inaccurate. Only then, as we drove around in circles, with the echo sounder showing a mere four to five feet (1.2 to 1.5m) beneath the keel, with white water all around us in a Force 4 and hopelessly lost on a falling tide, did the true significance of conditions on the Goodwin Sands and our predicament really strike home. Thirty minutes later we sighted the *SE Goodwin* navigational buoy! We had in fact unwittingly crossed the full width of the South Sand and were now on its eastern face, even further from Ramsgate than ever, with the fog even more dense. Prudently, we steamed south along the edge of the sands, following the line of breakers, right down to the *SW Goodwin* buoy, close to the South Goodwin lightship, then turned north by which time the fog had lifted and we were out of danger, and fortunately, not out of fuel!

The experience of being shipwrecked on the Goodwins is not well recorded, but must have been traumatic in the extreme. If a vessel was wrecked there in a storm, as the tide fell and the water shallowed, so the size of the breakers increased until the surface was a mass of white water as far as one could see. As the tide continued to fall, so parts of the sands would dry out as the water drained away, and soon the surface was firm enough for men to leave the wreck and walk about, perhaps lighting fires or waving to attract the attention of those on the distant shore. Only on the flood tide would their dreadful predicament become apparent, as the upwelling mass of water caused the particles of sand to go into semi-suspension, and the deceivingly firm surface slowly gave way to a quicksand. Caught any distance from their only sanctuary, the wreck itself, men would literally be swallowed up; if they returned aboard, the sands would slowly engulf the ship itself over a number of tides as it 'swaddled' down, taking the men with it unless there was a quick rescue. It must be that buried deep in the Goodwins, where the sand meets its chalk base, there are literally generations of shipwrecks compressed and 'concreted' into a solid mass, holding an unbelievable treasure house of gold, silver, tin, jewellery, copper, brass and other valuables, probably forever inaccessible.

8

The salvage and recovery of more mundane items, such as anchors and cannon, were once a regular occupation of what were called the 'wrack fishers'. In fact the first recorded salvage diving in England took place in the Downs, and the first named diver as such, Jacob Johnson, lived in or around Sandwich in the 1620s, possibly as early at 1611, operating a Sandwich registered hoy named *Charity*, employing five seamen. A Dutchman, from Enkhuizen, a seaport famous for its 'wrackmen', Jacob Johnson was probably an Anglicised version of Jacob Johanson or Jansen, who brought his trade to England, and very quickly established a good reputation, finding a patron in George Villiers, the Duke of Buckingham. Possibly the last letter written by the Duke, dated 22nd August 1628, the day before he was stabbed to death in Portsmouth, was addressed to Johnson, and commences, 'To my verie Loving friend Mr Jacob Johnson, the Dyver', a remarkable opening address from a man second only to the king, to a commoner.

Presumably using a diving-bell, since there is no record of the nature of his apparatus, Jacob Johnson must have been a brave man indeed, to dive the Goodwins area in such primitive equipment, with its strong tides and poor underwater visibility. At low water slack, as the tidal current falls off from its normal 4-5 knots, the sand in suspension drops to the seabed, and a diver may well be able to see for 50-60 feet (15-18m), but after 45 minutes or so the flood sets in, picking up sand particles as its strength increases, until you cannot see your hand in front of your face for a further twelve hours. No one knows how many historic wooden shipwrecks uncover and recover again, unseen, over the years. In the text of this volume there are several references to whole or partially intact warships, such as HM men o' war *Stirling Castle, Northumberland* and *Mary*, all lost in 1703, or the submarine *U-48*, reappearing and being snagged by fishermen, only to disappear again. Whilst I have never seen it personally, there is an intact, copper sheathed, sailing ship hull, complete with figurehead, upside down in the western part of the Kellett Gut, which has been seen several times by other divers, but remains unidentified, and a new discovery, slightly to the west, recently yielded some interesting finds.

Punctuating the changing fortunes and decline of the historic Cinque Ports — the erection and decline of coastal defences around the Downs; the building of the old naval dockyard at Deal; wars; trade and shipping; attempts to mark the Goodwin Sands with beacons and refuges for shipwrecked mariners; lifeboats; storms, and dozens of bizarre incidents — have been shipwreck after shipwreck, sometimes as many as half a dozen in a single day. The exact number will never be known, since many happened at night, passing unseen and are best summarised in a message signed by Capt John Spicer, master of the Dundee brig *Fairy Queen*. She is thought to have been lost with all hands on 10th November 1877, since no identifiable wreckage ever came ashore. This scrap of paper, sealed in a bottle and washed ashore at Sheerness in the Thames, stated poignantly and simply, 'How many vessels alas, lie buried beneath these fatal sands.'

This then is a book simply about shipwrecks and the Goodwin Sands. In its first edition, published in 1977, the final sentence read 'A recent indication of the wealth of artefacts which lie hidden beneath the Sands was afforded when, in October 1976, a bucket dredger working on the South Goodwins on behalf of the Dover Harbour Commission brought to light forty-one trade tokens of the East India Co.' Little were we to know that my wife and I were to spend most of the summer of 1984-85 working with a team of Ramsgate divers, recovering the largest hoard of coins ever salvaged from a shipwreck anywhere in the world — in excess of 1 million. These came from the broken remains of the Honourable English East India Company's ship *Admiral Gardner*, lost in 1809. A 'sister' ship, the HEIC *Britannia*, in the same convoy, was also lost the same night with an equally valuable lading. Whilst not positively identified, she too may have recently been found.

Charlestown, Cornwall 1992   Richard Larn

Chapter One

THE SHIP SWALLOWER

Four miles offshore from the Kentish town of Deal lie the Goodwin Sands, a great series of sandbanks whose formation and many secrets — not least the origin of its name — have fascinated men for centuries. Its capacity to claim ships and then seemingly to break and swallow them without trace is legendary, as is its ability to change shape and position. The Goodwin Sands and the Downs — the latter a four-mile wide channel partially enclosed to the east by the sandbank — have been the setting for many sea battles, rescues, shipwrecks by the hundred and tragic loss of life dating back to the time when men first ventured to sea around the British Isles. Certainly, of the countless thousands of natural obstacles which represent a hazard to shipping in the western world there is no single headland, island, rock, sandbank or bar which has earned such infamy or been more feared by seamen than the Goodwin Sands. Only constant and meticulous surveying ensures that continuing changes in the positions of the sands are recorded and published and only now, after 200 years of this work, is it possible to discern something of a predictable pattern in their movement. Situated as they are in the Strait of Dover a more unfortunate location for such an obstacle can hardly be imagined. With the seaward face of the Goodwins reaching out six and a half miles from the Kent coast into what is almost the narrowest part of the English Channel, it is little wonder that Trinity House finds it necessary to mark their outline with no less than three lightships and fifteen buoys; for this strait is still the busiest shipping channel in the world.

A true history of the 'great ship swallower' cannot be that of the sandbank alone. Although it serves as a massive breakwater for the enclosed anchorage of the Downs it can also be a fearful place for a vessel to be caught in the event of a gale from the north or south. Hence the coastal towns of Ramsgate, Sandwich, Deal, Walmer and Kingsdown, going from north to south, must also be included, as it was they that provided the seamen and small boats associated with pilotage, provisions, fresh water, rescue and salvage. Indeed it has been said that this part of Kent bred a race of hereditary pilots and salvagers, and certainly the history of salvage diving in the British Isles has its roots here. The area concerned in this book therefore embraces approximately seventy square miles, including Ramsgate, the Goodwin Sands and Downs, to the South Foreland.

Prior to the inauguration of a national lifeboat service, rescues and similar work were carried out by local boats normally engaged in fishing, smuggling, wrecking, salvage or the business of 'hovelling', which included the lucrative recovery of ships' anchors and cables or the provision of them to ships which had lost their own as a result of a storm. Such boats were generally luggers, wide-beamed sturdy craft that earned a living for their owners and crew as 'maids-of-all-work'. When a vessel was seen to be in distress, perhaps stranded on the Goodwins or dragging its anchors in that direction, as many as a hundred or more boats would put out from Deal and Walmer and race each other to the scene. This enthusiasm, it should be added, was not solely humanitarian, the main driving force being money.

The attitude to saving life from a shipwreck depended entirely on the period, circumstances and whether or not there were hostile witnesses. During the sixteenth and seventeenth centuries, and even later when the law decreed that 'a vessel was not a wreck as long as a man or dog survived', this was an open invitation to destroy rather than save life, or at least do nothing to preserve it. Fortunately there were men to whom the saving of life took priority over the saving of material goods and no doubt their personal circumstances dictated their generosity. Nevertheless, the main objective governing these mad scrambles to reach a wreck was the possibility of a salvage award if the vessel, or at least part of its cargo, were saved. Seldom were the rescuers unrewarded for their services, either by the Admiralty, the Board of Trade, a grateful owner or shipping company, any one of a dozen charities, a monarch or head of some foreign state, or in later years the Lifeboat Institution. Mercenary though their motives may have been it must be remembered that these men were often desperately poor and risked not only their lives but their very livelihood, for their boats probably represented their sole source of income. There was no compensation if a boat was damaged or lost other than perhaps a few pounds raised by local subscription or appeal. With the Goodwin Sands a notorious 'widow-maker', it is not surprising that on more than one occasion the men refused to accept a reward, not out of loyalty or devotion to duty but simply because the sum was considered insufficient. Consequently the competition betweel local boats could be fierce but it was nothing compared to that which existed between different beach areas of the Downs.

All through the centuries until as recently as the late 1930s, fierce rivalry existed where, in fact, an outsider would imagine there was only harmony. The coastal towns opposite the Goodwin Sands were basically considered as four separate beaches, namely Deal North End, Deal South End, Walmer Road and Kingsdown. Since they were some distance apart there was no bad feeling between the boatmen of North End and Kingsdown and only a somewhat strained relationship between North End and Walmer, but between the Deal men themselves — the North- and South-enders as they were known — there was open and bitter hostility. The dividing line was the point where the Royal Hotel now stands and boatmen living on either side were at open war with each other. With as many as a thousand men involved overall, it is little wonder that, at the first hint of a wreck or vessel in distress, they raced each other, cutting across the bows of rival boats or 'taking their wind' by sailing close on the windward side, in an attempt to be first to put a man aboard. It was here that the need for 'sets' of boats became a recognised practice since a fast rowing galley, which could be first to reach a wreck and 'claim' it, was not necessarily a suitable boat to lay out a kedge anchor or to salvage cargo. Therefore small organisations existed, consisting of both large and small boats and usually operating in great secrecy so that the rival would not know which boats were involved. These groups often had one or more financiers prepared to put up money to pay for salvage material or wages and who in return took a share of the profits. Often these faceless men who invested in such enterprises had good reason to remain anonymous, being senior customs officers, local officials, workhouse masters or even clergymen.

The first lifeboat to be stationed in the Goodwins area was the prize-winning *Northumberland*, built by James Beeching, which was purchased privately for £210 by the Trinity Board for use by the Ramsgate harbour commissioners in 1852. It was not until 1857 that a similar boat was installed on a beach closer to the Goodwin Sands, this being the first Walmer boat, named *Royal Thames Yacht Club* and provided by subscriptions from that organisation. Eight years later it was replaced by an official craft of the Royal National Lifeboat Institution, with a new boat going to Ramsgate and North Deal in 1865 and another to Kingsdown the following year. By 1866 there were four lifeboats stationed on a ten-mile stretch of coastline, an indication of the frequency of shipwreck and its attendant problems in the nineteenth century. The provision of four lifeboats in addition to others at Broadstairs, Margate and Dover, plus a very large number of local boats, would appear to have been a complete solution to the problem whereas, in fact, it brought new and unforeseen difficulties. Some of the most heroic and spectacular lifeboat rescues on record are accredited to the Goodwins and the men involved often went to sea in conditions nothing short of appalling, facing dangers far greater than at any other stations in the country. When the cannon on the lightships, or the maroons, boomed out in the night, half if not all the lifeboat crews were invariably already up and dressed, keeping watch from the foreshore, this being the practice when bad weather threatened. All the lifeboats except for the one at Ramsgate were beach-launched and with a heavy sea running there was very real danger for the crew from the moment the boat was afloat. Should the wreck be on the eastern face, better known as 'back of the sands', then lifeboats and hovellers alike faced not only the hazards of sea and weather but the risk that they, too, might become victims of the sands.

After the Goodwins became marked by lightships — the first of which went on station in 1795, the scheme being finally completed in 1874 — it was more often than not the lookouts on these who first sighted vessels in distress. Their signals summoned the lifeboats to sea and the boats would make for the lightship that had initiated the call to establish at first hand where the casualty lay. This in itself necessitated rowing or sailing anything from five to fifteen miles, perhaps deliberately crossing some part of the sandbank or navigating its channels and swatchways. Having then searched for and located the victim there was the

The Walmer lifeboat *Civil Service No. 4*, placed on station in 1897.

(RNLI archives)

hazard of getting alongside, or perhaps having to wait for several hours until sufficient water covered that particular bank. The rescue completed, if indeed there was anyone still alive to be rescued, they then ran the gauntlet of the return trip, perhaps deep laden with survivors, the coxswain either chancing his luck on the shingle beach where a man could hardly remain upright if there was any surf or else making for Ramsgate. If the wind or tide was unfavourable, and Ramsgate harbour was always a notoriously difficult place to enter in bad weather, they might make for Margate, perhaps not returning home for several days.

It was the presence of four lifeboats in such a confined area, plus three others in the immediate vicinity in addition to the hovellers, that brought the new problems best summarised in the old proverb, 'too many cooks'. When a light-ship indicated that a lifeboat was required at sea or some keen-eyed boatman sighted a vessel in distress, the age-old instinct to be first aboard prevailed and so competition continued, only now the squabbles were more often between the lifeboats. One solution which suited the more daring boat owners was to remain at sea during bad weather in anticipation of a wreck. Hence many a weary lifeboat crew arrived alongside a vessel, having fought hard to reach her, only to find their fellowmen, perhaps relations, already aboard and claiming salvage. Despite some basic rules and guide lines issued to lifeboat coxswains, two, three or even all four boats would launch to the same wreck, which was obviously a wasted effort. This led to continued bad feeling between the various beaches and was prejudicial to the basic function of the service, especially if more than one wreck occurred at a time. In the 1870s the basic instructions issued to lifeboat coxswains of the Goodwin Sands stations stated:

'In really bad weather, the action of several lifeboats will not be scrutinised too closely, but, as a general rule, the windward boat is to be launched, the lee boats are not to launch unless the coxswain considers it absolutely neces-sary. In fine weather, the windward boat of the group is to be the only one launched. If the wind is offshore, the boat in the most advantageous position with regard to wind and tide, and distance from the casualty, is the only one to be launched.'

In theory these instructions were adequate, but practice called for agreement between the various stations on each occasion the crews were summoned. In the absence of any telephone or radio communication each coxswain acted on his initiative, probably influenced to some extent by outside pressures and the opinion of his crew. The result was that lifeboats continued to put to sea need-lessly and it was 1912 before a special local meeting was held to consider the life-boat service in the area generally. At this meeting, each station having stated its case, it was proposed that the Walmer lifeboat should be removed and despite strong local objection in July of that year the general committee of the RNLI in London decided upon closure of the Walmer station and it did not reopen until 1926. Today, of the original quartet, only the Ramsgate and Walmer stations

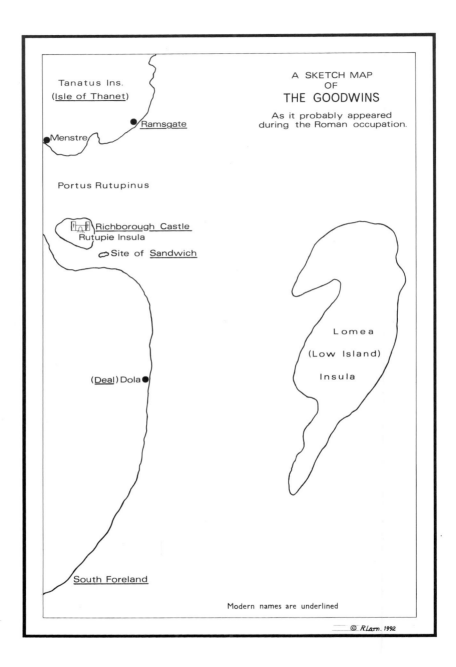

A SKETCH MAP
OF
THE GOODWINS
As it probably appeared
during the Roman occupation.

Tanatus Ins.
(Isle of Thanet)

Ramsgate

Menstre

Portus Rutupinus

Richborough Castle
Rutupie Insula

Site of Sandwich

Lomea

(Low Island)

Insula

(Deal) Dola

South Foreland

Modern names are underlined

© R.Larn. 1992

remain open, even the latter having suffered a period of closure during the Second World War. The reasoning of the RNLI in closing the Walmer station in 1912 was probably justified, although it caused a great deal of bad feeling locally. Its first boat, the *Royal Thames Yacht Club*, ten-oared and bought for £156, saved fifteen lives from the barque *Reliance* on its very first rescue, but in the following six years of service it rescued only one more person. Its namesake was launched twenty-three times between 1863 and 1871 to save five lives on one occasion and although the next lifeboat, the *Centurion*, had a better record, the *Civil Service No 4* boat, sited at Walmer in 1884, made fifty-six launches in eleven years, bringing back a total of six survivors. One unfortunate incident in 1907, which did nothing to help the situation, occurred when the Walmer lifeboat crew went on strike and refused to man their boat until they had received adequate payment for a previous launch. Obviously, the Walmer coxswain was always in a most difficult position, his boat being the centre one of the three beach-launched lifeboats. If the wind was offshore, or in the case of incidents during bad weather and at night when the location of the wreck was uncertain, his sense of duty dictated that he launched and worried about the consequences later. Fortunately, the situation was resolved before the outbreak of the First World War when the lifeboat service was stretched to the full, especially in this area.

The origin of the Goodwin Sands and its name have been the subject of much speculation. It is probable that the truth concerning both matters has now been irretrievably lost, although a geological solution to the former may evolve from the evidence of various submarine surveys now being conducted in connection with sand waves. Meanwhile the only existing evidence is that contained in sources already well researched, supported by the indisputable fact that Thanet was once an island. In common with other early writers interested in the Goodwins, Gattie, in his 'Memorials of the Goodwin Sands', was unable to quote with authority any evidence to support the theory of 'Lomea' — an island which deteriorated to the extent it is now only a sandbank.

Throughout history there are continuous references to three islands, said to be close to or nearly opposite the Roman *Portus Rutupinus*. Of these, the one to the north was said to be *Tanatus* (Thanet); the south island was *Rutupiae* or *Roochini Insula* (Richborough), leaving one more which lay to the south-east and was known as *Infera Insula* (Lomea, or Low Island). The earliest printed reference to this can be found in a book written by John Twyne (1501-81). A schoolmaster/antiquary and a citizen of Canterbury, Twyne became sheriff, alderman and finally Member of Parliament for that city, so that his evidence handed down to the present century in *De Rebus Albionicis Britannicus* must be accepted as the work of a scholar and not without foundation. Twyne writes:

'Of Lomea, or as it is now called Godwin Sands...this isle was very fruitful and had much pasture; it was situated lower than Thanet from which there was a passage by boat of about three or four miles. This island in an unusual

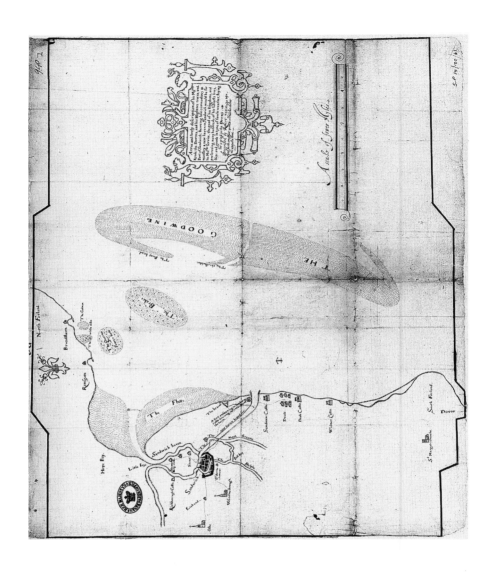

tempest of winds and rain and in a very high rage of the sea was drowned, overwhelmed with sand, and irrecoverably converted into a nature between that of land and sea…sometimes it floats, while at low water, people may walk upon it.'

Whether or not this is a direct quote from one of the early writers to whom Gattie, for example, makes reference, is not known. No other historical work concerning Kent written in that century offers anything to support this theory, so that any proof of the existence of *Lomea* would appear to rest on the evidence of Twyne alone.

Although this part of the English coastline has undergone immense change over the centuries as a result of both erosion and siltation, if Caesar and his invading Roman army did, in fact, land hereabouts in 55 BC — and there is some evidence to support this — it is probable that they saw the Goodwins very much as they are today. Before new evidence to support this is offered it is necessary to understand what has happened to the former island of Thanet, and also to consider some known facts as well as legends. At the time of the Roman invasion Thanet was completely surrounded by water, separated from the rest of Kent by the Wantsum Channel. Centuries of drifting sand and inland silt have now so completely blocked this passage, which once offered a vessel a short cut to and from the Thames estuary, that it is difficult to believe it ever existed. Siltation on this scale is a slow process, and the remains of Roman pottery, coins and other artefacts which have been found deep in the shingle of Stonar Bank suggest that this was already a severe navigational hazard during the first century BC. At that time it would have partially blocked the eastern entrance of the Wantsum. Today there is considerable evidence to show that the sand which blocked the Wantsum, isolated Sandwich, and that which today is slowly filling Pegwell Bay originated from the Goodwin Sands in a series of 'break away' banks which migrated shorewards. These migratory banks were a recognised natural phenomenon long before the eleventh century, which is the approximate time in history when legend would have us believe that *Lomea* was inundated and destroyed. It should not be forgotten that identical legends and stories of great floods and storms exist all along the French and Flemish coast as well and hence may have an element of truth.

One of the many legends concerning the Goodwin Sands tells us that the inundation took place in AD 1099. Following its complete and sudden submergence the first victim of the obstruction was the Earl Godwine who, returning home at the head of his fleet, was wrecked and drowned there. It was

Opposite: A chart of the Downs and Goodwin Sands, including the North and South Forelands, drawn by Robert Jager in 1629. The legend in the decorative panel reads: 'A true and lively description of his Majesty's Roade the Downes and his Highness towne and Port of Sandwich, shewing how commodious & necessary a new haven would be for his Majesty's service, the good of his Kingdom, and preserving many hundreds of his subjects lives, ships, and goods in tyme of fowle weather, staying for a wind in the Downes'.　　　　　　　　　　　　　　　　　　　(Crown Copyright, Public Record Office)

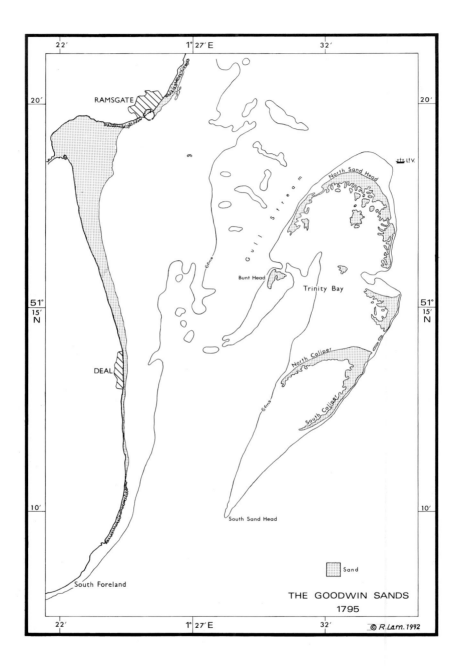

THE GOODWIN SANDS
1795

Sand

Ramsgate, Deal, South Foreland, South Sand Head, Bunt Head, Trinity Bay, North Calliper, South Calliper, North Sand Head, Gull Stream, Lt.V.

© R. Lam. 1992

common practice for rocks and sandbanks to take their name from a vessel or individual who came to grief as a result of wreck and if the Goodwins had derived their name in this manner the story would be credible. Unfortunately, more reliable sources of history tell us that Godwine met his death by choking whilst dining with Edward the Confessor at Winchester in April 1053, some forty-six years later. Another legend suggests a connection between the sandbank and Tenterden church. It seems that Earl Godwine, fleeing from his enemies, made a holy vow that, if preserved from death, he would erect a great steeple for the church in thanksgiving. There are two conclusions to this legend; one states that the island was destroyed by divine intervention as a punishment for the Earl's failure to keep his promise. The other tells us that the Earl spent so much money on the steeple that the sea defences of *Lomea* were neglected and it was engulfed by the sea. Whoever perpetrated this particular legend failed to check the facts, since Tenterden did not acquire a steeple to its tower until the middle of the sixteenth century.

The area covered by the Goodwins is of considerable size. From the three-fathom line at the North Sand Head to its equivalent at the South Sand Head the distance is about ten and a quarter miles and, at its widest point, four and a quarter miles. During low water of a neap tide nothing of the sands shows above the surface and even on a spring tide only a relatively small proportion is exposed. With an average tidal range of 16 feet and the Goodwins covered to an average depth of 12 feet at high water, the highest point of the bank today is only some 4 feet above sea level. It is impossible to define exactly the area left dry twice each twenty-four hour period of a spring tide since both wind and sand movements produce varying results but, roughly speaking, some twenty-one square miles of sandbank dries and remains so for something less than three hours at a time. Despite the intensive survey work conducted over the past 150 years, and the availability of deep-drilling, seabed, equipment, very little is yet known about the composition of the Goodwin Sands. The sum total of our knowledge of its geological structure comes from a boring made in 1849 under supervision of Sir J.A. Pelly, Deputy Master of Trinity House. Great controversy had raged over exactly what lay beneath the top covering of sand, yet less than half-a-dozen attempts have been made to solve the mystery. Smeaton, the well known engineer, carried out a survey of the Goodwins in 1789 and stated '...although they are of the nature of a quicksand, clean and unconnected, yet the particles lay so close that it is difficult to work a pointed iron tube into the mass more than to a depth of 6 or 7 feet'.

Test borings carried out during 1817 by Trinity House while searching for bed rock on which to install a beacon found the sand to be only 15 feet deep, after which the drill encountered blue clay, followed by hard chalk. In 1840 Admiral Bullock found the sand so dense that at a depth of 7 feet 6 inches hand tools just broke off. His workmen then used a solid iron bar, 3 inches in diameter, but having reached a depth of 13 feet found it took forty-six blows from a 112 lb

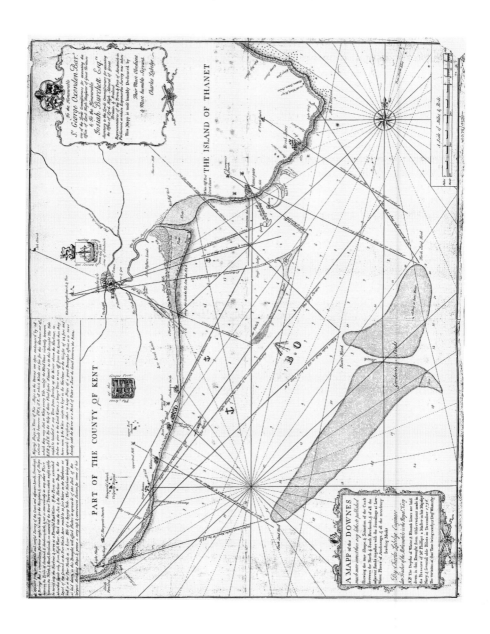

22

hammer falling 10 feet to drive the bar one inch deeper. This sort of evidence, whilst interesting, is unfortunately of little value, since there is no record of the point on the Goodwins at which these experiments were conducted. Geologically, there is every reason to suppose that clay and chalk are present beneath the entire bank but this appears to rise and fall as isolated pinnacles or loose deposits.

Only a series of trial borings spread across the entire area would reveal the true structure and in the absence of these the experiments carried out by Trinity House in 1849 represent the deepest drilling of the Goodwins to date. In the July of that year an iron tube, 2 feet 6 inches in diameter and in 10 feet lengths, was forced down by atmospheric pressure to a depth of 60 feet at the first attempt and then abandoned because no chalk or rock foundation had been established. A second attempt in October found chalk at 78 feet, with clean bright sand for the first 46 feet. Between the sand and chalk base, successive layers of small stones, broken shell and chalk nodules existed to 51 feet; decayed wood and shell to 67 feet, and pebbles to 72 feet. At no time was there any trace of mud, soil or decayed vegetation to support the theory of a drowned island.

A great many learned gentlemen have made a study of the Goodwin Sands in an attempt to find an explanation for their existence or to prove a particular theory. In a report to the Geological Society in 1838, a Mr Morris wrote:

'...the chalk base of the Ramsgate cliffs continues out towards the North Goodwin, deepening gradually at 60 feet. Then the mound of the Goodwins rises above low-water mark and extends outwards for two miles, terminating precipitately, and two miles still further out will be found at a depth of 210 feet; the Brake Sand is another such chalk mound.'

Five years later, the distinguished engineer James Walker put his opinions in writing:

'If the Goodwin Sands were ever cultivated land, they must have been in the first place originally reclaimed from the sea, and the extreme difficulty of doing this, either then or now, is to me convincing argument against it. I consider the sands as the natural consequence of the peculiar formation of the place, and of the cross tidal currents upon it, just as any other sand may be formed. Between Dover and the French coast, the channel is narrower, the set of the tide direct, and there is no sand, but the bottom is rough stone and

Opposite:
A survey of the Downs and Sandwich Haven made 'By Charles Labelye Engineer, late *Teacher of the Mathematicks in the Royal Navy, December 1736'*. The map claimed to be 'much more correct than any hitherto published' shows 'the True Shape and Situation of the Coast between the North & South Forelands and of all the adjacent sands together with the Soundings at Low Water, Places of Anchorage, & All the necessary Leading Marks.'   (Crown Copyright, Public Record Office)

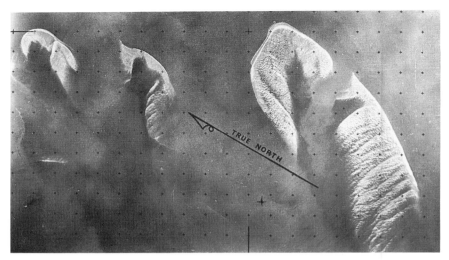

An aerial view of the Goodwin Sands from a height of 10,000ft. The Kellett Gut is the wide channel in the centre.   (Ministry of Defence, Royal Air Force)

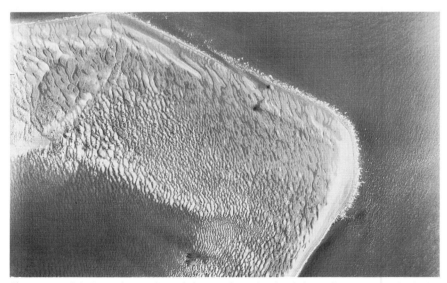

Close-up aerial view of a section of the southern bank of the Kellett Gut in which the remains of at least three wrecks are visible.   (Ministry of Defence, Royal Air Force)

chalk. Northward, the channel widens, and the currents crossed; there is also a bay or hollow in the coast, extending from the South to North Foreland, with the projection of the latter, may account for the peculiar formation of the Goodwins and of the Margate Sands around the Foreland. I consider the loose sands of the Goodwins as an exact balance of the currents upon it at the time, and that the different changes that take place in it would, if we could apply them, be found to be very minute and a fine measure of disturbing forces, namely winds, floods, and tides, and with a body so easily moved as sand, this is sure to be the case.'

Although both Morris and Walker had made a special study of the subject, it was over a very limited period and neither of them had continuous personal contact with either the Downs or sands, as did Capt Kenneth Martin, harbour master at Ramsgate during the late nineteenth century. Neither did they have the same scientific approach or facilities as Dr R. Cloet who, as head of the Unit of Coastal Sedimentation, carried out the most scientific survey of the Goodwins to date.

Capt Martin's opinion of the Goodwins formation was that:

'...they were originally a ridge of chalk forming an inclined plane, showing a little deviation in the Gull Stream, with the nearest shore of the Isle of Thanet; the several small shoals and patches, together with the Brake Sand, being similar ridges of chalk, together creating the many eddies which have been the means of clothing their summits, in some places with flint boulders and shingle, and at others like the Goodwins, with a clean live sand, of many miles extent, without a particle of extraneous matter.'

The evidence put forward by Dr Cloet and his team of divers, who actually measured the height and progress of sandwaves on the seabed, is, however, by far the most decisive. They first collected all the previous hydrographic surveys of the Goodwin Sands carried out between 1844 and 1947. These were then redrawn to a common scale and superimposed. The result was a 'stability chart' which showed those areas of the Goodwins in which the depth of water had not increased since 1844. There are, of course, many earlier charts of the area but, generally speaking, these are unreliable and hence unsuitable for transfer to a modern navigational chart, which has a high degree of accuracy.

With the sea at its present level the possibility of an island having once existed here, sufficiently dry and stable to be inhabited by man prior to about AD 400, is very remote. During this period of the Dark Ages the Dunkirkian transgression occurred which raised the level of the sea by about 18 feet, so that whilst the presence of an island on the site of the existing Goodwins is conceivable prior to this event it would still have been covered at high tide to a depth of at least 10 feet. This supports Holmes' theory that 'an obstacle existed here in Caesar's time'. There is some evidence to suggest that the inundation of 1099, to which reference has already been made, was only of a very local nature. If, therefore,

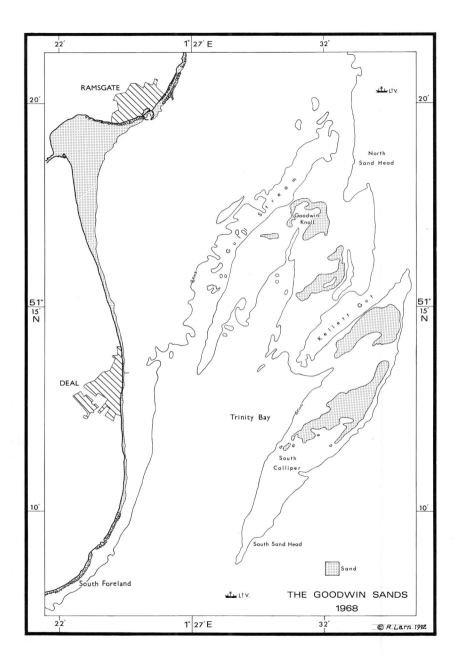

THE GOODWIN SANDS
1968

© R. Larn. 1992

as legend would have us believe, the site of the Goodwins was once an island proper it had probably been destroyed some 800 to 1,000 years previously.

The fact that the Goodwins were not stable in their position was commented on as long ago as 1848 when Admiral Beaufort, the Admiralty Hydrographer, stated in a minute to the Lords Commissioners, 'Within these few years, since the Goodwins have been surveyed with scrupulous accuracy, it appears that they have all had an annual movement to the westward, constantly tending to narrow the Gull Stream, although the Brake Sand is also approaching the shore.' Allied to this movement is the somewhat remarkable appearance and disappearance of a channel known as the Kellett Gut. It was found to be an open channel navigable by quite large vessels in 1926, during a survey by HMS *Kellett*, yet neither of the previous surveys carried out in 1865 and 1896 found any such channel. The famous Dutch navigator, Lucas Waghenear, gave no indication of the Gut in 1584 but Robert Fager shows a 'swatch' in his chart of the Downs, as did Pieter Goos in 1666. The Goodwins continued to be drawn as two separate areas divided by this deep channel in Labelye's chart of 1736 and also in that by Ross in 1779, and it is recorded that in 1795 the sand had been scoured away leaving a hard chalk bottom only at a depth of 78 feet. The Gut was still open to shipping in 1850 but already beginning to silt up and fifteen years later it had completely disappeared. It remained blocked for forty-five years, when it was again deep enough to be used by small vessels, especially minesweepers, throughout the First World War. Although the Gut remains open still there are positive indications that it is shoaling and at some time in the near future will again be closed.

Although the overall length of the Goodwins is less now than in 1795 they have been steadily increasing since 1840 at the rate of approximately 4,000 feet a century. The width is also increasing but at a much slower rate. Dr Cloet, in summarising his arguments and evidence concerning the sands, states:

'I have advanced some arguments suggesting that the Goodwins consist of an accumulation of sediment resting on a fairly even chalk surface. The existence of a former island is doubtful, and the only evidence is of legendary and questionable value. However, the sands, though subject to an appreciable amount of movement, have probably existed in their present position for a considerable time. The reason why the Goodwins do not move either into the Straits of Dover or farther into the North Sea is thought to be the interplay of an ebb and flood channel system of transportation. Because either one or the other stream is locally stronger on different parts of the same sandbank, the addition of sediment seems to produce a widening of the feature, where the opposing stream is least able to counteract the tendency. This continues until a new balance is temporarily achieved. Superimposed on it is the differential effect of two flood channels on the enclosed ebb channel of the Gull Stream. The ebb is weaker as a sediment carrier than the flood in Trinity Bay, while it does more than keep in check the expansion of the Small Downs flood channel. It has been suggested that the formation of the Kellett Gut is a response to the widening of the Goodwins.

It may be that we can go still further, and surmise that eventually the whole arm of the fork may be severed from the Goodwins, while a new North Goodwins develops from that part which is north of the Kellett Gut, and the Brake Sand merges with the shore. This brings us to the larger conception of sediment circulation on an open shore, which may possibly be a closed cell circulation within each limb, between ebb and flood channels, superimposed on a slow drift of the sandbanks towards the shore as their sediment content is slowly increased. This latter drift is not likely to be continuous, but probably consists of a growth to unstable proportions, followed by a severing from the parent bank. The formation of the Kellett Gut may consequently either be an attempt to redress the balance between ebb and flow, or the beginning of a more drastic change culminating in the origin of a new Brake Bank.'

If this hypothesis is correct, and there is no reason or evidence to think otherwise, it may well be the explanation of the disappearance of the Wantsum Channel, the siltation of Sandwich and Pegwell Bay and the pendulous movement of the Goodwin Sands. Meanwhile it is a fact that the Brake Sand has moved in a south-westerly direction a distance of 1,000 to 2,000 feet during the past fifty years and that the drift continues.

The term 'ship swallower' for the Sands has been handed down from William Lambarde who, in 1570, quoting the Scottish historian Boethius, described the Goodwins as 'a most dreadful gulfe and shippe swallower'. Daniel Defoe, while languishing in prison, wrote an account of the Great Storm of 1703 and referred to 'the awful celerity with which a wreck can disappear'. The fact that shipwrecks do literally disappear beneath the surface of the sands is understandable if one considers the Goodwins for what they are — a form of quicksand. At low-water springs, when vast areas are exposed and dry out, the falling level of the sea causes water to drain down through the sand particles so that they move closer together and present a tightly packed surface. As the tide returns on the flood the water finds its way back up through the sand, causing the particles again to drift apart. At this stage any object, large or small, provided it is more dense than the mixture of sand and water, will displace the material on which it rests and slowly sink. With varying depths of sand over a chalk underlay whole ships will settle down in a matter of days until they are completely engulfed and continue to sink until a chalk base is encountered. In places where the sand is less deep a wreck will settle on a chalk outcrop or pinnacle and perhaps remain partially exposed for many years. Alternatively, the strain imposed may break the vessel in two, each part sliding down the gradient imposed on the sand by the hidden chalk strata. At present there are the remains of at least two steamships showing above the surface of the Goodwins and these have undoubtedly reached a hard base and will there remain until knocked down or eventually disintegrate by corrosion.

Speculation concerning the total number of ship losses in the area varies considerably. One author has attributed to the Goodwins '50,000 lives and £200m in shipping over five centuries'; another claimed that 'at least 5,000 ships have been lost'. In fact, both are exaggerations, and no such figures could be reliably advanced unless a very full wreck index had first been compiled. The wreck index at the back of this book is the result of very intensive research and is certainly the most comprehensive yet produced for this area. Even so, it still represents only some two-thirds of the probable total, since all research sources have not yet been exhausted. It does, however, represent every wreck incident in the 'Calendar of Domestic State Papers'; the majority of those contained in 'Lloyds List' from 1743 to 1850; Admiralty and Board of Trade Returns from 1843 to the present day; 'Lifeboat Journals' from 1850, and other sources, principally some three dozen Kent newspapers and the Burney collection. Listing, as it does, approximately 1,000 shipwrecks between 1298 and 1975 — even if this is, in fact, only half the true total — the figures are impressive but much lower than has previously been suggested.

Periodically an old wreck becomes uncovered as the sand moves but it will have disappeared again in a matter of days at the most. An example of this was the uncovering of the German submarine *U-48* which was sunk during the First World War and seen during 1921 and again in 1973. Two sets of masts showing above the surface are all that is now visible of the *Luray Victory* and the *North Eastern Victory*, both steamships wrecked within a short distance of each other during 1946. On the sands or in the Downs bronze cannon, old weapons, ships bells, anchors, even Roman amphorae have been recovered and there are countless well-documented accounts of valuable cargoes and great treasure entombed for ever. The Goodwins exercise a strange sort of fascination and have been the setting for many treasure hunts, eccentricities, stunts, cricket matches, races on horseback, on foot, and more recently between go-karts. Huge picnics, parties, even firework displays have been held on the Goodwins; the brother-in-law of the famous diarist, Evelyn, was interred there in a lead coffin in 1705; also one Francis Merrydith, in 1761. The remains of the former no doubt still lie buried deep in the sands but poor Merrydith finished up in Hamburg, his coffin having been 'taken-up' by the anchor of a French ship.

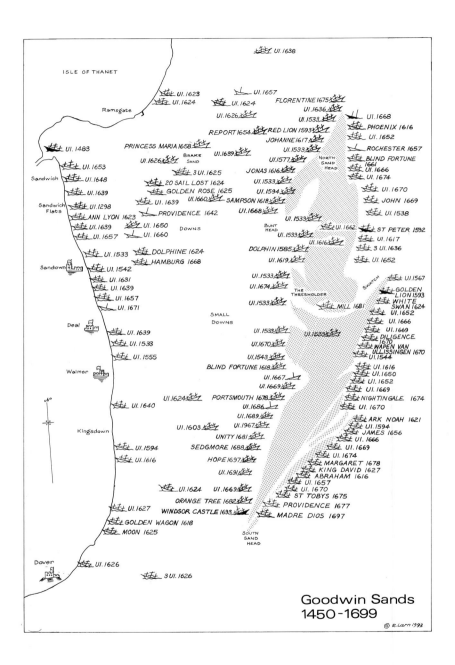

ISLE OF THANET

UI.1638

UI.1623
UI.1624
UI.1657
FLORENTINE 1675
Ramsgate
UI.1626
UI.1636
UI.1533
UI.1668
PHOENIX 1616
REPORT 1654 RED LION 1593
JOHANNE 1617
UI.1652
UI.1483
PRINCESS MARIA 1658
UI.1639
BRAKE SAND
UI.1533
ROCHESTER 1657
UI.1626
NORTH SAND HEAD
BLIND FORTUNE 1661
UI.1653
3 UI.1625
JONAS 1616
UI.1666
Sandwich
UI.1648
20 SAIL LOST 1624
UI.1533
UI.1674
UI.1639
GOLDEN ROSE 1625
UI.1594
UI.1670
UI.1298
UI.1639
UI.1660
SAMPSON 1618
JOHN 1669
Sandwich Flats
ANN LYON 1623
PROVIDENCE 1642
UI.1668
UI.1538
UI.1639
UI.1650
Downs
UI.1533
BUNT HEAD
UI.1662
ST PETER 1592
UI.1657
UI.1660
UI.1533
UI.1616
UI.1617
UI.1533
DOLPHINE 1624
DOLPHIN 1585
3 UI.1636
Sandown
HAMBURG 1668
UI.1619
UI.1652
UI.1542
UI.1631
UI.1533
UI.1567
UI.1639
UI.1674
SWATCH
GOLDEN LION 1593
UI.1657
THE THRESHOLDER
WHITE SWAN 1624
UI.1671
UI.1533
MILL 1681
UI.1652
SMALL DOWNS
UI.1666
Deal
UI.1639
UI.1533
UI.1533
UI.1669
DILIGENCE 1670
UI.1533
UI.1670
WAPEN VAN ULLISSINGEN 1670
UI.1555
UI.1543
UI.1544
BLIND FORTUNE 1618
UI.1616
Walmer
UI.1667
UI.1650
UI.1669
UI.1652
UI.1669
UI.1624
PORTSMOUTH 1678
NIGHTINGALE 1674
UI.1640
UI.1686
UI.1670
UI.1689
Kingsdown
UI.1603
UI.1967
ARK NOAH 1621
UI.1594
UNITY 1681
JAMES 1656
UI.1666
UI.1594
SEDGMORE 1688
UI.1669
UI.1616
HOPE 1697
UI.1674
MARGARET 1678
UI.1691
KING DAVID 1627
ABRAHAM 1616
UI.1657
UI.1624
UI.1669
UI.1670
ORANGE TREE 1682
ST TOBYS 1675
WINDSOR CASTLE 1693
PROVIDENCE 1677
UI.1627
MADRE DIOS 1697
GOLDEN WAGON 1618
MOON 1625
SOUTH SAND HEAD
Dover
UI.1626
3 UI.1626

Goodwin Sands
1450-1699

© R.Larn 1992

30

Chapter Two

'TWOO SHIPPS THONE CALLED *GOLDEN LYON:'* 1298-1699

The Downs has passed through two distinct phases of history during which its maritime significance has been of the utmost importance to the British nation. The first period lasted approximately 400 years starting in the latter half of the eleventh century which saw the rise and fall of the Cinque Ports. This was followed by another but much shorter period of fame between 1750 and 1900, brought about by dramatic increases in exploration, trade, industrial development and the growth of sailing ships, not only in number but also in size. These, in due course, were eclipsed by the steamship which, after an initial period of development, had no use for such an anchorage.

In the Doomsday survey of 1086, only the ports of Dover, Sandwich and Romney had been granted any special privileges in return for their co-operation in the feudal principle of sea service. The Crown granted these 'up-Channel' ports immunity from certain taxes and duties provided they furnished, as required, a specified number of vessels and seamen to defend the coast. Another function of these ports, the importance of which cannot be over-stressed, was the maintenance of communications with English territories in France. Although it was not until the reign of Henry II (1154-89), 100 years after the Conquest, that the term 'Cinque Ports' was first used, the five towns concerned, namely Dover, Sandwich, Romney, Hastings and Hythe, had already received individual contracts from the king. It was John, the fourth son of Henry II and aptly nicknamed 'Lackland', who lost Normandy and the great wine-growing areas of Bordeaux to the French king in 1204; and a year later only a fraction of the great Angevin empire remained in English hands. The emphasis on seaborne trade and communication routes then moved to the west country and for this and associated reasons the importance of the Cinque Ports then began to decline.

It was no mere coincidence that the five ports chosen were those closest to the Downs with its natural breakwater in the form of the Goodwin Sands. It was an ideal assembly point for fleets to gather and the envy of many European countries. Not only was the water sufficiently deep for ships to remain at anchor in safety but they enjoyed the additional protection of shore batteries sited in various castles and earthworks, together with an escape route both north and south of the sandbanks. The English Sea, as the Channel was then called, is at its narrowest at the Downs and vessels waiting to cross to the continent would there await a suitable opportunity since their small tonnage did not allow them to venture across in bad weather. Up until the late 1400s Sandwich Haven, the only port actually within the Downs, was in consequence a very busy and important place, handling not only trade goods but a steady traffic of mail, dispatches and government officials. Even in those early years, however, great masses of sand had already drifted inshore, causing the river entrance to be deflected to the north-east, so that the 1,000-ton Venetian galleys which came from Flanders to trade could no longer enter the haven. Plans were then drawn up to cut a channel through that part of the coast now known as Sandwich Flats, so re-opening the town to the Downs, but this, too, would soon have silted up and the project was never started.

The first reference to shipwreck in the Downs is to be found in the Calendar of Patent Rolls during the reign of Edward I. The name of the vessel is not given nor the exact location of the wreck other than that it was 'near Sandwich'. Her owner, William Martyn, appealed to the king on 7th June 1298, informing him that whilst returning from Flanders laden with armour and other goods, his ship had been cast away and plundered and requesting that a jury be appointed to investigate his complaint. Details of another early wreck are brought to our attention by Leland, the celebrated chronicler of Henry VIII's reign. Recording the loss of a great Spanish ship in 1483, he wrote: 'The Caryke, that was sonke in the Haven in Pope Paulus time, dide much hurt to the Haven (Sandwich), and gather a great banke there'.

Since natural silting was already well advanced, and trade rapidly declining as a result, a wreck or similar obstacle in the river or its entrance must have been a major disaster for the impoverished town.

Exactly who had the right to wreck on the Goodwins was never clearly established either then or for several centuries to come. There was no shortage of individuals who claimed, pretended or assumed it was theirs and it must have been a lucrative form of income, since there were legal squabbles, court cases and inquisitions every time a ship was wrecked. In 1602, for example, the Lord Warden claimed that as Admiral of the Cinque Ports, 'he enjoyed all wreck of the sea, and in his absence, this went to the king'. But this was contrary to the principle that the Crown was entitled to a share of all wreck and the entitlement of the lords of manors seems to have been conveniently forgotten. These gentlemen often owned great stretches of coastline, with an hereditary entitlement to wreck as well as other privileges granted to the family in earlier centuries. William Ward, sergeant of the Admiralty for the Cinque Ports, the Droit Gatherer General, and the Clerk of Dover Castle were all jointly charged in 1613 with 'embezzling the profits of wrecks at sea and usurping, a gross betrayl of their authority'. In their defence all three claimed they had the right to wreck on the Goodwins and elsewhere. Another Lord Warden of the Ports, in a letter to the king dated 22nd January 1533 was accused of having unlawfully claimed wrecked goods. The letter read:

'Twelve ships have been lost this winter on the sands with divers merchandise, and when men of the port (Dover) have gone out for their safeguard, the servants of the Lord Warden have taken from them their "Findalls" contrary to their libities. Certain kyntletts were found by divers persons and were taken from them, and only a crown was given them as a reward, though some of the kyntletts were full of wine and gold, and they are supposed to be treasure ships. All this has been witheld from the owners. When men have been found on the sea-sand their garments and their purses have been taken from them, and their bodies left unburied, and eaten by hogs and dogs.'

In fact, all wreck was treated the same — fair game to those who could lay the first claim and no thought for the rightful owner. A hoy barque carrying wheat and iron was lost on the Goodwins on 18th February 1542 and looted. She was followed by a Portuguese vessel in 1543; three vessels at the same time the following year, several unidentified wrecks in 1555, 1567 and 1577 and the *Dolphin* in 1585. All were total losses and the subject of 'wrecking' charges. An interesting addition to the list would have been a vessel of the Spanish Armada alleged by some to have been wrecked in 1588, but there appears to be no historical evidence to substantiate the claim. In his history of the sands, Gattie states that the commander of one of the six ships provided by the Cinque Ports was a Deal man who, well acquainted with the shoals and banks of the area, is said to have lured a great Spanish galleas ashore, where she was burnt. As recently as 1973 a diving expedition was on the Goodwins searching for her remains but they left empty-handed as had many others before them.

There was great excitement in the coastal towns of south-east Kent during November and December 1592 when three great ships, two Dutch and one English, were wrecked. All three were very rich wrecks indeed and were plundered to such an extent that the Lord Warden ordered several courts of enquiry to be set up. The first of the wrecks was the *St Peter* of Amsterdam, stranded on the Goodwins on or about 15th November, after which she was systematically stripped over five days. Many original depositions made during the enquiry proceedings survive and in them personal grievances, loyalties and a general resentment of authority are clearly evident. The first court hearing was convened by order of Lord Cobham and among the gentlemen present were Edward Peak, Mayor of Sandwich; Richard Cryshe, the younger; Mark Polcknam and others. Original documents such as these are seldom easy to read and are made all the more difficult by frequent deletions as deponents changed their minds while giving evidence. It is not difficult to conjure up a picture of the clerk, quill pen in hand, giving a sigh of resignation as he crosses out yet another line of carefully recorded evidence. Although the bulk of the cargo of the *St Peter* was spirited away, it is obvious from the many items landed and declared, that she was outward bound from Holland with a cargo of typical Dutch merchandise. Among the goods it included were: '...tapestrye, stockinges, lynen, black stuff, growgreyn, lead, fustyans, lattern pannes, pack needles, great knyves, thimbles, pynnes, kersey, dubleting, brass kettles, copper, rolls of wire, bookes, whiteplate, razors and nayles'.

Under oath and close examination as they were, it was impossible for the deponents not to implicate others and some may even have welcomed the opportunity to settle old scores. Despite admissions that they themselves were present at the wreck and that some had taken items of cargo, the majority conveniently professed ignorance of what became of the goods once ashore! One witness, whose name is illegible, testified that:

'...he and his company in his boat saved and brought thence xvij Keteles, Tenne copper plates being bottoms, a fyrken of white plates, ij Remnants of coarse white Dubleting mad uppe in one gold, cout about xv yards, one peece of growgreyn or Rasse, and ij peeces of Sayes which lykewise they have shared amongst the company, about xxx peeces of (illegible) or xiiij lattern pannes, wyer, paper of flatt gold, j bundles of pynnes, but what as becam of them he knoweth not. In the hands of Mr Moondey the mynyster, iij or iiij Razers and a payer or ij of knyves, j doosen payer of spectacles or more.'

Prominent in the salvage were boats belonging to Robert Wasteles and John Baxes, both of St Peters; John Knowles, Thomas Coppyns, and Henry Shelbyies of Ramsgate. Although Deal boats and men are mentioned, not one is implicated or named — a truly remarkable absence, bearing in mind their centuries-old reputation for wrecking.

Another deposition, this time by Shelbyies, one of the boat owners mentioned above, states:

'Henry Shelbyies, aged fifty-one or thereabouts — that he was on the Goodwynes on Wellensdaye the xxth of November last, and went not abourd till about xij of the clock that daye. To the second (question) he sayeth that he went abourd in his owne boat and there went with him in his company in the same boat, Richard Harvye, Wm Knowles, Vyncent Underdowne, Richard Bennett, Arthur Cowell, of Ramsgate aforesaid...when they came abourd they found not any man abourd, for all they that had byn abourde before were gon from her before they came abourd, and he sawe the Boats of Deale, St Peters and others of Ramsgate going from the shippe, but who was in them or what they carreyed away he cannot tell.'

What happened to the crew of the *St Peter* is not recorded but it is probable that there were survivors since, during the month following the incident, Guido Maleparte and Roger Van der Colyn, both Dutch merchants, and other persons of Middleburg were interrogated regarding the loss of the ship and her cargo.

Less than a month later, on 17th December, the *Golden Lion* of Middleburg and the *Red Lion* of London were also lost on the sands. Both vessels went to pieces and were quickly engulfed in sand, so that nothing like the same amount of cargo, or so we are led to believe, was salvaged. These two wrecks were probably the richest ever to fall into the hands of the locals. At the inevitable inquisition, held in March 1594, an incredible fifteen months after the incident, Richard Bassett of Ramsgate, 'sailer aged xxviij yeres or thereabouts', stated that he went to the 'twoo shipps thone called Golden Lyon' about four times in all. He could not actually get on board the wreck, since she lay underwater, but was able to salvage a case containing some thirty to thirty-two pieces of striped canvas. This was divided into about forty shares so that some of the men received seven yards, others eight. Bassett took ten yards for himself and a further twelve for the boat. Several sowes or pigs of lead were saved, which would have weighed about 300 lb each, one of which Bassett admitted selling to John Duck of Rye for 23 shillings and 10 pence. It is almost conclusive that the *Golden Lion* was yet another outward-bound East Indiaman and hence carried a great treasure in the form of silver coin, all of which remains buried to this day beneath the Goodwins.

Other investigations into the disposal of salvaged goods held at Dover between 17th and 19th July 1594 related to material from wrecks on the North and South Sand Head, also at Deal and Sandwich. Another vessel which provided the men from Dover with 'findalls' was a tragic reminder of the hazards of seafaring in the sixteenth century. This was a homeward-bound East Indiaman, on board of which famine had forced the crew to cannibalism. Weakened and debilitated, the crew were unable to help themselves when struck by a squall off the South Foreland and the ship went down with the majority of her crew.

Commencing in 1616 a decade of spectacular wreck incidents followed which gave rich pickings to the locals and involved the courts in innumerable charges of wrecking and concealing goods. First to succumb were three Dutch vessels wrecked on the Goodwins on 4th January. It was Thomas Fulnetby who brought news to the Lord Warden, Lord Zouch, that the *Jonas*, the *Abraham* and an unidentified ship were all lost and their cargo being landed illicitly. In a written reply, Lord Zouch informed him that the Dutch States Ambassador, Sir Noel Caron, had already solicited that such goods should be kept safe for their rightful owners and reminded Fulnetby that he must see the goods placed in the custody of the mayor of Sandwich. A protracted argument followed concerning the right of wreck, as it did every time anything of value came ashore. In this instance Richard Younge had something of an advantage since he had personal possession of all the items, 'having taken the goods and parts of the great ships cast on the Goodwin Sands, which are broken to pieces'. Among the contestants for ownership was no less a person than the Lord High Admiral of England who based his claim on the grounds that the wrecks had occurred in the Narrow Seas. The Warden of the Cinque Ports was equally convinced that they belonged to him and in this he at least received some local support. This came from the mayor of Dover who submitted a statement claiming that: '...the Downs, Goodwin Sands, and other places on that coast are within the Lord Warden's Admiralty jurisdiction; that the Vice-Admiral of that county has always received all manner of wrecks of the seas and other casualties happening in the King's Channel'.

The English West Indiaman *Belina* stranded and breaking-up on the Goodwin Sands, 23rd November 1824.   (City Art Gallery, Plymouth)

In response to these claims a Mr Fane produced contrary evidence to the effect that the Cinque Ports were exempted from the Lord Admiral's juris-diction, but the old men of Sandwich still insisted that, in their recollection, all wreck between Beachy Head, Sussex, to the Shoe Beacon, Essex, appertained to the Lord Warden and not to the Admiral of the Narrow Seas. Also that the mayors of the ports were entitled to punish offenders concerning ship matters provided that the vessel could be reached on horseback at low water. In the case of both the *Jonas* and the *Abraham* it was Deal boatmen who were charged with disorderly conduct, of having violated their agreement with the respective captains, and of opening and rifling 'merchants packs and goods', accusations which were to be echoed and re-echoed in the Downs for a further 300 years.

One year later almost to the day, with arguments concerning the previous wrecks still unsettled, three more vessels were wrecked, one of which sent Lord Zouch and his retainers hurrying to the parish of East Dean, on the other side of Beachy Head. A Dutch vessel had gone ashore at Burlingate, Sussex and, not surprisingly, the lessee of the manor and foreshore, a Mr Payne, claimed the wreck and her cargo. The vessel carried a large quantity of silver specie and in a blatant attempt to get the treasure for himself the Lord Warden, while admitting that the liberty of Cinque Ports wreck extended only to the east side of Beachy Head, argued that 'anciently, the right used to extend beyond Seaford, near Newhaven'. The Dutch factor, Jas Sutton, realising that swift action was needed if his principals, the Vereenigde Oost-Indische Compagnie, were to regain their property, applied directly to the Admiralty Court for recovery of the cargo. As a result, the money reverted to the rightful owners and Lord Zouch was left embarrassed, angry and without the £50,000 which he had hoped to add to his not inconsiderable fortune.

Also at about this time the bark *Johanne* of Bordeaux was lost near the Downs. Monsieur Beauvois, the French merchant concerned, was forced to pay six pounds to regain possession of the vessel's best cable and anchor which the Lord Warden had already claimed as his royalty. The third large wreck, another Dutchman, also lost on the Goodwins with a cargo of deals, netted Lord Zouch £800, the sum put up by Cornellison Bestever of Medenblick to recover his own property!

As trade with the Far East increased so did the numbers of East Indiamen lost en route, a not inconsiderable number of which were wrecked on or around the Goodwins. During the early months of 1618 the *Golden Wagon* was stranded near Dover and the *Blind Fortune* on the sands. Also the *Sampson* of Hoorne, which netted the Lord Warden a further £8,000, and the *Ark Noah* of Hamburg, from which forty casks of cinnamon, four bags of pepper and £4,000 in coin were saved. But these and many others which were to follow were all over-shadowed by the *Anne Lyon*.

In this incident, which occurred in November 1623, Thomas Fulnetby, now sergeant of the Admiralty Court of the Cinque Ports, took possession of some £9,000 in specie, salvaged from the wreck near Sandwich, which he deposited in Deal Castle for safe keeping. Looting of the wreck went unchecked and when requested to use his influence, even Sir Henry Mainwaring refused to help recover goods stolen by the inhabitants of Deal and Sandwich. Indeed, he himself went to Deal Castle in an attempt to persuade the sergeant to cut open the bags of money and so mix the contents that when the owners arrived they would be unable readily to identify their property. It is some indication of the value of the position of Lord Warden that, in the case of the *Anne Lyon*, Lord Zouch received £1,100 for merely returning a quantity of Brazil wood to the owners and a further £2,000 for sugar, cinnamon and other goods. In contrast, when a merchantman was stranded on the Goodwins a month later, but was got off and saved after a week's work by men from Ramsgate, they received £90 between them for their labours.

Not for the first time, several European countries were expressing concern about the numbers of ships being lost on the Goodwin Sands. A beacon or light was first proposed in 1623 and the Dutch, who had lost at least twelve vessels in five years, offered to contribute towards the cost. Secretary Conway instructed Sir Dudley Carleton to inform the States that the Lord Admiral was willing to

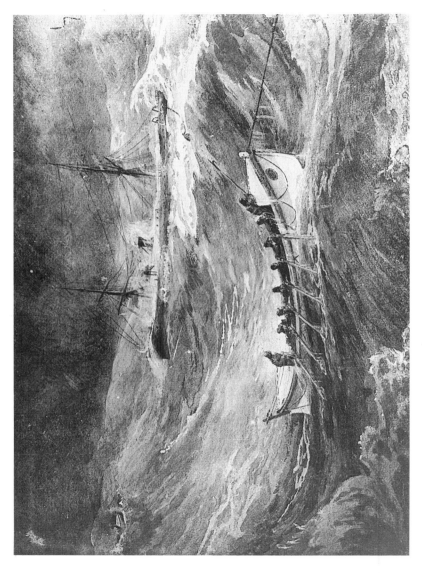

The most famous Kingsdown lifeboat rescue, in which the crew of the s.s. *Sorrento* were saved on 17th December 1872. The Walmer lifeboat *Centurion* (top left) waits in the lee of the wreck.　(RNLI)

erect and maintain a beacon, but since they would derive the greatest benefit, having lost the most ships, they should pay the greater part of its cost. The Dutch were far from happy with this suggestion and perhaps it was as well that nothing came of the scheme since the fearful storm which swept the Downs during 3rd/4th October 1624 would certainly have demolished any such structure.

In this gale, described at the time as 'most terrible, the like of which was never seen', many of the 120 vessels at anchor in the Downs were wrecked and twenty completely vanished. Before the storm had abated, one of two Dunkirk men o'war left in the Downs under guard attempted to escape and was engaged by the flagship of the Dutch Vice-Admiral, Moy Lambert. The Dunkirker, also with an admiral aboard, blew up and was lost with 200 of her crew. Shortly afterwards, the Dutch ship, holed below the waterline, also sank but happily without loss of life. The sinking of these two valuable warships in addition to those lost by storm left the Downs strewn with ground tackle and cannon. Although some Deal men took up six great anchors of 1,000 lb each by 'sweeping' with cables, the cannon required the service of a diver and while there is no documentary proof that this early diver was the Dutchman, Jacob Johnson, there is some evidence to support the belief. Certainly the record of the storm of 1624 contains the first mention of the word 'diver' to be found in the Calendar of Domestic State Papers, and since Johnson used a boat named *Charity* belonging to Sandwich and lived for a time in Kent, this and his later connection with the Duke of Buckingham and salvage operations provides sound grounds for the assumption.

At the time of the storm Lord Zouch was still Lord Warden but was in negotiation with George Villiers, Duke of Buckingham, to sell the appointment for '£1,000 in hand, and £500 a year for life' — another indication of the potential value of the post. Although the warrant for the transfer had not then been signed, Buckingham sought to take immediate advantage of the position by claiming all wreck within the rape of Hastings. Thus when the family of Pelham, hereditary owners of the manor there, instructed Richard Bourne to seize all the wreck that came ashore in their area during the storm, Buckingham claimed it for himself. Whereupon, risking the Duke's wrath, Sir Thomas Williams intervened, reminding the Duke that the patent of transfer had not yet been executed and that until he was officially Lord Warden the matter of wreck was not his concern. A similar dispute arose over the *White Swan* of Hamburg which was wrecked in early July of the same year with a valuable cargo of tin ingots, to be followed soon afterwards by the London ship *Dolphin*. In the case of the *Golden Rose*, another Hamburg vessel, the salvors claimed that she was worth only £4,000 in an attempt to deceive the Lord Warden, but unfortunately for them Buckingham obtained a copy of the original manifest which showed her to be worth nearer £40,000.

Although the Duke of Buckingham enjoyed the proceeds of wreck from the Cinque Ports for only four years before he was assassinated on 23rd August

Remains of stranded wreck on the foreshore north of Sandown Castle. The figure in the photograph stands alongside the stempost. The wide 'pot-bellied' shape and size of timbers suggest a vessel of some size and antiquity, possibly fifteenth – sixteenth century.
(Author's photograph)

Deal boatmen, posing in rough weather oilskins around a beach capstan. One has a 'spyglass' and is on the lookout for wrecks, another smokes his clay pipe upside down.
(Author's collection)

1628, during that time he made determined attempts to establish his rights as Lord Warden in perpetuity. Since he was already Lord High Admiral of England, there was a conflict of maritime jurisdiction which he thought could be used to his advantage. In 1625 he therefore requested, through Sir John Hippisley, to have sent to the Admiralty all records 'bearing upon the extent of the Admiralty jurisdiction of the Cinque Ports; believing it to be from the Shoe Beacon in Essex to Rednore in Sussex. The Admiralty Court in London wish to judge on matters of wrecks in the Downs and deny the Lord Warden's right to floating wrecks unless they are near enough to land to be reached on horseback. The cause is now to be finally determined. Hopes to prove the Lord Warden's rights.'

At the time it was said that Sir George Newman could produce records to prove that the Warden had the right to all goods taken from the sea within 100 miles of the Downs, but there is no evidence of these ever having been produced. Buckingham's concern over floating wreck was brought about by the wreck of the *Golden Rose*. She was carrying wine from St Lucar in Spain and since a dog survived on board she was deemed a derelict and not an actual wreck. Sir Richard Bingley had already made an agreement with the ship's master to take up the ship for a quarter of her profits, which amounted to £10,000, and it was this apparent loss of income that upset the Duke. History reminds us that Buckingham died heavily in debt, so it is little wonder that his main concern was finance.

The surviving records of wreck for the seventeenth century are unfortunately concerned more with ownership than the vessels themselves, so that little detail survives. It is known, however, that of a fleet of five English East India ships returning with indigo, pepper and calico the *Moon* was lost near Dover about 25th September 1625. Buckingham made use of Jacob Johnson, the diver, to salvage the wreck but warned others, 'he is not to be trusted'. It is also on record that the 'greatest ship belonging to the Archduchess has been blown up with a Hollander in the road, also another great ship, laden with victualls', but apart from this entry, dated 21st June 1626, no further details are known.

Another offer to maintain a beacon for the guidance of shipping in the Downs was made in 1629 in the form of a petition to the king. It was presented by Sir John Sackville, William Boswell and others who undertook: '...to erect and maintain a light on the main, on or near the Goodwin, and pray for a grant by patent for forty years, with power to levy certain rates on all vessels passing through the Downs, with salvage on ships delivered from wreck'. Presumably, nothing came of the offer since it is now generally accepted that the first beacon here was the one placed at the North Sand Head in 1795. Meanwhile, wreck continued to follow wreck at regular intervals, usually as the result of storm, and 11th October 1639 saw at least twenty-five vessels lost following a sea battle. Martin Harpertzoon Tromp, the Dutch admiral, was no newcomer to the Downs. During the January of 1637 he was there at anchor with 'twenty sail of tall ships, and two pinnaces', looking for a fight with the French. Two years later the Earl of Suffolk informed the Secretary to the Admiralty, Mr Windebank, that:

A bow view of the wooden barque *Vega*, stranded on the beach at Deal, c1880, believed to have been refloated and saved.   (Franklin Studio, Deal)

'At this instant the Spaniards and the Hollanders are in a bloody fight in the Downs. The Admiral of Holland began the fight, and there are already run ashore six Lubeckers, with more to follow...there are some ships come on shore near the castles, and I saw two of the Spanish on fire close under Walmer Castle ...a list of Spanish ships ashore, burnt or sunk, they number twenty-five, including the Vice-Admiral Royal sunk.'

Thirteen years later a similar battle took place between the English fleet, commanded by Blake, and the Dutch, led by De Ruyter and De Witte. It began at 3 p.m. on 28th September 1652, off the North Foreland, when the Dutch were chased to the back of the Goodwins. In all, three Dutch men o' war were sunk and one blown up but the victory cost the English 300 dead and as many wounded. After this engagement the Dutch returned home but were back again with seventy-seven new warships under the command of Van Tromp on 29th November the same year. A severe storm delayed the second battle for one day, after which the fleets closed and the Dutch were defeated for a second time with a fearful loss of life on both sides, a total of three vessels being sunk.

Although a great many warships were to fall victim to the Goodwins during the next three centuries there is only one instance of a man o' war being lost on the Brake Sand, just south of Ramsgate. This was the 38-gun *Princess Maria*, captured from the Dutch in 1652. Commanded by Captain Grymesditch, she came into the Downs on 8th February 1658 to collect a pilot to take her to Harwich. A Deal man, William Knight, came aboard but in getting the ship to sea he failed to notice a change in the wind and the tide stranded her on the Brake. Being old and worm-eaten she soon bilged and sank in a position easily accessible from the shore. Searchers were appointed to visit every house in Deal to look for pieces of the wreck and some were found as far afield as Broadstairs and Margate. Before she sank her masts were cut away and, once overboard, were immediately seized by wreckers who, with a boat at each end, proceeded to cut away as much as they could carry. Her guns after salvage were valued at £800 and the salvors were awarded one-sixth of this figure.

Other wrecks in the latter half of the seventeenth century included three ships lost on the Goodwins in January 1669. One of these, the *John*, carried wine from the Canaries, two chests of gold dust, elephants' teeth and dye wood. Homeward bound for London from Guinea her crew took to the boats, leaving an Irish and a Negro boy aboard to their fate. Later, the wreck caught fire and local boats were able to reach her and save the two youths.

Of the other vessels lost at the same time, one was from Ostend and carried a rich cargo which included linen cloth. One of her passengers who managed to reach shore in the ship's boat was a governor on his way to Madrid as a prisoner to be charged with high treason. In November 1670 a Dutch and a Flemish East Indiaman were both lost on the Goodwins. The name of the Flemish vessel is not recorded, but the Dutch VOC ship was the *Wapen Van Vlissingen*, an outward bound vessel of 725 tons, of the Zeeland chamber, carrying a considerable quantity of gold specie, which was never recovered. Three months later, in

The barque *Vega* stranded on the beach at Deal, c1880. (Franklin Studio, Deal)

March 1671, during test firing of cannon recovered from the wrecks at Deal dockyard, one of them burst. Metal was sent flying over the houses in all directions but no one was hurt. Another warship, the 5th rate *Nightingale*, became a total loss on the Goodwins on 18th January 1674, along with a Dutch caper of twelve guns which the *Nightingale* had captured in the Channel on the previous day. In the following year, on 24th August, the *Florentine* of London stranded and was lost on the west face of the Goodwins but whether or not her cargo of lead was salvaged is not recorded. Her loss is thought to have been caused by a freak tidal movement such as occurs during earth tremors. She came into the Downs at about 11 p.m. and anchored in four fathoms of water, only to find an hour or so later that the water had disappeared, leaving the vessel lying on clean sand. This so strained her timbers that she filled and sank on the flood tide and within two hours her hull was completely submerged, not even her masts being visible. Her cargo was thought to be stock-fish en route from Bergen to the Straits but her master and owner, Capt Gould, told the locals that she was also carrying some thirty tons of lead in ingots of over 200lb each.

One of the many secrets concerning the Goodwins and shipwreck is that of HM frigate *Sedgmore*, a 4th rate 50-gun ship which stranded near the South

Foreland on 2nd January 1689. The weather precluded any immediate assistance being sent and she went to pieces. A London newspaper, the 'Orange Gazette', reported that she carried almost £200,000 in merchant's bullion which was being brought to England from Spain. Salvage reports, however, while stating that her crew, guns and rigging had been saved, made no mention of any money. Four years later and less than four miles from the same location another English warship came to grief. This was the much larger *Windsor Castle*, a 90-gun 2nd rate built in 1678. On passage from the Nore to the Downs, she ran aground on the South Sand Head on 29th April 1693 solely because of carelessness on the part of her pilot. Although no lives were lost, she became a total wreck after the greater part of her stores and provisions had been salvaged.

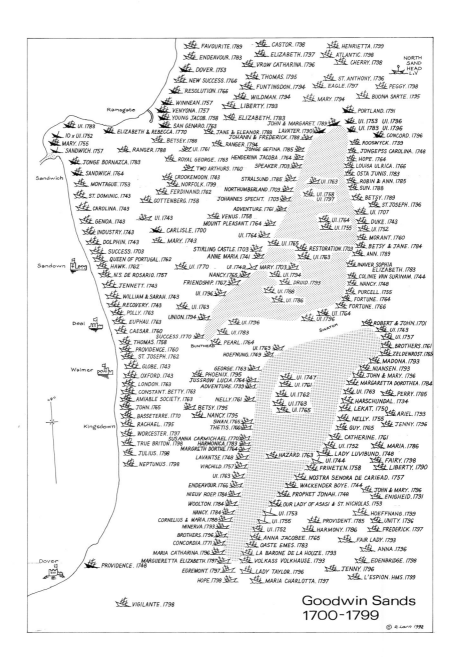

Goodwin Sands
1700-1799

© R. Larn 1992

Chapter Three

'THE LATE TERRIBLE TEMPEST': 1700-1799

At 8.30 a.m. on 19th September 1700 Richard Hitchcock, the gunners' servant on board HMS *Carlisle*, reached the frigate's mizzen topmast head, and started to haul down the ship's pennant as ordered by the duty officer. All around other warships were at anchor, the decks of some deserted, others busy as Admiral Sir George Rooke prepared to lead part of the fleet up river to Sheerness. On board the *Carlisle*, a 48-gun ship of 700 tons and one of the vessels ordered to remain in the Downs, all was quiet. Of her complement of 164, thirty-two were ashore on ship's business including Capt Francis Dove; Christopher Short, senior gunner; James Oswald, carpenter; William Hampton, surgeon; and the Rt Hon Burton, purser, the latter at Dover inspecting provisions and stores. On deck Symond Flew, the ship's sailing master, and his son, a lieutenant in the same vessel, were keeping watch together while Midshipman Pearsey was in charge of the ship's boats. These were under orders to go to Ramsgate within the hour to collect the captain and some fresh vegetables. This left approximately 128 men engaged in various duties throughout the ship, the majority between decks, and it can only be presumed that it was one of these who was responsible for the ensuing disaster.

Having completed his task and wrapped the flag around his waist in readiness for his return to the quarterdeck, Hitchcock paused for a last look at the coast, some four or five miles distant. Then suddenly without warning the entire ship exploded beneath him with a tremendous roar and he was hurled from his lofty perch in a great sweeping arc to fall into the sea some distance clear of the wreck. The entire ship vanished in an instant and the stunned crews of the boats, which having been some distance from the warship at the time fortunately survived the blast, returned to rescue the survivors seen struggling amongst the mass of floating timber and rigging. Of the 128 men aboard at the time, a total of 124 were killed outright. The cause of the disaster was never established but it was assumed that someone had been in the magazine, stealing gunpowder, and at the subsequent court martial held on board the 48-gun 4th rate HMS *Hampshire* in the Downs on 27th September the captain, officers and men were completely exonerated. It is worth noting that prior to the reduction of the navy as an economy measure after the Peace of Ryswick in 1697, every warship carried a yeoman of the powder room. He was completely responsible for all explosives and apart from the ship's gunner was the only rating allowed inside the magazine. The position was re-established on 26th September, the day before the court martial and as a direct result of this unfortunate disaster.

Following the inquiry the Admiralty requested Trinity House to carry out a survey of the wreck to establish its exact position and condition and to make recommendations as to its dispersal. The survey was completed and a report submitted on 11th October 1700. It read as follows:

'...we having, with all exactness we were capable of at this season, sounded upon and about the said wreck, do humbly report to their Lordships, that the said wreck lies in about seven fathoms at low water. The ground, a kind of blue clay, with a few stones on the top of it; with her stern to the southward, and lying North and by West, and South and by East, the South Foreland bearing South and by West ½ West, and the North Foreland, North and by West. The leading mark to find the wreck is, to keep the Upper Deal windmill a little open to the southward of that castle. The thwart mark is a reddish brick stable at the North end of the town, which is to be kept half a ship's length open to the southward of a windmill standing up in the country, and called Wingeham Hill.

'That the after part of the said wreck as far forward as the bulkhead of the quarterdeck, we judge to remain whole, the taffrail being but 4 feet under water at a low ebb. The rest of the ship forward, we believe to be blown abroad, excepting the floors and some of the futtocks, which do remain about 12 feet above the ground. That the said wreck, in the posture it is at present, must needs be dangerous to ships passing into and out of the Downs, as lying in the best of the Road. That it may be expected the sea and tides, if it happens to blow hard from the north or south upon spring tides will, in some short time, break away the upper works at least, of the said wreck as it hath, in a manner, wholly done those of the merchantmen sunk by the storm in the year 1689/90, though some remains thereof, or of some others, are sometimes met with by those that sweep for anchors, which must doubtless cut or damnify the cables of ships lying in that Road.

'That the after part of the wreck which yet sits whole, or at least, the upper works, may be blown up, which in our opinion ought to be done as soon as may be, and that the bottom, or what part afterwards remains, may be swept, and being lifted as it may, by four vessels of about 100 tons each, may be carried into shoal water. And when that is done, if not before, her guns and cables may undoubtedly be taken up in a proper season of the year. But what the charge of blowing up or weighing the said wreck as proposed, it is impossible to make any reasonable calculation of, since there is no answering for the weather or other accidents that may attend a work of this nature. In the meantime...a distinguishable buoy be laid on the broadside of the wreck, if not one on each side.'

The name *Carlisle* was promptly branded by the fleet as being unlucky, since the frigate lost in the vicinity of the North Sand Head was only a little over four years old, having replaced a namesake wrecked in January 1696 on the

Shipwash. Since those two disasters the name has only once been given to a British warship.

To attempt comparison between the strength and ferocity of individual storms is always difficult and if a century or more has elapsed between particular gales it is impossible to relate them, simply because methods of assessment as well as the materials and methods of construction of vessels and dwellings have drastically changed in the interim. Nevertheless, it is possible that the British Isles has never before or since experienced a storm to equal that of November 1703. At the time it was described by reliable witnesses as 'the greatest, longest and most severe storm that ever the world saw'. Recalling the devastation wrought by tropical cyclones and hurricanes, this statement is, no doubt, an exaggeration, but there is no questioning the fact that the great storm of 1703 left a trail of death and damage throughout England and the Low Countries the like of which had never before been seen.

Although he was in prison at the time, it was Daniel Defoe who published a record of that disastrous week and in his booklet 'The Storm' he describes it as 'the late terrible tempest'. In Kent alone one thousand dwelling houses and barns were blown flat; chimney stacks came down in their hundreds of thousands, killing a great many people in their beds; whilst in Holland, where the tide rose 6 to 8 feet above normal, over a 1,000 lives were lost and cattle beyond number died in the inundation. Parts of Yorkshire and Lincoln suffered severe earthquakes, tremors were felt the length of the country and for a whole week the wind blew with incredible force. At sea the damage to shipping and on the coast could only be described as phenomenal and among the many victims was the famous Eddystone lighthouse which was completely destroyed along with its designer and builder, Henry Winstanley. In the Thames ships were blown all the way from Execution Dock to Limehouse Hole and all but four finished up ashore in the Bight. Here they were thrown together bow to stern, one upon another, until they ground each other to pieces in such a manner 'as one would have thought to be impossible', to quote a London broadsheet. Above London Bridge no less than 500 wherries were lost and sixty barges sank in the vicinity of Hammersmith alone. Meanwhile in the city itself so many tiles were stripped from the rooftops that their prices rose overnight from a guinea a thousand to over £6.

As to events in the Downs and on the Goodwin Sands, the most detailed eye-witness account surviving is that of James Adams. He was a passenger aboard a merchantman at anchor in the Downs, awaiting an opportunity to sail for Portsmouth and thence to Lisbon. Adams recorded not only events concerning his own ship but others around him and it was he who witnessed the destruction of so many naval ships. The duration of the storm overall was thirteen days, with gales beginning on Friday 19th November and lasting for approximately three days. This was followed by a period of relative calm, with the wind decreasing to probably force 4/5 by today's reckoning, then increasing steadily from Thursday

The *Star of the Ocean*, one of 47 sailing vessels blown ashore or wrecked in the terrible gales of November 1877, which lasted for two weeks. This wreck took place south of Walmer Castle, 23rd/24th November.   (Deal Maritime Museum)

25th November onwards so that it was not until the 31st that conditions returned to a seasonal normal.

Thinking that the worst was over, a fleet of English men o' war under the command of Sir Clowdisley Shovell came into the Downs on 25th November and anchored. There was a little rain that morning, with the wind between south-by-east and south, veering to south-west as night fell and steadily increasing in strength. Several warships then put to sea rather than risk being blown onto the Goodwins but at least one vessel, a Dutchman, was lost with all hands on the sands that night. During the morning of 26th November the warships rejoined the fleet but still the wind increased until the strength was such that it seemed inconceivable it could get any worse. The ship from which Adams witnessed the storm had only recently been launched and at first her new anchors and cables were able to hold her in position. He reports that whole seas — not just breakers — went clean over her so that the crew feared she would founder where she lay. As that day progressed and the wind strength continued to increase, every warship struck her topmasts and rode at anchor with her two best cables connected end on end, prepared for the worst.

Then, at about 1 a.m. on 27th November, several ships began to drag their anchors. Some cut away their mainmasts in a vain attempt to reduce wind resistance, but with the wind now at hurricane force there was nothing else they could do to help themselves. By 2 a.m. distress guns were booming out from all directions and lights were shown calling for assistance, but to no avail. Adams personally witnessed the *Northumberland* and the *Mary* disappear as they dragged onto the Goodwins and were lost, but he appears to have missed the *Restoration* even though the sky was now ablaze with sheet lightning and some events were as clear as if seen by day. The *Northumberland*, a 3rd rate man o' war carrying seventy guns and commanded by Capt Greenaway, was wrecked with the loss of every one of her 253 crew. A smaller 4th rate, the *Mary*, originally built as the *Speaker* in 1649, was flying the flag of Rear-Admiral Beaumont. She also went to pieces on the sands that night, taking with her 272 men including the admiral. Her captain, Edward Hopson, and the ship's purser were both ashore at the time and only one man escaped from the wreck alive.

No sooner had the *Mary* gone down than another man o' war, driven before the wind, narrowly missed the merchant vessel on board of which Adams was clinging to the shrouds. This latest victim of the storm was the dismasted *Stirling Castle*, another 3rd rate of seventy guns, which continued to fire a cannon as a distress signal every half-minute right up until the moment she struck. She also became a total loss and only seventy of her crew of 349 were saved, including her 3rd lieutenant, chaplain, cook, surgeon's mate and four marine captains.

Thomas Atkins, a seaman from the *Mary* and her sole survivor, had a most remarkable escape. He was washed clean off the *Mary* as she broke up and whilst in the water clinging to a piece of timber saw Rear-Admiral Beaumont leave the ship's quarterdeck and drown. A freak wave then flung Atkins bodily on to the upper deck of the *Stirling Castle* as she drove past. Minutes later she too went ashore and Atkins was shipwrecked for a second time in as many minutes. Once again the sea hurled him overboard, only this time he fell directly into the one ship's boat still intact and eventually reached the shore almost unconscious from exposure.

At what time the *Restoration* came to grief is not known as there were no survivors from her crew of 386. Commanded by Capt Fleetwood Emes, she also was a 3rd rate armed with seventy guns and it was not until the storms abated and men were able to search around the Goodwins that her shattered hulk was located. At the same time as the *Stirling Castle* drove past Adams's vessel two merchantmen broke adrift from their cables; one of them struck a pink and the two ships sank with their rigging entangled, but the other managed to make it to the open sea.

Aboard the vessel from which Adams had seen so much destruction the crew had already cut down her masts, but it was obvious that her cables would not hold much longer. She therefore slipped her anchors and, with only a tarpaulin flying from the stump of the mizzen ran before the wind, since crippled though she was the open sea was preferable to the certain death offered by the

An unidentified wreck off Deal beach in 1896. Little can be gleaned from this photograph except that she was a 3-masted square-rigged wooden vessel, with painted gunports, her name obscured by the stern boat.   (National Maritime Museum)

Goodwin Sands. For four days they were blown northward with no idea as to their position, nor any sight of land. Eventually, a small pilot boat was sighted ahead, the master of which informed them that the coast of Norway was only a few miles to the east of them. They were assisted to an anchorage where they spent several weeks repairing the storm damage before returning to the Downs and, later, resuming their original voyage.

The navy in particular suffered terrible losses as a result of the storm. On the Goodwins alone four major ships and 1,190 lives were lost, whilst in the Yarmouth Roads the *Reserve* was wrecked and 258 drowned. In Holland both the *Vigo* and the bomb vessel *Mortar* were lost with eight men between them. The *Eagle*, advise boat, at Selsey, and the *Resolution*, at Pemsey, both sank, after their crews had been saved; as did the *Newcastle*, near Chichester, with 229 dead and the *Canterbury*, near Bristol, with the loss of her captain and twenty-five of her crew. Other victims included the Portsmouth at the Nore, with the loss of forty-four men, and the *Vanguard*, overset at Chatham. The grim total was thirteen ships and almost 2,000 officers and men, the greatest single loss by storm or battle in the entire history of the Royal Navy. And the toll might have been greater had not HMS *Prince George* (Vice-Admiral Leake), *Essex*, *Shrewsbury, Eagle, Content, Chatham, Assistance, Mary*, galley, and the fireship

Hunter all escaped to the open sea. The 80-gun 3rd rate *Nassau*, to be wrecked on the Kentish coast three years later, survived the storm by having her mainmast cut down, whereas the *Guardland, Dunwich* and *Postillian* lost all their masts. Of the 160 sail at anchor in the Downs on the day prior to 27th November, only seventy were still afloat twenty-four hours later and many of those lost could be seen floating keel uppermost.

In particular, the 2nd rate *Association* had a lucky escape. At the height of the storm she was at anchor off the Long Sand Head, in the Thames, under the command of Capt Canning, with Sir Stafford Fairborne, Vice-Admiral of the Red, aboard. She broke adrift from her two bow anchors at 5 a.m. on the Friday morning and drove towards the Galloper Sand. In the shallows where at times there was less than 12 feet of water between her keel and the seabed, a tremendous sea struck her starboard side breaking in several gun half-ports and the main entering port, snapping her tiller and, minutes later, tearing her rudder clean off. The admiral ordered the sheet anchor to be dropped and her mainmast cut down and for a time she rode more easily. Then her cable parted and she drove clean over the Galloper, leaking so badly from seams and damage that four chain and one hand pump had to be manned and kept going day and night. In this crippled condition the wind blew her across to Flanders, then up the coast to Holland until she managed to anchor off Heligoland at the mouth of the River Elbe. Some six days later, on 4th December, the *Association* met with another storm almost as violent as that encountered in the Thames and again lost her anchor and cable and went adrift. Again, she was drawn north and not until the coast of Norway had been sighted did she eventually manage to put into the Swedish port of Gottenbourgh, now known as Göteborg. She was by then in desperate straits, being without a single anchor or cable, lacking firewood or candles, and the crew rationed to a quart of water per man. It was 23rd January 1704 before she arrived back at the Nore having lost twenty-eight men through sickness since leaving the Thames and long since given up by the Admiralty as lost.

So little detailed information survives of what can only be described, because of their frequency, as 'common everyday shipwrecks' during the eighteenth century that such record as remains is little more than a monotonous list of incidents and dates. Thus almost a whole century of shipwreck history, with all that it implied, has virtually been lost and only occasionally is the corner of the veil lifted, perhaps in a letter or an Admiralty report. Only then do we get a brief glimpse of the suffering and hardship inflicted upon families when either the bread-winner or a close relative was drowned. Or of the financial ruin which so often followed a shipwreck as the cargo of yet another vessel spewed out over the Goodwins to join countless others that had gone before. One can only assume that with shipwrecks so numerous and life so cheap there seemed little point in those days in bothering to record the details.

Although the privateer lost on the sands in December 1707 with the death of all sixty of its crew was a Dunkirker, the greater proportion of wrecks in this

The three masted barque *Richard & Harriet* from which the Kingsdown lifeboat saved seven lives on 11th January 1871.
(Franklin Studio, Deal)

period were Dutch-owned. Two such losses were the *Harschundal* in 1734 and the *Rooswyck* in 1739. The latter, bound for Batavia, was lost with every one of her 200 passengers and crew, as well as a large quantity of specie. Many pieces of wreckage were found floating in the Downs, including packets of letters addressed to Vereenigde Oost-Indische Compagnie officials in the Far East. An interesting brass bell, marked *Johannes Specht*, hung in the belfry of the 'Feed My Lambs' school at Deal for 130 years. In 1960 when the structure collapsed the bell was put away in a coalshed and forgotten. It reappeared only when it was donated to the museum at Deal and for a time was thought to have come from a wreck, but this is unlikely.

Although in no way comparable with the storm of 1703, another fearful gale, this time from the north-east, struck the east coast and Kent on 23rd/25th February 1743 causing the total loss of at least twelve vessels in the Downs. Two convoys were at anchor when the gale struck. One was bound for Gibraltar and the Straits, the other for America, and both had been delayed because escorts were not available. Of the southbound vessels, all carrying cargoes of victuals for the garrison on the 'Rock', the *Oxford*, Capt Lamont, the *Genoa,* Capt Sinnot, and the *Carolina*, Capt Spillman, were victims. In addition to the three captains, a total of forty-nine men were lost. Five ships of the American convoy were driven ashore between Sandwich and Walmer, these being the *Globe*; the *William & Sarah*; the *Mary*; the *Industry* and the *Crookendon*, all of which had sailed from London.

During 1744, there were more Dutch ships lost on the Goodwins, these being the *Colinie Van Surinam* in January and an unidentified dogger and the *Wackender Boye*, both on 26th October. The crew of the former managed to scramble into one of their own boats and get clear of the wreck, but were then driven out to sea where they spent two miserable nights and days adrift in the Channel until picked up by a Genoese vessel and landed at Portsmouth. Of the few personal stories that emerge from such wrecks one worth recording concerned the *Fanny*, an English ship, and a large French privateer of some thirty guns. Early in 1747 a collier was taken by the Frenchman as a prize off the coast of Kent and, after transferring passengers and crew, sent to the bottom. Four days later she sighted the *Fanny* and gave chase. Capt Blakeley evaded capture for over eleven hours, finally taking his ship clean over the Goodwins at high water. In close pursuit the Frenchman followed him, became stranded and was finally wrecked. Only thirteen survivors from the two crews on board escaped and one can well imagine the astonishment of the English captain of the *Fanny* when he discovered his wife amongst them, she having been a passenger aboard the collier taken earlier.

Although the local boatmen were active at these and many other wrecks, helping others when they could but first and foremost helping themselves, they did not always come off best for every hand was against them. On many occasions Deal and Ramsgate boatmen lost companions, even their boats, in boarding a wreck but such were the rewards that the risks were considered worth taking. If not engaged in fishing or wrecking, the only alternative was smuggling and the Downs men were notorious for bringing in contraband at every available opportunity. In fact it was almost impossible to resist becoming a smuggler in the Downs. It was only a two-hour passage across the Channel by galley to France or the Channel Isles, and the occupation was considered so commonplace and lacking in odium that the very first entry in the register of deaths for St George's 'Chapel of Ease' at Deal describes a man's profession as that of 'smuggler'. Even as late as the twentieth century there was open war between boatmen and customs officers and on one occasion Thomas Adams, nick-named 'Julia' Adams, a well known character and pilot and the last of the old heavy-weather boatmen, was under suspicion of smuggling and of having caused the death of an excise officer. This official was said to have been picked up by his ears and then hurled down a flight of steps.

The church of St George has its roots deep in the Downs, since it was the large seafaring population of Deal in 1706 that brought about the need for a new place of worship. Until then the parish church had sufficed but it was more than a mile from the town, a distance sufficient sorely to test the piety of residents and seamen alike. The Navy in particular were keen to see a new church built at Lower Deal and several wealthy admirals and commanders offered to contribute towards the cost. A strong advocate of the proposal was Thomas Powell, mayor of Deal for many years, but he was far from popular with some factions and both he and the local boatmen were vilified in a savage satire similar in theme to that of Daniel Defoe's, who in 1705 wrote, '…lending to vessels in distress a predatory succor, more ruinous to them than the angry elements that assailed them'.

The satire, entitled 'Deal in an Uproar', read:

> 'In sight of treacherous Goodwins' faithless sands
> An impious and remorseless town there stands,
> Peopled by men whose cruelties of mind
> Make them the savages of human kind:
> Wretches abandoned to the worst of crimes
> That e'er were practised in most guilty times:
> Deal is its name, to mariners well known,
> Where there is not a vice but what's its own:
> But fraud, oppression, theft and rapine reign
> With every act of wickedness for gain
> As hatchets they with justice bibles call
> Rising by shipwreck that makes others fall…'

Yet had it not been for Powell's entreaties to the Lord Archbishop of Canterbury in 1703, the money even to start building St George's might never have been raised. A promise by the bishop to donate the sum of £100 was sufficient to encourage local subscriptions and money was also promised from the fleet once the building had reached a height of 9 feet above ground level. Unfortunately the death of Sir Clowdisley Shovell by shipwreck amongst the Isles of Scilly in 1707 denied them his promised contribution which would have been substantial and thereafter all work ceased for the better part of two years. Then Powell again went to London, visited Lambeth Palace for the second time and was rewarded with a renewed assurance that the £100 would be available when required. Building then recommenced and eventually the new town church was completed, to be used by countless generations of seamen ever since.

Of the dozen or so Dutch and English East Indiamen known to have been lost on the sands, three VOC ships went ashore from the same outward bound convoy on 19th February 1736, of which only one escaped. The 600-ton *Buis*, Capt Hendrik Orsel, was particularly lucky, having left the Texel for Batavia on 12th December but in company with the other vessels was forced back by bad weather. They sailed again on the 18th, going ashore on the Goodwins the following day. The *Buis* lost 102 seamen, forty-four soldiers and nine tradesmen — a total of 155 of her complement of 190. The Dutch records suggest that many of these men in fact deserted, so got ashore in boats presumably. Weather conditions must have been exceptional that year, since the *Buis* remained on the sands intact for over a month before being refloated, when she anchored in the Downs. Whilst there 111 replacement Dutch seamen and 28 soldiers joined, and she sailed for the Far East, still badly damaged, on 5th May 1736. The 850-ton *Loosdrecht*, of Amsterdam, Capt Willem Vroom, and the 850-ton *Meermond* also of Amsterdam, Capt Jakob Gosen Hoogstad, were less fortunate, both being lost with some 250 men each and their valuable cargo and specie. Four years later the Amsterdam merchants suffered yet another loss when the outward bound 850-ton *Rooswijk*, Capt Daniel Ronzieres, was lost with all hands and yet more gold, silver and cargo.

Although the loss of one particular Spanish ship near Sandown Castle on 20th December 1757 was in itself no more significant than any one of the other forty-five known losses since 1750, it is worthy of record for the ship's name alone. On passage from London to Terceria, the *Nostra Senora de Rosario, St Anna, St Antonio et St Almas* was stranded and bilged in a gale, eventually going to pieces where she lay. Surely no other wreck in the Downs ever had so splendid a title? Five years later another Spanish-built vessel came to grief in the Little Downs. This was the 60-gun 4th rate *San Genaro*, a man o' war captured by the British at Havana in 1762. The cause of her loss is obscure as she appears to have sunk while at anchor. Among foreign vessels lost on the Goodwins during that century Dutch ships continued to predominate and among them were two from Amsterdam carrying corn and bale goods, to and from Surinam respectively, both lost on or about 20th December 1763. A total of nine English HEIC (Honourable East India Company) ships have been lost around the Goodwins and the Isle of Thanet, of which only the 499-ton *Earl of Holdness* was wrecked in the Downs. She drove from her anchors in a gale on 11th January 1764, whilst outward bound for Madras, and was lost on Sandwich Flats. Of the Dutch ships, the *Henderina Jacoba* was lost on 10th October 1764; two more, both

The dismasted barque *Ornew* at anchor off Deal beach, after having been ashore on the Goodwin Sands July 1895 and refloated. She was later towed to Ramsgate and repaired.
(National Maritime Museum)

unidentified, on 21st November of the same year; the *Zeldenrost*, with glass from Dieppe, on 15th May 1765; a snow, carrying wine and brandy, on 10th September, and the *Anna Jacobee* some seven days later. One particularly rich wreck was the *Oostereem*, of 1,150 tons, a hired-in VOC ship, previously named the *Venus*, which left the Texel under the command of Capt Axel Land on 17th January 1783 flying her old Prussian flag in the hope the disguise would save her being captured by the English as a prize. Between 7.00 and 8.00 p.m. on 21st January she went on the sands and was obliged to fire distress guns. The Deal boatmen went out in their hundreds, but were prevented from boarding by the armed soldiers on board, so that her cargo of bale goods, gunpowder, war stores, cannon, pistols, muskets and almost £20,000 in pillar dollars remained intact. Capt Land and her crew remained aboard for a day and a night; then, with the weather deteriorating and the ship literally going to pieces beneath their feet, they took to their own boats, bringing with them all the specie which they placed in the charge of the Dutch Consul. That same night the *Oostereem* became a total wreck, and virtually nothing of her cargo was saved.

Incidentally, the authors of two earlier books on the history of the Downs and Goodwin Sands area state that another rich Dutch East Indiaman, the *Osta Junis*, was wrecked there on 12th July 1783. One author states 'she was likewise salvaged by Deal boatmen who found that she contained more than three times the amount of specie saved four months earlier'. In fact, however, Deal boatmen did not salvage the treasure from the *Oostereem* nor is there any reference in official records or contemporary newspapers to any such incident as the wreck of the *Osta Junis* which would hardly have gone unnoticed. Since it is altogether too much of a coincidence that two such ships should be lost more or less at the same time and place, the similarity between their names suggests they are one and the same.

Ten years in time and forty-two shipwrecks later the *Madona* was lost on the Goodwins. Although she was a large ship, in common with so many hundreds of others almost nothing is known about her. In fact, the only reference is preserved in a letter dated 13th November 1793 from John Iggulden, who wrote from Deal to Messrs Cobb & Co, bankers and agents at Margate, informing them: 'Nothing of any consequence has been brought on shore at this place from the ship *Madona*. Some of the rigging and a few articles of that kind are to be sure being landed, but so trifling is it that I did not deem it worth the trouble of claiming'.

Perhaps the *Madona* and many other vessels might have been saved had the Goodwins been marked at night with some sort of beacon or light. True that the Brake Sand was buoyed in 1791 with a red float at the southern end and a black one to the north, but despite early attempts by the Dutch merchants in 1623, and by Lord Killigrew sometime later, nothing was done to illuminate this hazard until 1795. In that year Trinity House placed the first light vessel at the North Sand Head, reputedly at the suggestion of a Henry Taylor, and as the Brethren paid him the sum of £500 there must be some truth in the matter though his idea was hardly original. Since a much smaller proportion of the ships using the Downs entered and left by the south channel, thirty-seven years were to pass before a similar light was placed on the South Sand Head. During that period at least seventy-four vessels came to grief here including the *Hoeffnang*. This was a large Dutch vessel bound from Hamburg to Malaga with a cargo of staves which went onto the Goodwins on 13th June 1799. A Ramsgate mackerel boat, already at sea, went to her assistance and in their haste to lay hands on anything of value her six crew left their small boat unattended, which broke adrift leaving them stranded. That night the wind increased and in the early hours the *Hoeffnang* went to pieces leaving twenty survivors clinging to wreckage. A Deal boat found them drifting out to sea and landed them safely at Dover.

The closing months of the eighteenth century saw two more ships lost: the *Norfolk*, Master Riley, from King's Lynn to Bridport, which struck Ramsgate pierhead such a blow whilst entering that she stove in her bows and sank after drifting clear. The other wreck was the frigate *Espion* which had previously belonged to the French. Originally named *Atalante*, this 36-gun 5th rater had been taken as a prize off Cork by the *Swiftsure* on 7th May 1794. At 1 a.m. on 17th November 1799, while in charge of a pilot, she stranded on the sands at high water and as the tide dropped had to be shored up with spars and other timbers to prevent her falling on her beam ends. She carried a large number of Russian troops and these were all ferried across to the troopship HMS *Roebuck* and the *Overyssel* by Deal boatmen. The wreck remained upright until 2 p.m. when the flood tide swung her round, her bow now pointing north, after which she began to heel over. Her loss was a serious matter as the English were hastily withdrawing troops from the continent, the 63rd and 69th Regiments of Foot and the 7th, 11th and 15th Dragoons having arrived the same day as the Russians. By 11th November the *Espion* was lying on her side, bilged and a total loss. Her stores and some guns were taken out and she was then abandoned to the winter gales. A court-martial was convened aboard the *Overyssel*, a 3rd rate Dutch prize, from the deck of which the wreck of the *Espion* could be seen only too clearly. Although Capt Rose was acquitted, an unfortunate ship's master was suspended and the pilot, found guilty of gross neglect, was sentenced to six months and one day in prison and forbidden ever to act as a pilot again.

Chapter Four

A LIGHT FOR ALL NATIONS: 1800-1854

By the closing years of the eighteenth century, the British army had been driven out of the Low Countries to the sound of the Marseillaise. The navy, for a time at least, had lost the nation's confidence, having twice mutinied as well as being virtually excluded from the Mediterranean and 40,000 English troops lay dead in the West Indies. With Bonaparte in Egypt, and having captured Malta in passing, and intent on opening an overland route to India, it took a British victory at the Battle of the Nile to reverse the Emperor's oriental ambitions and to restore Britain's mastery of the seas. There followed many years of uncertainty; of blockade and counter-blockade, war and peace, in which the British navy alone stood between England and Napoleon's invasion fleet.

Throughout this period the Downs was an anchorage of inestimable value, a 'bolt-hole' for warships blockading the French ports should weather or enemy prove too strong. It was also a point from which the 'narrows' could be closely guarded and where ships could form convoy before venturing out into the Channel. The volume of seaborne traffic increased a hundredfold almost overnight as frigates, transports, huge men o' war and despatch boats alike arrived and departed almost hourly, so that at times as many as 400 sail lay at anchor. At the same time coasters in their hundreds passed through the Downs, hugging the coast, and keeping the fleet and the royal dockyards supplied with provisions, beer, pipe staves and armament stores. Two such vessels were the brig *Bell* and the ship *William & John*, both from Deptford and bound for Plymouth. A great gale from the south-west caused both ships to part their cables on 24th January 1800, the *Bell* going ashore near the old No.2 Battery, north of Deal, and the *William & John* on Sandwich Flats. Although the *Bell* was eventually refloated and taken to Ramsgate, the *William & John* could not be saved despite Capt Jackson having ordered both main and mizzen masts to be cut down. The wreck went to pieces in the shallows where some 4,000 bags of ship's biscuit and 22,000 staves floated out to be fought over on the beach by local wreckers. A Deal man, John Barnett, whose boat had been alongside when the ship parted her cables, was the only casualty. In his haste to return aboard his own craft he slipped, fell into the sea and was drowned. Before the year was out a succession of vessels of all nationalities had fallen foul of the Goodwins, including the *Grasston Bothmer*, about 8th April; the *Indiana* on 14th April; the *Lord Donoughmore* on 20th May; the *Little John* on 24th October; the *American Hero* on 11th November and the *Niagra* and the *Amphion*, both about 19th December.

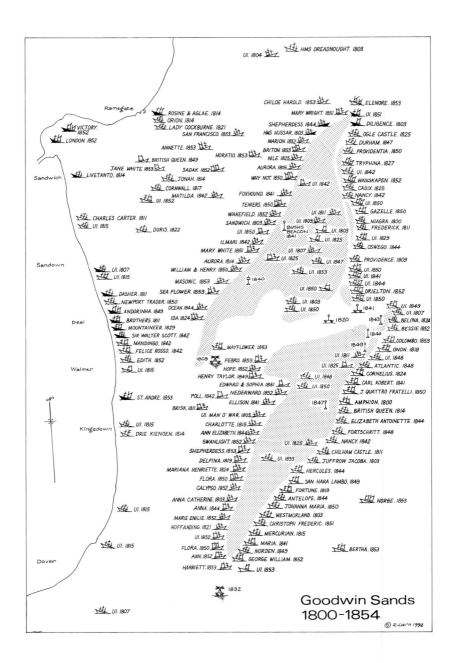

Goodwin Sands
1800-1854

As the blockade of French ports intensified so demands on men and ships increased and although the almost continuous seatime thus involved kept the English fleet at the peak of readiness — a fact shortly to be proven at Trafalgar — it was a soul-destroying duty for the crews who became both weary and despondent. It is not therefore surprising that a fair number of warships and other armed vessels were among the casualties that became stranded or met an untimely end in the vicinity of the Downs. The 5th rate frigate *Hussar* of 1,043 tons and carrying thirty-eight guns was one such victim. She went ashore on the inner face of the North Sand Head during the forenoon of 29th May 1803. Although refloated without suffering serious damage two tides later, after which she continued towards Brest to join the offshore fleet, none of her crew were to see England again. In February 1804 she was wrecked in the Bay of Biscay with the loss of all hands. An entry in the 'Gentleman's Magazine' of 1803 reports, 'The old frigate *Dreadnought* foundered three leagues due south of the North Foreland', but this report cannot now be substantiated. No vessel of this name appears in fleet lists of the period, though there was a 4th rate, the sixty-gun *Dreadnought* built in 1742, which was sold out of service in 1784. If she was the vessel in question then it is possible that she had been converted into a privateer. The stated position of the loss of this then sixty-year-old warship is clear of the Goodwin Fork, somewhere in Trinity Bay, a location where any wreck would quickly become engulfed by sand. A Dutch warship was also reported as having been 'cast-away' at the same time and place but no details survive except that her entire crew were saved.

Examples of blatant and outright 'wrecking' can be quoted for almost every mile of coastline throughout the British Isles, yet to this day there are some who will insist, often forcefully, that any such accusations are false. The fact remains, however, that wrecks were consistently looted by all and sundry and if some unfortunate victim of shipwreck was murdered in the process or nothing was done to preserve a life, such actions, though inexcusable, were a part of the way of life in those days. Offerings from the sea were considered as much a birthright of the men of Kent as those of Devon and Cornwall; the only difference, if any, being that the men of Deal had been doing it for a far longer period. Then, as today, even the rumour of wreck goods for the taking would bring people from all walks of life hurrying to the foreshore, intent on keeping anything they could find.

The maritime history of the Goodwin Sands is full of such incidents, the best documented for this particular period concerning the West Indiaman *Endeavour* and a Deal boatman, Peter Atkins, who was eventually sentenced to death for his 'wrecking' activities. Homeward bound, the *Endeavour* went onto the Goodwins at 3 a.m. on 8th February 1805 while carrying a cargo of rum, sugar and coffee valued at £23,000. This was jointly owned by the vessel's owner, Henry Wildman, being produce from his Jamaican estate, and his agent, John Kneller, who was aboard as a passenger. Atkins, who appears to have been something of a local celebrity, got aboard the *Endeavour* at daybreak and,

The scene one mile south of Walmer Castle after the gale of 25th November 1877. In the foreground, the brig *Star of the Ocean*, with the *République* and the *Mohely* to the north. Scattered wreckage is from the *Haabet* and the brig *Amine*.

(Franklin Studio, Deal)

realising that the ship could not be saved, volunteered his services to ensure that the cargo was landed safely. His offer having been accepted, Atkins went to the ship's side and hailed a number of Deal boats which were lying off, the crews of which were soon clambering aboard and breaking open the ship's hatches.

Eight puncheons of rum were the first items recovered and these were stowed aboard Atkin's boat, the *Noble*, which made for the beach. This trip was repeated three times and on the final one, made just before nightfall, both Kneller and Atkins were aboard. This time the boat was carrying four hogsheads of sugar, the property of Wildman, two tierces of coffee, owner unknown, a small cask of rum, which was Kneller's, and the ship's compass. When still a mile from the shore, Atkins ordered Kneller into another boat, saying that he would only see too much 'since the prads (horses) were waiting'.

A Mr Iggulden was appointed to act as agent at Deal for the owners and all salvaged goods were ordered to be delivered into his safe keeping, but of the original cargo only £500 worth was ever handed over. Wildman's son then arrived at Deal from London intent on looking after his father's interests and, accompanied by Kneller, questioned Atkins in the agent's office and again in the Three Kings inn. At first Atkins denied ever having been at the scene of the wreck at all, then insisted that everything he had salvaged had been surrendered. Eventually he 'confessed' that he had kept the small cask of rum brought ashore on that last trip on 8th February, his excuse being that he intended to sell it to save the owner having to pay the duty. When asked what had happened to the coffee he declared that it had been shared out amongst the crew of his boat.

Far from satisfied with such obvious lies the owners placed the matter in the hands of the police and HM Customs. On 17th February police searched Atkins's house in Beach Street, Deal, where they found two sacks of sugar but no sign of the 'wrecker' himself. A warrant was issued for his arrest but it was May before he was found hiding in the attic of his home. Bow Street runners were sent down from London to arrest him but, heavily outnumbered by the hostile local boatmen, were forced to invoke the aid of the resident cavalry unit to secure their prisoner. Atkins was taken to London where he appeared before an Admiralty Court at the Old Bailey on 26th June charged with 'felony and piracy on the high seas, within the jurisdiction of the Admiralty of England, in plundering the cargo and tackle of the ship *Endeavour*, stranded on the Goodwin Sands'. It took the jury exactly fifteen minutes to find him guilty and he was sentenced to death by hanging. In an age when death sentences were seldom commuted, Atkins was fortunate in that his wife worked as housekeeper at Walmer Castle and that her mistress, Lady Hester Stanhope, thought highly enough of them both to intervene and have the sentence reduced to transportation. Atkins was sent to Brazil where he worked for the Admiralty at Rio de Janeiro in charge of naval stores. He later settled in Guernsey, then Calais, where he kept an inn for a time, finally returning in the mid-1800s to Deal where

The schooner *Flores* off Walmer beach on 12th January 1911 having dragged her anchor until she is in danger of being blown ashore. (A. Webber, Deal)

he died shortly after at the age of eighty-four. In this particular case it was the individual who was punished rather than the community as a whole, as happened in January 1784 when a regiment of soldiers was ordered to set fire to the many Deal hovelling luggers pulled up on the beach as a reprisal against the owners for general smuggling and wrecking activities, a harsh and senseless punishment for those to whom the boats represented their livelihood.

A period of almost eighteen months then elapsed before another wreck of any consequence occurred. This was the Admiralty hired transport *Aurora*, carrying the commanding officer, staff and 250 troops of the 26th Regiment of Foot. On Monday 16th December 1805, an alert lookout at the masthead of HM Sloop *Cygnet* reported to Capt McLeod that wreckage and floating stores could clearly be seen on the seaward face of the Goodwin Sands. A boat was lowered to investigate and returned with several chests belonging to army officers, as well as the bodies of a number of uniformed soldiers. Since there were no survivors among either crew or passengers, neither the precise location nor the cause of the loss was ever established. Among the army officers lost that night were a Major Davidson, Captains Hoggins and Cameron, Ensign Dalyell, Quartermasters Campbell and Robertson, Lieutenant Hopkins and Surgeon Deval.

Two months prior to the wreck of the *Aurora*, an old brig was deliberately destroyed off Walmer Castle in the course of an unusual experiment. It was hoped that the French fleet in Boulogne harbour, then under constant blockade, could be successfully attacked with a new explosive device and it was one of these that was detonated beneath the hull of the moored vessel, blowing her to pieces to the great delight of thousands of spectators gathered on the foreshore. There is no record of the nature of the device nor of it ever being used in action. A form of incendiary rocket was, however, later tried against the enemy but, when fired from warships moored out of cannon shot of the French, the rockets failed to find their target and succeeded only in wrecking the rooftops of a number of houses.

A particularly severe gale on 18th February 1807 wrought havoc among the many ships at anchor in the Downs. A barque, unidentified to this day, lost her ground tackle and was blown ashore at Kingsdown with the loss of all her crew, while other ships were seen to founder or go to pieces off Sandown and Down. Many merchantmen known to have been at anchor when the storm broke were never seen or heard of again and it can only be presumed they either sank or broke up on the Goodwins. Three English men o' war in the Downs, the *Railleir* (ex-*Henry*), a sloop of sixteen guns; the *Devastation* (ex-*Intrepid*), a bomb vessel of eight guns and the *Saleby*, a prize, all had to cut away their masts and were fortunate to survive the huge seas which went clean over the sands even at half tide. Some thirteen vessels were cast ashore between Deal and the South Foreland, resulting in a heavy loss of life and property, and at least twenty-three others were wrecked. The entire coastline between the forelands was strewn with wreckage and other valuable material and a contemporary report of the storm states, '...the country people fought like animals over the smallest piece of wreck'. Other less fortunate locals who lived close to the beach were too busy drying out flooded houses and shops to join in the scramble. Seven months later, on 30th September, an unusually high tide completely flooded the town, drowning cattle and destroying crops, and even covering the entire marshland area to the north of Deal. Fortunately the many differences that had existed between the local boatmen and the Commissioners of Salvage had been settled before another series of gales struck the Kent coast in 1811, wrecking the transport brig *Brothers* on 4th January on Deal beach; the *Brisk* off Kingsdown on 13th January; the *Chilham Castle*, the *Charles Carter* and two others on the Goodwins on 13th April, and putting the *Dasher* ashore at Deal North End and the *Frederick* on the sands on 25th September and 20th October respectively.

One of the worst accidents to befall the HEIC was the loss of two East Indiamen, the *Admiral Gardner* and the *Britannia* at the same time on the west face of the South Goodwin Sands, on 25th January 1809. The *Admiral Gardner*, 816 tons, Capt Eastfield, and the larger *Britannia*, Capt Jonathan Birch, had set out from Blackwall some three days earlier on their voyage to India and the Far East, anchoring off Gravesend to take on additional crew and passengers, and at Deal to allow the company waterman, a Mr Granger, assisted by his two

The crew of the schooner *Flores* are brought ashore by breeches-buoy. (A. Webber, Deal)

sons, to bring out casks of fresh water. Accompanied by the *Carnatic*, all three Indiamen left the Downs on 24th January but on reaching the South Foreland, anchored until the tide changed. A near gale got up from the north-west, and the pilot on board the *Admiral Gardner*, thinking that her anchor was dragging, went to cut the anchor cable with an axe, but in so doing cut off two fingers of his left hand! Suffering from shock, he was taken below to a bunk, where he quickly became delirious.

During the night she parted from her small bower anchor, and drove ashore at about 3.00 a.m., where Capt Eastfield ordered both main and mizzen masts cut down to reduce her roll. At about the same time, the *Britannia* also lost her anchor and went ashore, a mile to the north-east. It was 3.30 p.m. the following day before Deal boatmen could get out to them to save the crew and passengers, so rough was the sea, by which time eleven men had drowned from the two ships. A degree of salvage was possible on both wrecks, some cloth, iron goods and ship's stores being saved, after which they disappeared into the sands and became forgotten.

In October 1976, 167 years later, a bucket dredger bringing sand ashore at Dover from the South Goodwin for a harbour extension, picked up a quantity of copper 10 and 20 Cash coins of the East India Company, all dated 1808, known to have been on board both the wrecked Indiamen. A 'new' wooden wreck was then snagged in 1979 by a fisherman, and investigation by divers revealed a very large vessel which had been carrying copper ingots, barrels of nails and musket flints, iron bar, grapnels and anchors, iron cannon and vast quantities of the copper Cash coins. A diving team and project was assembled, and over two summers the wreck was surveyed, excavated and identified as the *Admiral Gardner*. Considered by the authorities as being of historic importance to the nation, the site was designated a Protected Wreck by the Secretary of State, then de-scheduled when it was found it was outside of the UK three mile territorial limit, only to be re-scheduled when some two years later the limit was extended, bringing it back into UK waters. From this wreck site was recovered the largest quantity of copper coin ever found in any shipwreck site in the world, which included an intact 'treasure' barrel, holding 26,000 of the historic HEIC Madras currency. Since then the Goodwins have taken back the *Admiral Gardner* wreck, since it has remained almost completely buried since 1986.

Apart from the occasional locally-owned lugger or cutter there was seldom any feeling of personal loss amongst the locals with regard to wreck, but following the loss of the *British Queen*, a Margate-owned packet vessel, almost the entire population of the east coast of Kent went into mourning. The skipper of a Ramsgate cutter first brought news of the disaster on 19th December 1814. While sailing along the back of the Goodwins that Saturday afternoon he sighted a new wreck embedded in the sand and at no small risk had ventured alongside and secured a line to some loose material, which he towed ashore for examination. It proved to be the gaff, mainsail boom and upper part of the stern of the *British Queen* which had sailed from Ostend on her regular twice-weekly packet service between there and Margate on 13th December and must have struck the Goodwins in driving snow. There were no survivors among passengers or crew, the victims including Capt Lashmer and his son and the two sons of the vessel's owner, a Mrs Lanning, who suffered not only this bereavement but also the loss of her livelihood, since the vessel, a total wreck, was uninsured. But for his late arrival at the quayside an hour after the packet had sailed the list of passengers would also have included Lord Percy, a prominent social figure of the time.

The *British Queen* was not the only victim that night, a number of other vessels also finding themselves in distress. Ramsgate is a notoriously difficult harbour for sailing ships to negotiate in certain tidal conditions so it is not surprising that of the many ships that ran for shelter that day, four at least missed the entrance and were driven ashore on the nearby rocks. The principal strandings included those of the Dutch galliot *Drie Kienden*, en route from London to St Michael; the *Orion*, a Prussian ship, Memel to Cork; the French brig *Rosine & Aglae* and the *Livetanto*, a Portuguese brig, London to Oporto. Of these, the former was refloated and taken to Broadstairs for repair after discharging most of her cargo where she lay. The second and third both bilged

The pathetic remains of the steamship *Ashley*, lost on the Goodwins in 1924.
(John G. Callis, Deal)

and filled and probably became total wrecks, whilst the *Livetanto* miraculously remained intact on Sandwich Flats, having lost only her mainmast and bowsprit. Another brig, the *Aurora* of Milford, bound from Calais to London with flour, went on to the Goodwins that night and before daybreak was smashed to pieces. Her crew landed at Dover in their own boat, but in considerable distress and partially undressed as most of them had been in their bunks when the vessel struck.

As the nineteenth century progressed so the annual total of wreck incidents in the Downs increased and hardly a week went by when the sands were not strewn from end to end with timbers and rigging. With the peak years for shipping losses still some forty years away, the annual number now began to escalate during the 1830/40s to reach almost unbelievable figures and included among the victims were a number of rich Indiamen from both the East and West India Companies. The *Cornwall* was one such victim and although little is known of her loss except that she stranded on the Brake Sand, the wreck of the West Indiaman *Belina* is still spoken of as a classic amongst rescues by Deal boatmen. Shortly before dawn on 23rd November 1824 in a heavy gale accompanied by rain from the south-west the crew of the lugger *Sparrow* were assembled on the beach alongside the Rodney stage (so named after the inn bearing that name on the west side of Beach Street). As soon as daylight enabled the men to scan the horizon with their telescopes one of their number, Thomas Middleton, saw a new wreck on the sands. Knowing full well that the inevitable 'race' would shortly follow, the *Sparrow* was quietly launched with Edward Erridge as coxswain. Shortly afterwards the Downs guardship fired a gun to signal that they too had spotted the wreck and four more Deal boats put to sea.

Fighting every inch of the way, it took the crew of the *Sparrow* over two hours to reach the scene where they found the *Belina* already starting to break up. Fully aware of the danger of placing their relatively small craft alongside a wreck, the Deal men signalled their intent, then swooped down from windward and making a single pass under reduced sail were able to catch a rope thrown to them, by means of which the six remaining survivors, Capt Craig and five seamen, were drawn to safety. Only two bodies were recovered from amongst the fourteen lives lost in this wreck and these were interred in the sailors' burial ground, then known as the 'Strangers Nook', the entrance to which lay between the Jolly Sailor inn and the South Eastern Railway gates in Western Road. Edward Erridge received a well deserved medal from the shipping company in recognition of his bravery and Lord Liverpool, then Warden of the Cinque Ports, ordered a special engraving of the rescue to be published. In all, Erridge and his crew were instrumental in saving more than 100 lives from wrecks on the Goodwins over the years.

Another incident in which they were involved concerned the brig *Crown*, part of whose crew were stranded on the Goodwins for three whole days. It was George Pettit who first caught sight of ant-like figures on the sands at low water and with the aid of their telescopes the Deal men could clearly see men running about and waving their arms before being forced to retreat into the upper rigging of a mast as the tide rose. When finally rescued by the crew of the *Sparrow* the survivors, frost bitten and suffering from exposure and starvation, presented a pitiful sight to the onlookers at Deal who, not waiting for the capstan, quickly beached the boat by hand. Indeed there were so many willing helpers that between them they could have carried the *Sparrow*, survivors and crew alike, shoulder high up the beach with ease. It was an incident such as this that inspired J. Deveson, a local poet, to write:

> 'Though they oft heave a sigh for their wives and their home;
> Still fearless they plough throu' the ocean's white foam;
> Mid the roar of wild waves no danger they feel;
> For to succour distress launch the boatmen of Deal.'

A year later almost to the day the *Ogle Castle*, an English East Indiaman, also fell victim to the Goodwins with a tragic loss of life. During the night of Wednesday 2nd November 1825, the wind blew with almost hurricane force, exceeding in strength even the great gale of 1st March 1818 in which the greater part of Ramsgate pier had been demolished. At dawn on the Thursday the 513-ton ship was seen drifting down towards the Goodwins and a number of hovellers went out to her assistance. In a full west-south-west gale, with waves

A guardian of the Downs, the *Gull lightvessel* marked the safe channel beween Deal and the Goodwin Sands. This one was run down by the liner *City of York* on 18th March 1929, causing it to sink with a huge hole in its port side. Raised in June 1930, she was beached at Deal for examination.

(Will Honey)

going clean over the wreck, there was nothing the Deal boatmen could do except watch and wait, praying that the wind would drop or the sea abate. As soon as the keel of the Indiaman touched bottom she was thrown over on her beam ends with her bow pointed towards the coast and her portside exposed to the full fury of the sea. She remained in this position for only twelve minutes, then pivoted, heeling over all the time as the upper deck now took the pounding seas. Her bow was quickly engulfed by sand and within half an hour her mast tops, now only 12 feet clear of the surf, broke off and the *Ogle Castle* started to disintegrate. Her passengers and crew implored the boatmen to help them but they could approach no closer than two cables lengths and, gradually, in groups of a dozen or so at a time, the sea plucked them off the roof of the saloon, from the stern, and from the rigging until none remained. The vessel's name was not known at the time, but was eventually established from a fragment of sail cloth which, along with some bales of cotton, was recovered from the sea and forwarded to Lloyds for identification. On 4th November the Dover sloop *Aera* brought ashore several more bales of both wool and cotton as well as some silk and despatches, all of which proved to have come from the *Ogle Castle*. Exactly how many people lost their lives that day will never be known as no crew or passenger list survived but it was certainly well in excess of one hundred. A few days afterwards a short paragraph in 'The Times' reported: '...only about 3 feet of the hull shows above the surface, as she is slowly engulfed in the middle part of the South Goodwin'.

When the call came to the scene of a wreck the beach at Deal was more often than not completely denuded of all men except for those too old or infirm to take part but occasionally they, too, would become involved, as in the case of the wreck of the *Mountaineer* on 24th November 1829. At the height of an easterly gale the vessel, one of several at anchor in the Downs, was seen to be adrift and driving down towards the beach. Several luggers, including the *Betsy* and the *Lark*, were launched to assist but their offer was rejected, not by the master of the *Mountaineer,* Capt Shiel, but by the pilot who thought he might lose his fee if the Deal boatmen were allowed to take charge. Shortly before 4.00 p.m. the brig took the ground near Deal Castle and began to bump very heavily. The *Lark* was laid alongside the wreck but this served only to aggravate the situation as the boat soon broke adrift, leaving some six local men marooned on the brig along with the crew. Onlookers on the beach built huge bonfires but even their light could not penetrate the blinding snow squalls that swept in from the sea and it was midnight before conditions improved. As the snow died away and visibility improved local volunteers manhandled the 2½-cwt Mamby mortar projector into place and at the first attempt managed to fire a 25 lb ball carrying a light line across the wreck. A heavier rope followed and soon the first survivor was on his way to the shore by means of a primitive form of breeches-buoy. Three men lost their lives that night; a seaman from the brig and a Deal boatman named May, both of whom died of exposure. The body of the pilot, who had jumped overboard in an attempt to swim ashore, was found partially buried in

A Thames sailing barge, the *British Oak*, stranded on Ramsgate Sands in 1936.
(F. Treweeks, Ramsgate)

the shingle next day. As the tide receded the entire foreshore was left covered with wreckage, animal horns, coffee, spices and wine, all of which quickly disappeared!

Public attention, already focused on the ever increasing annual toll of ships around these shores, especially in the vicinity of the Goodwin Sands, forced the government to form a Parliamentary select committee, known as the Select Committee on Shipwreck, to investigate every aspect of the subject, from the construction of the ships themselves, their manning, operation and even light-houses. Although this body may now appear to have spent much of its time and finances in producing a welter of statistics concerning the many causes of ship losses, it is to its credit that it instigated the Merchant Shipping Act, which in due course led to the passing of the Plimsoll Act and the introduction of many other safety measures. One of the committee's early reports, submitted to the House of Commons on 22nd March 1837, drew attention to the many salvage tasks performed in the Downs area and is an indication both of the extent of the salvage work and of the rewards which, bearing in mind the relative value of money 160 years ago, were considerable. For such assistance as, '...extricating the brigantine Anna, 170 tons, from a ship's hawse and carrying off an anchor and cable to her in rough weather in the Downs, sum awarded £105'. Of this total, £5 5s went as commissioners' fees, £3 8s as registrar's fees and 5s for the hire of the room in which the commissioners of salvage deliberated each claim. Similarly, '...for getting the brig *Corinthian* off the Goodwins in thick weather, £220'; or, '...for getting the ship *Gladiator* off the Main, opposite the town of Deal, and for carrying off two anchors and cables and rendering other assistance, the sum of £630'.

The next eight years or so saw much activity in connection with two distinct projects, the building of a pier at Deal and the permanent marking of the Goodwins by beacons, the latter proposition emerging from the Committee on Shipwreck. Perhaps the greatest single objection to Deal as a naval base was its lack of any harbour, breakwater, jetty or pier, so that the transfer of men and stores alike had to be conducted from an open shingle beach. Hundreds of small craft were swamped as a result and the total loss in lives and equipment is incalculable. In 1825 the Duke of Clarence, then Lord High Admiral, visited Deal to investigate the practicability of a floating pier but nothing more was heard of this scheme and it eventually fell to a group of private investors to take the initiative. This resulted in an Act of Parliament in 1838 authorising the formation of the Deal Pier Company with a share capital of £21,000. A plot of ground to the north of the Royal Hotel was purchased, corresponding to a position approximately 200 yards north of the present pier, and Sir John Rennie was commissioned to design a suitable structure 445ft long. Piling was eventually completed for a distance of 250ft offshore but then financial difficulties arose, work ceased and the pier was never completed. It remained in this part-built state until 1857 when the entire structure collapsed in a south-easterly gale. At auction, the remaining salvageable ironwork fetched exactly £50. Recently evidence of a very old wooden pier or jetty was uncovered in a position somewhat nearer Sandown Castle and partially excavated under the guidance of the late W. Honey, curator of the Deal Maritime Museum and a local historian. A considerable number of coins dating from the sixteenth century were recovered and can be seen in the museum, and it is likely that the site was that of a very early landing-place.

Reference has already been made to the first lightvessel installed to mark the North Sand Head in 1795 and as the majority of vessels entered and left the Downs via the northern channel of the Gull Stream, this was the obvious position in which to place another light. Following a highly successful trial period lasting fourteen years a second light was considered necessary and a new vessel, a wooden craft of 158 tons specially built and equipped for the task, was moored in the Gull Stream in eight fathoms on the 'inside' face of the sands in 1809. As with the North Sand Head light, the Gull Stream light immediately proved its worth, saving many ships from going ashore and offering a floating refuge for those less fortunate.

The next requirement was for a light to mark the South Sand Head, so another special-purpose craft was ordered, this time from a Blackwall yard, more generally associated with the building of Indiamen. A wooden vessel of 184 tons, she

An unidentified topsail schooner stranded somewhere in the Downs, c1913 and probably refloated and saved.   (Will Honey)

cost Trinity House £3,212 and went on station in 1832. Each of these lightvessels carried signal cannon in addition to a plentiful supply of rockets and in later years, following the introduction of lifeboats to the area, played a vital rôle in nineteenth-century 'search-and-rescue' operations by keeping a watch for ship-wrecks and taking aboard survivors.

With the outline of the Goodwins marked by three lightvessels and a buoy at each end of the Brake Sand there would seem to have been no good reason why anyone should now have contemplated expending huge sums of money on erecting fixed beacons on the sands themselves. Admittedly there was still need for an East Goodwin lightvessel, which was not forthcoming until 1874, but certainly little or no justification for a beacon, the more so when the monopoly of such edifices was invested in Trinity House who did not welcome intruders. Nevertheless there then ensued a period, commencing in 1836, when a great many such proposals were submitted and a number of 'monuments' erected, often at private expense as if the participants were engaged in some costly kind of competition.

Whilst there is no doubt that the first proposal for such a beacon in the 1800s came from the Deptford civil engineer, William Bush, it would seem that he had enemies, some of whom were determined to see him ruined if not disgraced. Bush was called before the Select Committee on Shipwreck to give evidence on

5th August 1836 and claimed to be the inventor of both a beacon and a lighthouse which could be erected on shoals or sandbanks for the preservation of life from shipwreck. He further asserted that such a beacon could be used on the Goodwin Sands and that '...the cost of each such lighthouse would be about £100,000'. According to the minutes of that meeting, his proposals were approved by Trinity House, but judging by the length of time he was subsequently kept waiting it is now obvious that this was a delaying tactic. In 1840 Capt Bullock, RN, put forward a similar proposal, except that his beacon was considerably cheaper to manufacture, and there were so many similarities between the two designs, that it would not be unreasonable to suggest that one was a product of the other. .

Both suggestions were basically for an upright mast or column resembling a ship's mast. Bush's with two platforms or 'cross-trees', Bullock's with only one. While Bush was still awaiting formal permission to erect the beacon seemingly approved four years earlier, Bullock's beacon was floated out to the sands on 10th September 1840 and erected with the help of HMS *Boxer* in a position described somewhat vaguely as 'seven miles from Deal'. This could either have been the North Sand Head or the most easterly part of the South Goodwins, probably the former. It would appear that Capt Bullock, who at the time was employed by the Navy to survey the south coast from Westminster Bridge to Lands End, was also not without influence, since neither of the beacons he eventually erected were criticised nor removed, as had happened to others.

Who actually paid for the first beacon is uncertain but it consisted of the jib-boom from a frigate, 13 inches in diameter and 40 feet in length. Eight stays or guys attached to 17-foot iron piles buried in the sand held the mast upright. Fitted to the top of the wooden boom was an hexagonal gallery of trelliswork designed to hold twenty persons. The inner face of the trelliswork held a number of boards on which were painted in several languages instructions to shipwrecked mariners to 'Hoist the blue flag'. This flag was housed in a canvas bag secured to the mast and, apart from a barrel of freshwater, was the only other item provided. There are minor discrepancies between the report in 'The Times' and Gattie's 'Memorials of the Goodwin Sands', the latter recording that bread and biscuits were also provided as well as a large basket chair to 'succour the exhausted', but both agree that the first man to climb the beacon was Lieut G.C. Boyes, RN, waving a Union Jack in the form of a handkerchief and calling for three cheers for Capt Bullock and Queen Victoria. Incredibly cheap and simple to construct, Bullock's beacon survived for almost four years until it was run down by a Dutch schooner on 5th August 1844. There is no record of it ever being instrumental in saving life but, if nothing else, it was a centre of attraction locally. On 30th November 1842, HRH Prince Albert made a special trip out to the sands to see this masterpiece and would no doubt have landed and walked on the Goodwins had the tide not been too high.

Perhaps the reluctance on the part of authority officially to approve Bush's beacon was in part due to misgivings concerning his overall plan for the

Goodwins. Assuming financial support could be found, Bush proposed to convert the entire sandbank into a 'haven or harbour of refuge'. This was to have been achieved by sinking a series of cofferdams linked together to form a continuous seawall. His masterpiece, however, was his 'Light for All Nations', which was to have been a massive lighthouse built in three separate sections, the lower portion consisting of a caisson to be sunk to a depth of 64 feet and then filled with 120,000 cu ft of granite. Bolted to the top of the caisson would be the cast-iron body of the structure, 86 feet tall, and surmounted by a 40-foot lantern-housing complete with gallery. In true Victorian style the lighthouse was to have had at its highest point a life-size cast-iron statue of Queen Victoria, whilst on the lower gallery set some 30 feet above the sea would be the legend, 'W. Bush, CE, 1843. A Light for All Nations'.

The installation of Bullock's beacon and apparent lack of enthusiasm for his own project caused Bush to seek sponsorship elsewhere and this he found in the Duke of Wellington. What financial agreement was made is not recorded but early in 1840 an order was placed with the Thorncliffe Ironworks, near Rotherham in Yorkshire, for construction of the huge 120-ton base unit on which the light would be built. Shipped to Deal in sections, it was assembled in the Admiralty dockyard and plans were made to install the first section in late September 1841. Extensive publicity had been given to the venture and when it was known that the Duke of Wellington was in Deal to witness the initial stage of erection a large party of gentlemen, including Lord Mayborough and several eminent engineers, arrived at the Royal Hotel. The weather proving unsuitable on the appointed day, 18th September 1841, Bush agreed to sink the caisson in 23 feet of water and in exactly five minutes it had settled on the seabed just clear of the pier.

Various dates were set for towing the device out to the sands and then postponed and it was not until 22nd October that things really began to move. On its way across the Downs the towing vessel, the steamer *Monkey*, ran aground and the caisson had to be cast adrift. Another steamer, the *Shearwater*, rescued it and towed it back to Deal where it promptly sank. Badly damaged in a subsequent gale, there it remained, close to the old wooden pier in front of the Star and Garter Hotel and a considerable nuisance to local boatmen.

Over the winter months it was salvaged, dismantled and rebuilt and was once again afloat and on its way to the sands on 28th July 1842. Reaching the appointed location on the North Caliper, the caisson was allowed to settle on the bottom and, apart from a slight list of about one foot in twelve, the designer was satisfied. Three weeks later it was found to have sunk 16 feet and by 12th September was down 25 feet. After successfully surviving a number of autumn gales and sinking deeper all the time it was struck on 15th October 1842 by what was believed to be an American timber ship, the *Nancy*, which not only disintegrated with the loss of her entire crew but also overturned the caisson. Undaunted, Mr Bush set about a reconstruction and when this too was destroyed down to the low-water mark by a gale in 1844, he still persevered. By

January 1845 the original caisson had been salvaged and replanted for a less grand project than the original 'Light for All Nations', and on the 19th of that month the designer and his guests partook of roast beef and plum pudding in the partly completed living quarters, some 50 feet above the sea. By July the structure was so close to completion that Bush, with his wife and son, slept in one of the chambers beneath the lantern room for several nights eagerly awaiting the time when 'the soft blue light from eight patent Vesta lamps' would shine out over the Downs.

Whether or not Trinity House had waited to see if the lighthouse would ever be completed before taking action is uncertain, but they now informed Mr Bush that his light was in a completely impractical position, in the middle of the sands where it would only lead vessels into danger and ordered him to dismantle the entire structure. Sir J.H. Pelly, Deputy Master of Trinity House, giving evidence before the Parliamentary Committee on Lighthouses in June 1845, had this to say: '...quite ridiculous where placed, it is a most dangerous structure, and ships approaching it must be wrecked on the sands'.

Whether or not Bush was harshly treated it is now difficult to say and if, perhaps, he had taken more notice of a formal letter sent to him on 24th September of the previous year ordering him to cease his activities, he might have been able to persuade the authorities that the chosen location had been dictated by the Admiralty and that the venture was not one of personal gain but for the benefit of all seafarers. Or perhaps it was because he had preferred to correspond with Lloyds, to whom he had written on 20th September 1844 as follows:

'The Light for All Nations'
Union Street, Deptford

Gentlemen - Having been engaged for several months in erecting on the site of the Caisson, sunk by me on the Goodwin Sands during the autumn of 1842, an iron column, with the two-fold object of fixing thereon a red light for the guidance of mariners and for boring the quicksand to ascertain its depth, with the ultimate view of erecting a more permanent lighthouse, I have fixed the column 9 feet above high-water mark and shall in the course of the next fortnight, weather permitting, carry it up to the height of 30 feet, and that on or before the 1st November I shall show at the top of the column, a brilliant red light. The true bearings of the other lights have not yet been ascertained accurately, but shall be furnished to you in the course of next week.

I have the honour to remain Gentlemen, your obedient servant.
Signed: W. Bush, CE.
To the Committee for Managing the Affairs of Lloyds.'

After five years' work, the expenditure of some £12,000 of Bush's private money and an unspecified amount belonging to the Duke of Wellington, the almost completed lighthouse was taken down. By June 1849 only a 7 feet high stump was showing at low water and, after further dismantling, the great

Returning to its station following a rescue, the Deal lifeboat *Charles Dibdin* on the beach over Whitsun 1926.   (Author's collection)

caisson, together with Bush's high hopes for 'A Light for All Nations', disappeared beneath the Goodwin Sands for ever.

But this was by no means to be the end of beacon-building on the Goodwins, which was to continue for several years to come. Capt Bullock's device, which it will be recalled was erected in 1840 and demolished by accident in 1844, had been replaced within less than a month but it too had long since disappeared, carried away by a gale on 23rd October 1847. Another contestant in this expensive pastime was a civil engineer named Steward who attempted to locate a beacon on the eastern edge of the Goodwins in a position best described today as the southern side of the Kellett Gut. This was in 1843, a year after Bush's first attempt to build a lighthouse, but Steward was also dogged by problems and when at last in September 1844 his beacon was erected on the sand it promptly capsized. A second attempt after modification and repositioning was no more successful and the project was then abandoned. Other beacons survived for considerably longer periods. That of James Walker, erected on 6th July 1844, lasted until 1850 when it was removed by Trinity House, not because they objected to it but simply because it had moved with the sand. In six years it had travelled over 450 feet to the west and sunk 9 feet in the process.

Despite the amount of effort and money expended on beacons and other means of marking the outline of the Goodwins there was no immediate reduction in the number of shipwrecks, nor was there for many years to come.

During the night of 10th/11th October 1841 a Swedish brig, subsequently identified as the *Carl Robert*, stranded on the sands and was smashed to pieces. The *Hope*, a Dover boat, found four Swedish seamen clinging to part of the coal-laden brig and got them to safety and a further three men were saved by a Walmer-owned lugger. In recognition of the fishermen's humane service, which had cost them a day's work, a local subscription was started and raised over £50, part of which was set aside for the victims of the wreck and the relatives of the three seamen who had been drowned. Collections of this sort were not unusual, for these people lived not only by the sea but off the sea and knew only too well the dangers involved in the work of rescue. Typical of their courage was that of the seven-man crew of the Deal boat *Poll* which, on 15th November 1842, went out in a full gale in answer to lights shown by a large steamship offshore. Their boat was totally unsuitable for such work or weather, being only 32 feet long, 1 foot 11 inches in depth and drawing no more than 10 inches. They managed to reach the steamer, which proved to be the Peninsular Steam Navigation Co's *Hibernia*, Capt Evans, and one of the crew of the *Poll*, Adam Lambert, went aboard. At that moment the vessel rolled over in the swell on top of the small boat, smashing it to pieces and throwing the crew into the sea. All six were rescued and taken on to another port and their feelings can well be imagined when they discovered that the *Hibernia* had never been in any difficulty and Capt Evans had merely wanted to land a pilot.

The year 1844 was a particularly bad one for shipping losses and it was fortunate that in the gales of 15th/16th January only two of the four vessels that went ashore locally became total losses. A Spanish brig, the *Anna*, her sister ship *Hercules*, the *Shepherdess* and an unidentified schooner all went ashore but only the latter became a total wreck in the Downs, the *Shepherdess* being lost on the Goodwins. A Bideford-owned brig, she was on passage from Newcastle to Plymouth with coal when she went ashore and several local boats went to her assistance, including the now famous *Sparrow*, the Deal lugger *Earl Grey* and a new *Poll*. Between them they saved all the crew under extremely difficult and dangerous conditions. At high water the wreck floated away and sank, and the 'Kentish Observer' of 25th January reported her as '...now lying on the North Sand Head, on her beam, and no mast to be seen'. The government made an award of £34 to the three boats, the *Earl Grey* receiving £18 to be shared amongst thirteen men, the remaining £16 going to the twelve crewmen of the other two boats — hardly a generous award but these men had long since learnt to expect little for their services.

Winter gales always brought their share of destruction and those of 1848 were no exception. A Bremen-registered emigrant barque, the *Atlantic*, must have been on the outer edge of the Goodwins for some time before being discovered by several Deal and Ramsgate luggers on 15th November. Although the weather was fine a huge swell made immediate rescue impossible and by the time conditions improved and those left on board could be rescued, Capt Foster, two passengers and the ship's boy had been swept overboard and lost. At almost exactly the same moment as the *Atlantic* was found another German ship, the *Burgundy*, Capt Hunt, with 300 emigrants aboard, was lost on the Long Sand, less than twenty-five miles to the north. Her passengers and crew were rescued without incident by HM Revenue Cutter *Diamond*.

Although in no way connected with shipwrecks, a particularly bizarre and strange smuggling incident was reported in December 1848. As Christmas drew near and the increased demand for duty-free spirit kept the local smugglers busy, the body of one of them, a master bricklayer named Watson of Margate, was found on the beach close to the Customs House with a rope around his waist to which were tied no less than seventy-two tubs of brandy. As he could not possibly have dragged that number ashore on his own nor swum in from deeper water towing such a weight, his death remained something of a mystery.

Two more ships were lost in the Downs before the new year. A Prussian brig, the *Fortschritt*, from Stettin to Dublin with brandy and zinc, got onto the Goodwins during the night of 15th December. Her crew had the good sense to remain aboard although the vessel was going to pieces beneath their feet, and at daybreak when the shore was clearly visible they abandoned the wreck, dragged their small boat across the sands and reached Ramsgate safely. Two months later, in February 1850, the Cinque Ports Admiralty Court passed a judgement concerning a wreck of a Russian ship about which little appears to be known. This vessel, on passage from Taganrog in the Sea of Azov, part of the Ukraine, had grounded on the Goodwins while passing through the Downs with a St Mawes pilot at the helm. All seventeen crew were saved by Deal boatmen who afterwards refloated the derelict vessel whose cargo of select furniture timber was valued at £3,000. The crews of the local boats who saved the Russians received £30 between them; £500, in addition to expenses, went to those who had saved the vessel and cargo, with an additional £40 to be shared amongst the boats that recovered floating stores, timber etc.

Nowhere in the British Isles has there been such an area as the Goodwins, where ships went aground and broke up so quickly that little was known of them except for the occasional clue gleaned from floating wreckage or corpses. Countless examples of this can be found in local newspapers of the period. On 16th May 1850 a stern board with the name *Newport Trader* picked out in yellow lettering was found on Deal beach, and that same day a log book from the *William & Henry*, Master Rider, bound from Hull to Exeter with coal, but where these two ships were lost was never established with any certainty. Other examples that same year included the 242-ton brig *Gazelle*. Reported missing in November by her owners following a south-westerly gale of at least force ten, the remains of this unlucky vessel were finally located embedded on the outer edge of the Goodwins. Many casks of tallow were recovered floating in the vicinity of the North Foreland but positive identification was not possible until a box containing outward-bound mail for Sydney was found floating in the Downs. What happened to the twenty people aboard is not known but they most probably shared the same fate as those on board two other wrecks in the same gale from which, again, there were no survivors, nor any trace apart from a complete stern and a figurehead washed up at Broadstairs.

With something like sixty-one lifeboats installed around the British Isles by 1850, twelve of which were provided by the National Institution for the Preservation of Life from Shipwreck, founded in 1824, and a further thirty-nine as gifts from private individuals, it seems incredible that none was provided for use on the Goodwins until 1852. The first reference to any lifeboat within reach of the sands can be found in the 'Rochester, Chatham and Surrey Gazette and County Advertiser' of 11th March 1851 which reported that an unidentified brig, later found to be the *Mary White*, a new vessel of 272 tons carrying coal to Southampton, went ashore on the North Sand Head and that the Broadstairs lifeboat had been stove-in during a rescue attempt. For their efforts the eight men in the crew each received a silver medal for gallantry from the Institution. Gattie names the wreck as the *Mary Wright* and states that she became a total loss but this is incorrect. The brig was eventually refloated and saved, but the price was the loss of her captain and two seamen from a complement of ten. It would appear that it was the Ramsgate hovelling lugger *Buffalo Gal* which rescued the seven survivors as well as saving the lifeboat, since she returned to port in triumph with the crews of both the brig and the lifeboat and with the damaged lifeboat in tow.

The first installation of a lifeboat on the Goodwins station was at Ramsgate in 1852. This was the 'prize' lifeboat built by James Beeching of Great Yarmouth, one of 280 plans submitted from all over the world in answer to the Duke of Northumberland's offer of a 100-guinea prize for the best model. Unlike the earlier Greathead boats built at South Shields since 1790, Beeching's model incorporated a self-righting ability and, purchased by the Ramsgate harbour commissioners for £210, was appropriately named the *Northumberland*. After only two years' use urgent modifications became necessary. Her water-ballast tanks were removed and an iron keel and solid ballast substituted under the supervision of the Lifeboat Institution following complaints from her crew that she was 'too tender' in a rough sea and that the shingle beaches in the Downs were damaging her bottom.

Not surprisingly, the Deal and Walmer boatmen were far from happy at the arrival of the lifeboat which they saw as another competitor added to the craft in which they went out to answer the frequent calls for assistance. In many instances a rescue was performed and the survivors safely back ashore before the crew of the lifeboat were even aware of the event and this situation was to continue for the best part of half a century before full co-operation was established. During a nineteen-day period in January 1852 alone, five ships were in trouble, three of which brought the *Northumberland* to sea performing meritorious service. These involved the *Edith*, stranded off Deal on the 10th; the Stockton brig *London*, ashore in Pegwell Bay the following day; and the Maldon-registered schooner *Victory* carrying coal from Sunderland, also ashore in Pegwell Bay on the 26th. Two incidents which the lifeboat missed concerned the

A later successor, the RNLB *Charles Dibdin* (Civil Service No.32) which served on the Walmer Station from 1959 to 1975. Continuous siltation of the shingle foreshore still necessitates beach-launching from this position. (Richard Larn)

Marie & Emilie on 15th January and the *Wanskapen* five days later. The former was a full-rigged ship carrying a large crew and 160 emigrants, bound for New York. Discovered aground on the Goodwins by the lugger *Charlotte Ann* of Ramsgate, whose crew managed to refloat her without taking off a single passenger, she returned to port with her prize and the passengers were accommodated at the Spread Eagle inn in the High Street while repairs were carried out to the ship. During that same period, on 20th April, the Milford schooner *Oxielton*, Master Williams, was run down and sunk in deep water near the East Spit. It was a fine clear night when the steamer *Bordeaux* from Rotterdam sliced into the port side of the sailing vessel, whose crew were able to scramble into their boat before the schooner sank.

The stranding of the brig *George William* on the South Caliper on 27th October of that same year is the first recorded instance of the Ramsgate lifeboat being taken out to the sands under tow of the harbour commissioners' steam tug *Samson*. This later became the accepted practice and spared the lifeboat crew what would otherwise have meant a row or sail of anything up to ten miles should a vessel be ashore as far afield at the South Sand Head and an equally arduous return journey. On this initial occasion the local boatmen were the first to reach the wreck, that of the *George William*, 264 tons, Quebec to London with deals and fifty casks of Canadian balsam, which had struck the Goodwins at about 2.00 a.m. It was mid-morning before the Ramsgate boatmen saw her and when the lifeboat eventually arrived on the scene, slipped her tow and crossed over the sands, the wreck was found to be deserted. On returning to harbour with the brig in tow they learnt that the Deal lugger *Diana* had beaten them to it, having taken off her master, his twelve-year-old son, and five seamen. The Deal men involved in this rescue were John Tapley, John, Arthur and Thomas Trott, Philip Files, Henry Kirkaldie, Henry Marsh, Edward Clayson and William Mackins, all of whom shared an award of £15 from the Institution.

The following brief synopsis of wrecks and incidents during the early part of 1853, as reported to the Receiver of Wrecks, today seems almost unbelievable.

13.1.1853	*Ann*, brig, of Whitby, Capt Stonehouse, Saldanha Bay to Berwick with guano, ashore on the Goodwins. Walmer boat *Garland* rescued all her crew.
17.1.1853	*Calypso*, London to Jamaica, stranded on the Goodwins.
24.1.1853	*Briton*, Shields to Bristol, total loss on Goodwins. The masts of another vessel, lost lately, are still visible.
27.1.1853	'It is said that forty bodies were last week seen by the men on the lightships, floating through the Gull Stream'
10.2.1853	*Sadak*, Smyrna to London, stranded, now washed off.
10.2.1853	*Jane White*, Hartlepool to Dieppe, ashore on the Brake Sand.
17.2.1853	*Masonic*, American-registered, Newcastle for New York. Stranded on the sands.
17.3.1853	The South Sand lightship has drifted one mile in the direction of the South Foreland.
24.3.1853	*Colombo*, brig, Italian, for Newcastle with sulphur, stranded on the Goodwins.
29.3.1853	*Victoria*, hovelling lugger, crew of four, cruising the Gull Stream, foundered in a snow squall, only one man named Thompson rescued by *Fawn*.
31.3.1853	*Febro*, brig, of Bremen, with Dutch emigrants, stranded on the Goodwin Sands.
28.4.1853	*Mayflower*, from Guernsey, coal, total loss on Goodwins. Unidentified — a large vessel wrecked on the Goodwins. Others wrecked on the Goodwins. An electric telegraph at 10.33 says a 300-ton ship on Goodwins.
12.5.1853	*San Francisco*, of Bilbao, stranded on the Goodwins. *Horatio*, Odessa to Bremen, wrecked on the sands.

Of these, the wreck of the *Sadak*, lying in seven fathoms, proved to be such a nuisance that Trinity House were obliged to place a green wreck buoy 120 feet eastward of the obstruction on 10th March. Some time later she was blown up as a navigational hazard.

Following the erection of so many beacons during the 1840s, the subject was not raised again until 26th April 1853 when another civil engineer, a Mr Smith, proposed the following scheme in a letter to the press:

'A Scheme for getting rid of the perils of the Goodwin Sands. In the 1st place it is intended to form a framed breakwater to protect vessels in the Downs when the wind is such that they cannot be protected by the mainland or by the sands. The structure is of a peculiar nature, since anything in the nature of a fixed edifice cannot be attempted. To be independent of the moving sand, it is intended to erect the breakwater in deep water in the chalk in front of the sands, starting near the South Sand Head. It will consist of a number of independent frames or gratings, each about 50 feet long and rising from the seabed to about 15 feet above high water. Each frame will be secured at the base by a suitable shackle to pile-heads for which Mitchells screw pile is peculiarly adapted. The frame, upright in the water, is restrained in its revolution about its base by jointed stays and holdfasts secured underwater in like manner. Thus upon a heavy sea striking the frame, the frame yields to the impact and the concussion expends itself in straightening the holdfasts. Immediately the weight attached to the stay will pull the frame upright again. Length of frames equals 2,000 feet, along which will be a roadway supported on pilings and connected to a tower, with a lighthouse and an asylum for wrecked mariners.'

It is fitting that amongst the last incidents to be recorded in this chapter should be two in which both Deal and Ramsgate boatmen, as well as the crew of the Ramsgate lifeboat, risked their lives under the worst possible conditions in a gallant attempt to save life. At about 10 p.m. on 8th November 1853 repeated cannon fire was heard on shore coming from one of the light vessels, followed by the thud of exploding distress maroons indicating that a ship was ashore. Several boats went out in conditions so bad that had it been daylight and the boatmen able to see the state of the sea offshore, they would surely not have tried to get afloat. Three luggers in all managed to reach the North Sand Head where the wreck proved to be that of the 79-ton French schooner *Elenore* (BOT Summary 1860/61; Gattie, p.175, *Eleanore*), Lulea to Dunkirk with tar in barrels and deal. Shortly after the luggers arrived the Ramsgate lifeboat appeared in tow of the *Samson* but the seas were such that not one of them could get close to the casualty. After cruising around for several hours waiting for conditions to improve the crew of the *Northumberland* made a pass at the wreck but missed and the lifeboat fell away to leeward. A Ramsgate lugger then put three men into a punt who attempted to row across to the sands but within seconds they had capsized and all were drowned. Having now been brought back into position by the tug, and listened to the cries of the shipwrecked crew for almost five hours, the lifeboat's crew made another desperate attempt, only to have their craft flung onto her beam, filled with water and then thrown bodily onto the sands. In pitch darkness and the storm still raging the crew managed to refloat their craft, resumed their places at the oars and made yet another attempt to reach the wreck, but once again they were swamped. Soon afterwards the wreck went to pieces and only her captain, M. Boom, managed to reach the nearest lugger, the *Ondine*, where he was hauled aboard completely nude. One passenger, a young man named Fevre, was also rescued, but not until the next morning when the crew of the *Charlotte Anne* went to inspect a bundle on the Goodwins and found him lashed to a spar and apparently dead. Fevre had survived the entire night and up until noon the next day, all the while exposed to the full force of wind and sea.

The master of the *Ondine* gave the following vivid account of his experiences next day:

'... I wished myself at home more than once, for I never saw anything so frightful all the times I have been near wrecks. The dark night, with such a terrible sea! The cries for help of the poor men! The roaring and smoke of the steamer! The lifeboat ashore on the sands, and every sea breaking sheer over and over her, tried our heart strings I assure you. And at day-break we could see nothing but the raffle of the wreck; and so we came away.'

The last but one noteworthy incident for this period is best described in the words of two Deal boatmen, William Spears of the *Briton's Pride* and John Bayley of the *Seaman's Hope*, both local luggers, whose statement to the 'Kent Herald' was printed on 12th January 1854. It concerned the loss of the Norwegian brig *Annette* of 160 tons, carrying a crew of seven and a cargo of salt from St Ubes to Stavanger.

'We launched at 3 a.m., rough gale from the north-west. About 6 a.m. saw flares and heard loud report of a gun, as if from a ship in distress. We bore down in that direction and by the light of a blazing tar barrel saw the brig on her beam ends on the Sands. After three ineffectual attempts due to heavy weather, we threw a rope which was secured and William Spears got aboard, but had hardly done so than the rope broke and the boat smashed into the brig, carried away its mizzenmast and knocked off her rudder. The brig later sank so that only the top of her masts showed. We left the wreck at 11.30 a.m. and reached the shore at 12.30. Two boats and seventeen men were involved in this service.'

The editor added this footnote: 'William Spears, with others, has saved the lives of thirty-nine on three occasions, these plus nine in this instance make forty-eight. We hope the philanthropic and humane will come forward with a helping hand and reward them for their bravery'. Well might the British public have taken that message to heart for Board of Trade figures released that same day showed that there had been a total of 1,115 ships stranded, foundered, or burnt the previous year around the British Isles, of which no less than 500 had been total losses.

In lighter vein, in that summer of 1854 a Mr Morris Thompson and a Mr Hammond conceived the idea of playing a cricket match on the Goodwins.

This was the first time the game had been played there but there have been many other matches in subsequent years, as recently as 1992. On 10th August Capt Pearson and a crew from one of the finest luggers at Deal, the *Spartan*, accepted the Thompson-Hammond challenge and at 5.00 p.m. both teams landed and set up stumps after walking for about a mile to find a suitable pitch. Play continued until most sunset, the winning team having scored fifty-seven runs.

To end the year there was the loss of the London barque *Devonia*, Master Lawson, during a full gale and snow-storms on Christmas Day 1854. Carrying almost 500 tons of coke from Shields to Aquilas, on the Mediterranean coast of Spain, the ship struck the sands without warning at 9.00 p.m. As she shuddered to a halt a huge sea crashed down on deck carrying Richard Boys and Allen Brown, two young seamen, overboard to drown. The rest of the sixteen-man crew, scrambling along the deck, managed to reach the roof of the poop deckhouse just as the barque broke up and were floated away on their precarious platform. For ten hours they lay exposed to sub-zero temperatures and the biting wind, during which time the coloured steward, John Caroline, and George David, the second mate, both died. Fortunately the wreckage and the survivors were sighted in the Channel at daybreak by the steamers *Lord Warden* and *Princess Helen*, both belonging to the South Eastern & Continental SS Packet Co, working out of Folkestone.

Chapter Five

FOUR LIFEBOATS FOR THE GOODWINS: 1855-1874

Between 1852 and 1861 the Ramsgate lifeboat *Northumberland* under coxswain James Hogben was instrumental in saving the lives of almost 150 persons from various shipwrecks either on or in the vicinity of the Goodwin Sands. If there had still been any lingering doubts as to the need for such a craft these were about to be finally dispelled as the volume of wreck incidents grew to almost astronomical proportions. By 1865 the toll had been such as to demonstrate the need for not one but four lifeboats concentrated on eleven miles of coastline, with a fifth at Broadstairs, a sixth at Kingsgate, and shortly after, others at Margate and Dover, a coverage unique in lifeboat history. But all this still lay ten years ahead and meanwhile the same old 'race' continued as local boatmen competed to be first aboard a shipwreck.

The first incident for 1855 concerned the schooner *Fanny* which took the ground at the North Sand Head on 19th January. Four cannon shots fired by the lightvessel there sent the Deal and Walmer men scrambling into their boats at daybreak and soon a veritable fleet of galleys and luggers was afloat, crowding on all sail as their crews strove to be the first to claim salvage rights.

But the *Fanny*, bound for the Crimea with government stores, was already beyond help, so that only her crew and a few bundles of military uniforms were saved, the former being given into the care of the Shipwreck Association and the clothing to the dockyard authorities at Deal. Whether or not the Ramsgate lifeboat formed part of this rescue fleet is uncertain but it is likely that she remained on her moorings at Ramsgate as the abundance of small craft suggests a calm sea, whereas the lifeboat was usually reserved for bad weather. In rough conditions, assisted by a steam paddle tug, the *Northumberland* had every advantage over conventional boats, and there was not another craft in sight when, on 4th February of that year, she set off in a blinding snowstorm to search for the wreck of a Dutch schooner. In this instance the Ramsgate men were not able to locate the wreck but did manage to intercept the schooner's crew rowing their own boat towards the Gull lightvessel.

What circumstances dictated the Broadstairs lifeboat's attempt to reach a wreck on the Goodwins on 20th March is not recorded, but with the larger Ramsgate lifeboat not only closer but with the advantage of a tug to get her to sea, it seems strange that the Broadstairs coxswain should have risked his crew and craft in a force nine easterly gale to reach the wreck of the 170-tons register Middlesbrough brig *Thomas & Anne* ashore on the North Sand. Unable to get

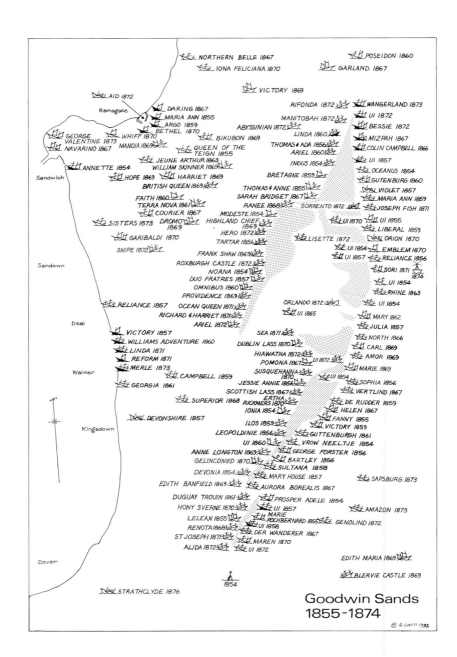

NORTHERN BELLE 1867   POSEIDON 1860
IONA FELICIANA 1870   GARLAND 1867

VICTORY 1869

Ramsgate
AID 1872   RIFONDA 1872   WANGERLAND 1873
DARING 1867   MANITOBAH 1872   UI 1872
MARIA ANN 1855   ABYSSINIAN 1872   BESSIE 1872
ARGO 1859   LINDA 1860   MIZPAH 1867
BETHEL 1870   THOMAS & ADA 1856   COLIN CAMPBELL 1866
GEORGE   WHIFF 1870   BIKUBON 1869   ARIEL 1860
VALENTINE 1873 MANOIA 1869   QUEEN OF THE   INDUS 1854   UI 1857
NAVARINO 1867   TEIGN 1855   OCEANUS 1854
JEUNE ARTHUR 1863   GUTENBURG 1860
ANNETTE 1854   WILLIAM SKINNER 1869   VIOLET 1857
Sandwich   HOPE 1869   HARRIET 1869   BRETAGNE 1859   MARIA ANN 1859
BRITISH QUEEN 1869   THOMAS & ANNE 1855 JOSEPH FISH 1871
FAITH 1860   SARAH BRIDGET 1867
TERRA NOVA 1861   RANEE 1868   SORRENTO 1872
COURIER 1867   MODESTE 1854   UI 1870   UI 1855
SISTERS 1873 DROMO   HIGHLAND CHIEF   LIBERAL 1859
1869   1869
GARIBALDI 1870   HERO 1872   LISETTE 1872   ORION 1870
TARTAR 1856
SNIPE 1872   UI 1854   EMBLEM 1870
Sandown   FRANK SHAW 1869   UI 1857   RELIANCE 1856
ROXBURGH CASTLE 1872   SORI 1871
NORNA 1854   1874
DUO FRATRES 1857   UI 1854
OMNIBUS 1860   RHINE 1863
PROVIDENCE 1869   ORLANDO 1872   UI 1854
RELIANCE 1857   OCEAN QUEEN 1871   UI 1865   MARY 1862
RICHARD & HARRIET 1871   JULIA 1857
Deal   ARIEL 1872   NORTH 1866
VICTORY 1857   SEA 1871   CARL 1869
WILLIAMS ADVENTURE 1860 DUBLIN LASS 1870   AMOR 1869
LINDA 1871   HIAWATHA 1872   UI 1872 MARIE 1869
REFORM 1871   POMONA 1867
Walmer MERLE 1873 SUSQUEHANNA   UI 1854
CAMPBELL 1859   1870   SOPHIA 1856
JESSIE ANNIE 1856   VERTLIND 1867
GEORGIA 1861   SCOTTISH LASS 1867
ERTHA   DE RUDDER 1859
SUPERIOR 1868 RICKMERS 1870   HELEN 1867
IONIA 1854   FANNY 1855
DEVONSHIRE 1857   ILOS 1859   VICTORY 1859
Kingsdown   LEOPOLDINIE 1856   GUTTENBURGH 1861
UI 1860   VROW NEELTJE 1854
ANNE LONGTON 1869   GEORGE FORSTER 1856
GELINCONIED 1870   BARTLEY 1856
DEVONIA 1854   SULTANA 1858
EDITH BANFIELD 1869   MARY HOUSE 1857   SAPSBURG 1873
AURORA BOREALIS 1867
DUGUAY TROUIN 1861   PROSPER ADELE 1854
HONY SVERNE 1870   UI 1857   AMAZON 1873
LELEAN 1855   MARIE
RENOTA 1868   ROCHBERNARD 1855   GENOLIND 1872
ST JOSEPH 1871   UI 1858
ALIDA 1872   DER WANDERER 1867
MAREN 1870
UI 1872   EDITH MARIA 1869
Dover
BLERVIE CASTLE 1869

1854

STRATHCLYDE 1876

Goodwin Sands
1855-1874

© R.Larn 1992

90

alongside the wreck due to a strong headwind, the lifeboat transferred eleven of her crew to the lugger *Fame*, already there when they arrived, and by this means five men from the brig's complement of six were saved, the other member having already drowned. For this service the two crews shared a reward of £22 donated by the Lifeboat Institution. Six weeks later the Ramsgate lifeboat was able to save not only the five-man crew of the sailing vessel *Queen of the Teign*, stranded on the 'off-part' of the Goodwins but, with the help of a Deal lugger, the ship as well. Bound from Antwerp to Liverpool with sugar, bark and seed she had stranded in such a position that by the time the lifeboat *Northumberland* arrived, the water was too shallow for her to go alongside and the master and four crew aboard the wreck were obliged to jump overboard and struggle through the surf to safety. Gattie records that it was the Deal lifeboat that went out, but there was no station at Deal until 1865.

The Ramsgate lifeboat was to be involved in three more rescues that year, in one of which she was so seriously damaged that she was very nearly lost. On 20th October the fishing smack *Maria Ann* of Colchester, attempting to enter Ramsgate harbour in a south-west gale, was hurled against the pierhead to founder within only a few yards of the stonework. One seaman escaped from the wreck by climbing up the mast, which for a brief period was touching the pier itself, but then the smack fell over on her side. Another member of the crew, struck on the head by the bowsprit, fell overboard and drowned leaving three others clinging to the rigging in full view of hundreds of onlookers. Repeated attempts were made to throw lines to the unfortunate men some thirty feet from safety, but the wind was too strong and the only hope lay in the lifeboat which incredibly enough had to be towed out to a wreck almost within the confines of the harbour. The tug was the twin-funnel paddle steamer *Aid*, only recently acquired by the Ramsgate harbour commissioners and the first of two such vessels to bear the name. Just as the lifeboat cast off from the tug a French gunboat, the *St Barbe*, also attempting to enter harbour, drove across the mast of the wreck and became fouled. Although this prevented the lifeboat from getting close to the smack, it did enable the three survivors to clamber to safety into the gunboat's rigging. The lifeboat then anchored and, dropping astern on a warp, had no sooner taken off one of the *Maria Ann*'s survivors than she struck the wreck a tremendous blow, causing considerable damage to her timbers. With water in the boat up to her thwarts, the lifeboat ran for Broadstairs and shelter and was later towed back to Ramsgate by the tug *Aid*, beached and repaired by torchlight, and was back in service by daybreak. In November the same lifeboat was launched twice in one day to the French brig *Marie Rochbernard*, since her crew could not find the wreck at the first attempt, while on 19th December they took the crew of the Fowey schooner *Lelean* not from off the wreck itself but from the Gull lightvessel on which they had taken refuge.

Between September and December 1856 the services of the Ramsgate lifeboat were required no less than six times, for the brigs *Jessie Annie* and *Bartley* in September, the *Tartar*, *Leopoldine* and *George Forster* in November, and the *Sophia* early in the last month. From the September incidents the *Northumber-*

Within a few days of the trawler *Ross Tarifa* being wrecked on the Goodwins in 1948, the 'great ship swallower' had already partially consumed her victim.

(Skyphotos, Hythe, and John G. Callis, Deal)

land saved a total of fourteen lives, the full crews of each of the two brigs. The *Jessie Annie* was already on her beam ends, dismasted and with her decks blown up by the time help arrived so there was no hope for the vessel itself, but the *Bartley* of Southampton, with a cargo of timber to help her remain afloat, was pulled off the sands by the *Sampson* on 25th September and saved. In the other incidents the *Northumberland*, assisted by one of her two powerful tugs, saved not only the crews but also three of the four vessels involved, only the Prussian brig *George Forster* remaining on the Goodwins to become a total wreck. It is therefore not surprising that the annual report of the Lifeboat Institution for 1856 had this to say of the Ramsgate lifeboat and crew: 'Indeed, there is no lifeboat in the Kingdom which has been brought so constantly into requisition during the last two years (1855/6) and none that is kept in a greater state of efficiency or more constant readiness for instantaneous service than she is, under the superintendence of the vigilant and active harbour master at Ramsgate, Captain K.B. Martin.'

To date, all the losses on the Goodwins or in the Downs had concerned only sailing vessels despite the fact that steam had been in use on the open sea around Great Britain since the late 1820s. But on 5th January 1857 the 'ship swallower' claimed its first steamship, the paddle packet *Violet*. A violent storm had raged all week and conditions were so bad in the Channel that shortly before the Royal Dover steam packet was due to leave Ostend all but one of his passengers chose to go ashore rather than risk the passage in such weather. Indeed, if it had not been for the company's mail contract it is doubtful if Capt Lymes would have decided to sail at all that day.

But sail he did with his crew of eighteen and one passenger and, shortly after 1.00 a.m. the following morning, rockets from the North Sand Head lightvessel alerted the Ramsgate lifeboat and tug crews and by 3.00 a.m. they were searching the back of the sands. Driving snow reduced visibility to only a few yards, and, finding no sign of a wreck, the cox'n took his boat well out to sea where it remained for the rest of the night. The search was resumed at dawn and only then did they sight the solitary mast of a new wreck sticking up out of the sea and sand. There was no immediate clue to her identity and no survivors but both questions were soon answered by the discovery of a bundle of clothing and human remains on a part of the Goodwins which dries at low water. The bodies proved to be those of three seamen, all lashed to one small lifebuoy bearing the legend s.s. *Violet*. It would appear that the 292-tons gross paddle steamer, built in 1843, had struck the Goodwins in poor visibility, that her crew had attempted to save the mail by throwing the sacks overboard, since most of them were recovered later, and that subsequently the 139-feet long vessel had gone to pieces. At low water on 6th January only the tops of her paddle boxes and one mast were to be seen as the Goodwins slowly and relentlessly engulfed yet another victim.

Despite the advantages of having a steam tug to take a lifeboat to sea, if a wreck should occur on the South Caliper of the sands, the relative distances

The Trinity House lightvessel *East Goodwin*, with the inshore survey vessel HMS *Echo* passing close by. With an ever changing outline, it is necessary to frequently re-chart the Goodwin Sands.   (Author's photograph)

between Ramsgate and Deal to the middle of the south sand are approximately twelve and five miles respectively. A second lifeboat located actually in the Downs would then have the advantage of proximity and sometimes the weather gauge of both the Ramsgate and Broadstairs boats. A branch of the National Lifeboat Institution was therefore formed at Walmer in January 1857 and the station was presented with a new 30 feet boat weighing two tons and built to the design of James Peake, master shipwright of the royal dockyard at Woolwich and a committee member of the Institution. Rowing ten oars and costing £156 to build, she was paid for by members of the Royal Thames Yacht Club, whose name she bore, half of the money raised coming from one gentleman alone. Reporting this splendid addition to the fleet the Institution described the *Royal Thames Yacht Club* lifeboat as being 'perfectly equipped both for rowing and sailing', while 'The Kentish Times' disclosed that the lifeboat 'master or cox'n, who is appointed by the Institution, is given a salary of £8 a year, and a retirement pension of £20, whilst the volunteer crew receive 3 shillings or 5 shillings a man, depending on the weather'.

The new boat had been on the beach for hardly a week when her services were required at the wreck of the barque *Reliance* of London and she proved her worth by saving fifteen lives on her first launch. The donors of the new life-boat were so proud of this achievement that they added £10 to the £13 awarded between the crew by the Institution.

After the *Reliance* had become a total wreck and was beginning to break up a large quantity of her cargo and stores was salvaged. To ensure a fair valuation of these goods, on which depended the reward payable by the owners to the boatmen, one of their number, named Pearson, went to London on 8th February 1857 as their representative. Amongst the goods laid out in the customs ware-house were what appeared to be several chests of soap and, as was the custom, each was opened, examined for condition and a pointed steel rod then used to probe the contents. One chest was found to conceal a smaller wooden box which, on being opened, disclosed a canvas bag inside of which was a human head, badly decomposed and having obviously been crudely severed from its trunk. The head was identified as that of either a Malay or Philippino male, but his identity, place of death, or the reason for the concealment of his head in such a manner was never established.

The closing months of 1857 saw a further eight vessels in distress and a great many lives lost. A gale on 10th October was so strong that the Ramsgate harbour master was quoted as saying, '...there has not been so fearful a gale since 27th November 1836', and at its height a fine American ship was seen to go ashore on the South Caliper. Her crew were rescued by Deal boatmen but no record of her identity, which must have been known at the time, appears to have survived. On 7th November the Dublin steam packet *Devonshire*, with passengers and cargo, ran ashore on the Main, off Kingsdown, but was able to refloat herself in much the same way as did the *Duo Fratres* the same day, before the Walmer lifeboat could be launched. This Norwegian brig, carrying coal from Newcastle to Barcelona, stranded on the Goodwins but was got off and taken to Ramsgate by a Deal lugger. On the 10th of that same month another addition was made to the lifeboat fleet in the Downs area. The first lifeboat to be stationed at Margate, she was donated by the inhabitants of Cowes, Isle of Wight, and built on the island. She was described as 'a noble boat, which without fittings cost an estimated £100. To complete her with appliances for saving life and the preservation of her crew another £50 will be needed'. Presumably this sum was raised locally, since a little more than a month later, on 17th December, she was launched for the first time, bearing the proud name *Friend of all Nations*.

Operating a lifeboat at night in shallow water under oars and sail only and in weather conditions when every seaman of choice would be ashore, demands not only a cool head and confidence but an expert knowledge of local conditions and fine seamanship. But most of all it calls for the freedom to act as circumstances dictate, without recrimination. For this reason the cox'n of the Broadstairs lifeboat was in no way held responsible for the loss of his boat on 26th November. It was almost midnight when two signal rockets from a light-vessel summoned the Ramsgate boat, under tow of the *Aid*, to sea in the teeth of a north-east gale. On arrival they found a brig on the face of the sands and, in

A change of sand level in Pegwell Bay on 6th February 1964 revealed the remains of a Second World War Lancaster bomber. Master Navigator Colin Walsh, RAF, stands on the mainplane touching a propeller blade. (Syndication International)

her lee, the relatively small Broadstairs lifeboat all five of whose spare hands were on board the brig attempting to refloat her. The officers and crew aboard the wreck steadfastly refused to abandon their vessel and as it was obvious that she could not be saved the *Northumberland* continued to stand-by until 2.30 a.m. when the brig started to break up. By then the Broadstairs lifeboat had been so badly damaged, having repeatedly struck the hull of the wreck, that her crew, in addition to the brig's, were all taken aboard the larger Ramsgate boat. With the crippled and waterlogged Broadstairs boat in tow the *Northumberland*, now deeply laden with some thirty men aboard, went over the sands to seek the shelter of the Downs before turning her bows north towards home. In the broken water covering the Goodwins, the two lifeboats collided several times and eventually the Broadstairs boat struck a sand bar so heavily that she filled and sank. If it had not been for the extensive modifications carried out to the Ramsgate boat in 1854, which included a new 4-inch, 15-cwt iron keel, she too might well have been lost that night.

Not all rescue attempts were so successful and in an incident involving the Walmer lifeboat and the sloop *Liberal*, the *Royal Thames Yacht Club* returned

Examining the Lancaster bomber's remains on Sandwich Flats at low water. The fuselage lies between the two intact propeller blades. (Author's photograph)

with only one survivor, although her crew had literally, for a moment at least, held another in their hands. This occurred on 15th April 1859 when the Wisbech sloop went ashore on the South Sand Head. Unable to get close the Walmer boat waited for the tide to turn but before it had risen sufficiently the mast of the wreck collapsed, throwing three men in its rigging into the sea. Of these, one drowned, one was taken into the lifeboat, while the third, Capt Richard Bonn, too weak to swim, was seized by one of the Walmer men, John Chadwick, who had jumped overboard to his rescue. He managed to get him alongside the lifeboat and, grasping the captain's wet clothing, the crew were about to heave him over the gunwale when the cloth split and he disappeared underwater. The gallant Chadwick himself also came close to drowning as he was several times thrown away from the lifeboat before he could be hauled aboard.

Although 1859 added a great many more names to the ever lengthening casualty list, information concerning them is scant; though it is known that at least eight of them became total wrecks. The lugger *Neptune* saved all four crew from the *Bretagne* on 22nd June, a rescue for which the Deal men concerned received £1 10s between them. From the French barque *De Rudder* there were no survivors when she was wrecked on 1st August but her remains must have

Six tugs vainly attempt to get the American steamship *Helena Modjeska* off the Goodwin Sands after stranding on 13th September 1946.

(Topix, Thomson Newspapers)

been both accessible and valuable since, within four days, two Whitstable smacks carrying four divers were salvaging some of her cargo from ten fathoms, including hides and tallow.

August is not a month normally associated with shipwreck, but that year, 1859, the brig *Victory* foundered on the 17th after striking floating wreckage and only a week later the Norwegian barque *Ilos*, carrying iron from Newport to Helsingfors (Helsinki), was lost on the sands. A public auction of her stores and fittings was held at Deal on 2nd September, followed by that of the 'hulk of the said vessel, coppered and copper fastened, as she now lies on the Goodwin Sands'. The final incident of that year would almost certainly have taken the Walmer lifeboat to sea again had events not happened so quickly. Whilst at anchor off Walmer Castle within only a few hundred yards of the lifeboat station, the wooden brig *Campbell* was run down and sunk without warning on 16th November by the steamship *Foyle*, a packet vessel working between London and Dublin. Though the larger of the two ships, it was she that suffered the only casualty, one of her seamen being crushed to death in the collision.

A particularly severe equinoctial gale on 24th/25th September 1860 saw the *Northumberland* at sea twice in six hours. At 11.00 p.m. guns were heard from the direction of the Gull lightvessel and on the lifeboat's arrival in the vicinity burning tar barrels were sighted close to a wreck on the inner part of the North Sand Head. She proved to be the Whitby barque *Linda* of 300 tons, laden with railway iron and in the course of a spectacular rescue of her crew a lifeboatman, Henry Venion, was washed clean out of the boat by a huge sea but somehow managed to scramble back aboard. Shortly before daybreak the Ramsgate men again took the lifeboat to sea, this time under tow from the *Vulcan*, to see if it were possible to save the *Linda* herself. They found the hull full of water and the barque a total wreck but less than two hundred yards away from the *Linda* now lay another wreck which must have gone ashore unnoticed in the early hours. This proved to be the barque *Ariel* of Gottenberg, laden with deal planks and the lifeboat returned triumphant to its home port with thirteen more survivors. As a tribute to the part played by local boats in these rescues on the Goodwins, the only silver medal awarded locally that year for bravery was presented to Thomas Trott, a boatman attached to the Deal lugger *Diana*. Attempting to save the crew of the brig *Poseidon* in the same gale, the masts of the wreck and the *Diana* fouled each other and had it not been for Trott, who leapt over the side with a knife to cut them free, the loss of life could have been heavy.

It was on New Year's Day 1861, and not the previous year as recorded by Gattie, that a most tragic wreck took place resulting in the drowning of a Deal pilot, Henry Pearson, as well as twenty-three others, including six women. In thick fog accompanied by snow driven before a near hurricane force wind the Hamburg brig *Guttenburg* of 170 tons went on to the South Sand Head and later capsized. It was fortunate that the wreck had not occurred half an hour earlier when the *Guttenburg* was carrying fourteen survivors from the *Canton* which had been found dismasted and water-logged off the coast of Newfoundland. By

Trucks, tractors and machinery being unloaded from the wrecked bow section of the *Helena Modjeska* after she had broken in two. (Will Honey, Deal)

The stern section of the Liberty ship USS *Helena Modjeska*, beached in Sandwich Bay 28th October 1946. Both bow and stern sections were towed into the River Blackwater on 10th June 1947 and sold for scrap. (Author's collection)

chance the Walmer lugger *Cosmopolite* had fallen in with the German vessel off Dover and at her captain's request, since food supplies were now very low, had relieved him of the shipwrecked crew. After the *Guttenburg* struck, several distress signals were fired but in the exceptionally poor visibility these went unnoticed except by a small handful of watchers on the beach at Deal, so that Ramsgate and all three lightvessels were for a time unaware of the disaster. A Deal boatman, Stephen Pritchard, telegraphed Ramsgate to ask for the lifeboat to be launched and within minutes both the *Northumberland* and the *Aid* were ready for sea. Then, to everyone's astonishment, Capt Shaw, the Ramsgate harbourmaster, refused them permission to leave. His decision was based on the commissioners' inflexible rule that the lifeboat was not to go to sea unless specifically signalled or summoned by any one of the lightvessels, or a vessel was actually seen to be in distress. Since in this case the fog made it impossible for the Ramsgate men to see either the North Sand or Gull lights, let alone the South Sand, they argued strongly that the word of a responsible local boatman should be trusted but the harbourmaster was adamant. With the wind onshore from the north-east the sea state prevented any of the luggers, and presumably the Walmer lifeboat as well, from being launched, so the only hope for the wreck lay in the *Northumberland*. For three long hours, from 6.30 until 9.30 p.m., the lifeboat crew pleaded for permission to leave but still the harbourmaster refused, despite two more telegrams from Deal confirming the incident. His only comment was to say: 'If you must go, then go in your own luggers,' knowing full well that if this had been at all possible they would already have left.

Unbeknown to the Ramsgate men, an attempt had already been made from Dover to reach the crew of the *Guttenburg*, since a Mr Irons, presumably the local harbourmaster, had sent a tug out to the South Sand but it had returned empty-handed, having failed to find the wreck. At last the Ramsgate harbour-master heard the sound of distress guns fired from the southernmost of the Goodwins lightvessels whose crew had sighted the wreck when the snow had ceased and visibility had improved. The *Northumberland* was quickly released but on arrival at the scene the Ramsgate men found the vessel smashed to pieces and her captain, Mr Pearson, the pilot, and twenty-two others dead. For some time it was thought that no one had escaped the wreck but in fact two had been rescued by a Dover boat and a further five had managed to reach port in their own small lifeboat in an utterly exhausted condition. A charge of neglect of duty was brought against Capt Shaw for not sending assistance sooner but he maintained that he was only observing 'the regulations, or routine' and, since the trustees of Ramsgate harbour expressed their satisfaction with his conduct, the Board of Trade decided there was no call for an inquiry. Despite being exonerated by his superiors, Capt Shaw suffered the humility of a widely distributed satire entitled 'Routine — A Tale of the Goodwins', which left no doubt as the author's opinion on the matter.

The foremast and Samson-posts of the 7,607 ton USS *North Eastern Victory*, wrecked on the South Goodwin's Head 24th December 1946, as they still show today.

(Author's photograph)

It was this wreck of the *Guttenberg* that also brought about the premature retirement of the *Northumberland's* coxswain, James Hogben, who had been in charge of her since her arrival nine years earlier. James Hogben had been at sea all his life, at first in small vessels trading between London and Ostend, then in his own boat of some fifteen tons trading between Ramsgate, Dunkirk and Boulogne, followed by twenty years' hovelling around the Goodwin Sands. On the day the *Guttenberg* was lost Hogben had already been to sea in the Ramsgate lifeboat and was both exhausted and unwell. A knee injury incurred in the boat combined with the mental strain involved in the unfortunate *Guttenberg* incident proved too much for him and he developed some sort of nervous disorder so that he could not even walk along the pier for fear of falling over the edge. Following a partial recovery he was employed as a boatman in the harbour, then as a night watchman on the pier, but he never went to sea again. His replacement was Isaac Jarman, who also had had many years of seafaring experience, including being twice shipwrecked. He held the position for ten years, going to sea in the lifeboat no less than 132 times and saving between three and four hundred lives, but in the end he too became ill with severe bronchitis, a direct result of being out in the lifeboat nine times in one fortnight, five times in one week alone. When he was forced to resign, he was succeeded by Charles Fish, probably the greatest cox'n Ramsgate ever saw.

Three months after the *Guttenberg* incident there was a rather unusual affair concerning the 700-ton American ship *Georgia*. Missing stays on approaching the shore on 30th March 1861, she stranded near Walmer Castle and the local boatmen swarmed all over her in their enthusiasm to get her afloat until they discovered only one item of cargo — a coffin complete with corpse. Most seamen are superstitious on this score and the Deal and Walmer men being no exception, they hastily left the *Georgia* and refused to return until the 'cargo' had been landed. Sevenal tons of shingle ballast were then taken out and dumped overboard, the tug *Sampson* pulled the sailing ship clear and, after re-embarking the coffin, the *Georgia* resumed her passage to New York.

A contemporary newspaper account dated 23rd May 1861 states that 'the new lifeboat at Walmer, paid for by the Royal Thames Yacht Club, and allocated to the Downs by the National Lifeboat Institution, was taken out last week for its quarterly exercise under Capt Ward, RN, who reported that she was highly satisfactory, and that her crew approved of the 37-feet-long boat.' This would appear to contradict the general belief that a new replacement lifeboat at Walmer, also named the *Royal Thames Yacht Club*, was not supplied until 1863. There are also discrepancies concerning the date the *Northumberland* was replaced by the *Bradford* lifeboat. Reporting two wreck incidents during the spring of 1863, one newspaper records that on 6th April the large London ship *Rhine* went ashore on the Goodwins and broke her back. At 10 a.m. the following day the 102-ton French *Jeune Arthur* of Nantes, Master Charron, laden with coal, was struck by an American vessel in the Downs and foundered twenty minutes later. That same day at 3.00 p.m. an unidentified schooner was seen to go ashore on the Goodwins *to which the lifeboat 'Bradford' and her tug went out*. This is at variance with the accepted date of 1865, the year usually quoted as that in which the Bradford Exchange subscribed approximately £600 in one hour to build and equip the new lifeboat. The matter is further complicated by an account in the 'Kent Coast Times' of 6th January 1867. In a footnote to a long report concerning shipping losses in the area, there followed: 'a few months ago the people of Bradford paid for a lifeboat to replace the old *Northumberland* which, after having served for many years, saving 250 lives, was broken up for firewood. The *Bradford* has been to sea several times before but this occasion, the 6th January, was the first time she was called out to perform a proper service.' There can be little doubt that the *Bradford* was installed at Ramsgate in 1865 and the confusion may have resulted from the temporary introduction of a smaller lifeboat, the *Little Friend*, during the changeover period. Nevertheless, three different dates appear in contemporary records with evidence of a sort to support each.

During 1865 two more lifeboats were installed at new stations in the Downs, bringing the number of boats within easy reach of the Goodwins to six, counting Dover and Broadstairs. The first of these went to North Deal beach and was named *Van Kook* after E.W. Cooke, a famous marine artist who was responsible for collecting most of the £450 required for her construction. This boat was

A Russian grain-elevator barge, un-named, stranded at Kingsgate in September 1946, later refloated and saved. (Will Honey, Deal)

stationed on the beach, roughly 100 yards south of Sandown Castle, opposite an inn called the Good Intent. The second, a 33-feet self-righting boat rowing ten oars, went to Kingsdown under the name of *Onzio*, which was later changed to *Sabrina*. As with the North Deal boat, she also lay on the beach but within a year was properly housed in a new boathouse and remained on station until February 1873. From Kingsdown, she is variously reported as going to Newquay, in Cornwall, although the records of that station make no mention of this.

The *Van Kook* was not called to sea except for practice until 7th February 1866 when a full-rigged ship was seen to be in distress near the Goodwins. Within minutes the lugger *England's Glory* and the Deal and Walmer lifeboats were manned and launched. The lugger arrived first and after ensuring that the two lifeboats were close at hand she stood right in amongst the surf, passing the wreck as close as she dare. As she sped past, six of the lugger's crew flung themselves across the gap, found handholds in the ship's rigging and were able to scramble aboard. The *Van Kook* under Cox'n Wilds anchored some way up wind, veered out a cable and was able to get six of her men on board as well, but the Walmer boat in attempting the same manoeuvre fell away to leeward and was unable to regain her position. The ship was the *Iron Crown* and her position on the sands was such that she was in immediate danger of becoming a total loss. With her bows aground and huge seas coming up astern, any attempt to get her head to wind by dropping her anchors would have driven her over her own tackle and holed her bottom. Instead, the lugger's crew, displaying great skill and seamanship, managed to get a kedge anchor over the weather side, suspended from one end of the ship's foreyard. In this manner she swung round on the flood tide with the Goodwins right beneath her keel, and in no time the three waiting steam tugs had her in tow and on the way to safety in the Downs. The crew of the Deal lifeboat on this, its first service, comprised Cox'n R. Wilds, R. Roberts, E. Hanger, G. Pain, J. Beney, G. Porter, E. Foster, C. Larkins, G. Browne, J. May, A. Redsull, R. Sneller, T. Goymer and R. Erridge.

Although many charges of wrecking and plundering, some real but a great many more imaginary, have from time to time been laid at the door of both Deal and Walmer boatmen, no excuse can be made for their behaviour at the wreck of the North on Thursday 30th August 1866, a case so serious that a Board of Trade inquiry was held and its findings reported to the House of Commons. The North, of 1,238 tons, went ashore on the Goodwins about two miles north-east of the South Sand lightvessel. She had sailed from Liverpool on 28th June carrying coal for Aden, her captain being under orders to seek a return cargo as best he could. A quantity of rice was taken on at Bassein, in Burma, and on the return passage the North stopped for fresh provisions and water at St Helena and Queenstown, before proceeding up Channel for London. It was dark when she struck the sands and her captain and crew of thirty promptly abandoned ship in their own boats, seventeen in the ship's lifeboat, the remainder in the pinnace. All were saved, the former being found at sea by a Texel-based lifeboat and landed at Dover, the other fourteen by the lugger Reform which took them to Deal. In the confusion following the wreck the crew were able to save almost nothing of value, so that the ship's stores, instruments, fittings, furniture, tools and personal belongings were all left behind.

At daybreak on the 30th the wreck was clearly visible from every beach in the Downs and soon boats, including the two new lifeboats, were on their way out from every town and village in the area. Robert Hurst, keeper of the South Sand lightvessel, wrote in his log, 'As soon as the day come on, the boats were swarming.'

So, too, were their occupants who, clambering aboard in their dozens, completely stripped the North of anything and everything, whether of value or not. Her sails were stripped from her yards, her spare sets rifled from the lockers and with them went every inch of rope and wire, including rigging, even down to blocks, shackles and deadeyes, so that it was surprising her masts remained standing. Two of her crew who later returned to look for personal effects reported, 'There was not enough rope left to make a mop, nor sufficient canvas to tie round your finger if it had been cut.' Several tons of canvas vanished and with it some three-quarters of a ton of attached cordage, as well as four tons of hawsers. None of the ship's instruments was ever seen again, nor the carpenter's tools or a stitch of clothing and, of course, not a scrap of food. With nothing left to take from inside the vessel, as the tide fell leaving the North high

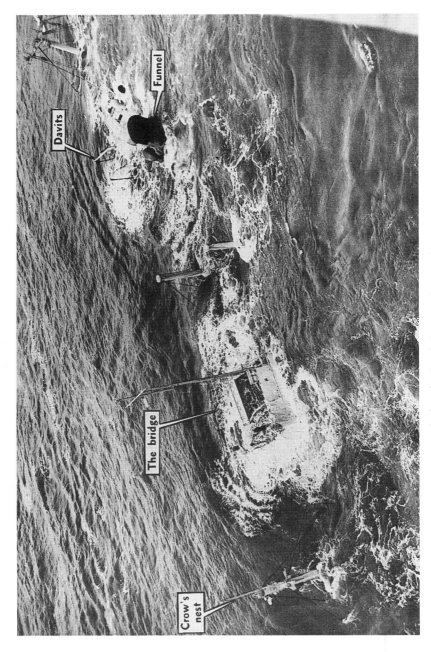

The Italian freighter *Santagata* wrecked on the Goodwins on 24th December 1950.

(Daily Graphic)

and dry, the boatmen turned their attention to her copper sheathing. This covered her entire lower hull from the keel to a height of 21 feet and over her 192-feet length represented 12,000 lb weight of metal, most of which was removed.

The stripping of the *North* was not in itself unusual since such activity had been commonplace for centuries, and from long experience the men of the Downs knew it was only a matter of days, if not hours, before the 'ship-swallower' would claim the wreck for ever. Nor was the removal of goods criticised, but rather the manner in which it had been carried out and the fact that almost nothing was surrendered to the Receiver of Wreck. The basic principle of the law of wreck and salvage as laid down in the Merchant Shipping Act is that salvaged goods shall be protected and where possible returned to their rightful owner. This point was quite clear in the subsequent Board of Trade report which stated: 'Had it all been returned to the Receiver, then the conduct of the strippers would not only have been legal but praiseworthy.'

Canvas, rope and blocks from the wreck were traced to marine dealers at Dover, named Dennis and Dowell, as well as one at Deal, by the name of Foster. Some of the stores even found their way to a firm of papermakers at River, near Dover, and later became the subject of a trial at Canterbury. Mr Montague Bere, who conducted the inquiry into the alleged plundering, wrote in his report, '...an inability to read and write seems to be considered a desirable qualification for a marine store dealer, whether in Deal, Walmer or Dover.' This was because he found Foster's book-keeping so neglected that there was no record as to the source of rope and canvas. None of the boatmen questioned at the inquiry professed to be able to remember the name of a single Deal boat other than their own, nor the names of men that went to sea, nor even the state of the wreck before and after their visits! Even the coastguards were suspected; Mr Bere commenting: '...their evidence clearly cannot be relied upon and in some instances was plainly and directly contradictory.'

The eventual outcome — a few minor convictions and the removal of certain officials — served only to demonstrate once again that the inhabitants of the coastal towns bordering the Downs were an exceedingly close-knit community. With everyone's attention focused on the wreck of the *North*, little heed was paid to her survivors and it was several days before it became known that of the fourteen men saved by the Deal South-End lugger *Reform*, eight were from the steam tug *Wellington* which had foundered while trying to salvage the *North*.

Four years later, on 16th January 1871, when the *Reform* herself was lost in a tragic accident just off the beach, the Deal town council had reason to regret having ignored an earlier petition by fifty boatmen for the removal of Deal pier as constituting a danger to navigation. In the early hours of that cold January morning, with a full south-west gale blowing, distress flares were seen in the Downs and the *Reform*, beached opposite the famous Time-ball Tower, was launched. While being pulled out through the surf on a running warp a loose piece of rope fouled the block and the sea threw the lugger against the iron

An artists impression of the wreck of the French schooner *Gustave*, which missed Deal pier by only a few feet on 24th November 1877, going to pieces on Deal beach watched by hundreds of spectators.   (Deal Maritime Museum)

piles of the pier, smashing the boat to pieces within minutes. Her crew of eleven were thrown into the sea but there were few about to help them. Two men leapt over the turnstiles and threw ropes towards them, while three members of the Deal lifeboat crew manned a small boat, but between them they could save only Thomas Baker, John Bailey and William Goymer. The bodies of all eight drowned were recovered and laid to rest in the cemetery of St Leonard's Church. A relief fund was started and was about to close, having reached £1,670, when the Deal galley punt *Hope* was lost in another salvage attempt and four more local men drowned.

Amongst the many reports of gallant rescues are others less complimentary. A letter in the 'Deal, Walmer & Sandwich Telegraph' of 7th December 1867 reads:

'The launching of the Walmer lifeboat was greatly delayed by the selfish conduct of some of the boatmen of whose bravery I had always heard so much. I was in hopes that the proceedings on that occasion were exceptional and of rare occurrence, but from what happened last Saturday night I am afraid delay appears to be the rule; for then I was startled to hear the boom of a gun labouring heavily through the wind, and the rockets flew to call assistance for the little band of hopeful fathers, husbands and sons stranded on the treacherous sands. Fear not, the lifeboat and her crew will come when your last signal has faded away. It is impossible that you could have sunk so soon, it was only a little more than half an hour she was getting off the beach, and then some of the crew were in the best of spirits as they had received all the help Bacchus could give them before they ran to get their belts, and very little time was lost in settling who should go coxswain (as the right one declined the honour).

'If things go on in this way it would be better to give the charge of the boat to the boatmen's wives, they could not possibly manage worse. Verily, God help the shipwrecked mariners while the Walmer lifeboat is launching.'

Signed: A Sailor's Daughter

Whatever the truth of the matter, the correspondent was obviously unaware that on returning from this episode the lifeboat capsized three times when off Deal pier, about a mile from shore. Fortunately a lugger was on hand and rescued the entire crew.

Of the countless rescues which have taken place around the sands two which will surely go down in history took place on 5th and 6th January 1867 when the Ramsgate lifeboat put to sea three times and was afloat for a total of twelve hours. Shortly before 8.00 a.m. on the 5th, in thick fog accompanied by a strong east wind, signal guns were heard from the direction of the North Sand Head or Gull lightvessel at five minute intervals and within ten minutes the Ramsgate lifeboat, under tow of the *Aid*, was clearing the harbour mouth. A sudden increase in the wind strength cleared the fog, so that a schooner could clearly be seen ashore on the off part of the North Sand Head. Arriving in the Gull Stream, having steamed through the Cudd channel, the lifeboat met with a ship's boat carrying eight men, the entire crew of the schooner *Mizpah*, Master Browning, which had been bound from Amsterdam to Genoa with sugar. This Brixham-registered vessel had got onto the Goodwins the previous evening but had been unnoticed in the fog. When the water in the schooner's hold reached a depth of almost five feet her crew were taken aboard the *Faith* of Boston, which was close at hand, but returned at daybreak before deciding to row ashore. The *Mizpah*, in fact, refloated herself that same day, so that four luggers were able to get her into Ramsgate. After landing the survivors the lifeboat again put to sea, this time in quest of a vessel reported to be on fire, but a thorough search revealed nothing.

The next day the lifeboat was out again, this time to the Danish barque *Aurora Borealis*, ashore on the south-east spit of the Goodwins. Her crew of ten were clinging to the mizzen rigging, soaked to the skin by a raging sea which threatened to pluck them from their perch at any moment. So bad were the conditions that five times the lifeboat was towed by the *Aid* into position and five times they fought to reach the wreck in the boiling surf, but each time they were defeated. Then the steam tug attempted a rescue, by manoeuvring sufficiently close to fire a rocket line over the barque, but the sea threw her onto the sands and she came very close to being lost. Drastic measures were now necessary if a rescue was to be carried out before the tide dropped, so the lifeboat was again towed into position and this time charged the wreck bows-on. As

The coaster MV *Berend N*, her starboard rail awash after her cargo shifted off the South Foreland, January 1954. She was taken in tow and saved. (H. Hayles, Yarmouth)

Driven clean through Deal pier after being blown ashore on 19th January 1873, the iron barque *Merle* could not be extricated and was broken up where she lay. There are at least 40 other vessels in the Downs in this photograph. (A.J. Langridge, Deal)

they struck the Danish vessel a terrific blow a lifeboatman heaved an anchor over the vessel's bulwarks and, hanging onto its hawser and that of a grappling iron at the stern, managed to pull alongside and embark the Danish ship's crew. The lifeboat arrived back at Ramsgate at 2.30 p.m. with her crew, especially the first and second coxswains, Isaac Jarman and Charles Fish, so exhausted that they had almost to be carried to the Sailors' Home in York Street.

The only other incident on that eventful day fortunately did not require the services of the lifeboat. At 6.00 p.m. the schooner *Garland*, Master Smurthwaite, Sunderland to St Valery with coal, sank some six miles off Dungeness. Her officers and crew, ten in all, attempted to reach Dover by boat, but when the tide forced them into the Downs they rowed to Ramsgate, where they arrived at 4.30 a.m. At first they could find no one to help them as almost everyone in the town was at the scene of a large fire in Stapelton's drapery shop at 79 King Street and it was some time before the shipwrecked mariners were able to explain their plight and be directed to the newly-opened Sailors' Home. In recognition of the bravery of the lifeboat and tug crews, the Board of Trade gave the twelve men a sovereign apiece, to which the King of Denmark added 200 rix dollars, so that they each received £3 9s — which they considered an insult to themselves and a reflection of the low value the King apparently placed on the lives of his subjects.

That same month Isaac Jarman, the Ramsgate lifeboat coxswain, suffered the loss of his brother who was drowned in a wreck, together with the rest of his crew, within sight of the town. Carrying coal from Hartlepool for use at Rams-gate by the various steam tugs stationed at the royal harbour, the schooner *Navarino* of Arundel, commanded by Capt T. Jarman, struck the Brake Sand on or about 22nd January while attempting to enter the port in a snowstorm. The body of her captain and that of a local boy named Dixon were washed ashore near No. 2 Battery at Deal, along with the ship's compass, a boat and papers, the vessel herself being later found on the beach in Pegwell Bay. In the pocket of the dead master was a letter from his brother Isaac, dated 9th January and written from 13 Frederick Street, Ramsgate, part of which read, '...we have had fearful weather here and a great many wrecks, but some of the poor fellows are saved.' There were, in fact, to be a great many more shipwrecks before the year was out including those of the brig *Courier*, sunk by collision with the *Star of the West* on 4th February; the *Sarah Bridget*, a brigantine, stranded on the Goodwin Knowl and also the *Pomona*, both on 21st March. The Plymouth smack *Daring* was lost with her crew of five off the end of Ramsgate pier on 25th April and other victims included the Russian man o' war *Vertland*, on 30th May; the *Der Wanderer*, a Norwegian barque carrying timber, on 9th October; the *Helen*, a Welsh schooner stranded four days later and, finally, the *Scottish Lass* which sank on 4th November when she struck the mast of a wreck and was holed.

A year later, in January 1869, there was a gale that lasted for the best part of three days and saw at least six more vessels fall victim to the sands. Of the many newspaper reports of the storm the most colourful was that of the 'Kent Coast

The Ramsgate lifeboat and a tug circle the burning tanker *Johannishus*, damaged in a collision east of the Goodwin Sands. (Evening News)

Times', which read: '...the scene from the cliffs shortly before 7.00 p.m. could be compared to nothing but a display of fireworks, rockets flying up in all directions from ships in the Downs, and soon flares were burning to such an extent, that the sky was quite illuminated thereby.' As the *Bradford* lifeboat cleared the harbour entrance heading for the scene, she narrowly missed colliding with a schooner that was sinking on the North Brake Sand. The calls for help from her crew could clearly be heard above the storm, but in the pitch darkness and with no flares to guide them it was impossible for the Ramsgate men to locate them and they drowned within earshot.

Out on the Goodwins the 854-ton barque *Highland Chief*, Master Beverley, was found aground with seas breaking over her deck. For four hours the lifeboat attempted to get close enough to save her crew and finally succeeded just as the barque went to pieces, and then only after three of the lifeboat's crew had waded waist-deep across part of the sands. Five of the shipwrecked seamen who had already got away in a small boat were never seen again but the remaining twelve, including a pilot and the captain's two-year-old Newfoundland dog which had saved his life on a previous occasion, were rescued. On the return journey the *Bradford* encountered the schooner *Tavistock*, derelict and adrift. Six of the Ramsgate men boarded her and earned a useful bonus by getting the schooner, which was laden with Penryn granite, to safety. As the storm continued a number of survivors from other wrecks rowed into Ramsgate harbour including the crews of the Colchester oyster dredger *Start*, the Rye sloop, *Thomas & Wilson*, the *Harriet* and the brigs *Hope* and *Amor*. The latter was German-owned, and several of her crew were rescued by the lifeboat, in addition to those who had saved themselves. In appreciation of this rescue the Grand Duke of Mecklenburg-Schwerin presented silver medals and certificates to Daniel Reading, master of the *Aid* and cox'n Isaac Jarman. Similar awards were made to the crew of the tug, namely, J. Simpson (mate), W. Wharrier (engineer), F. Lawrence, T. Nichola, J. Freeman and T. Tucker; and also to the crew of the lifeboat *Bradford*: C. Fish, J. Stevens, W. Gornham, S. Goldsmith, S. Penney, P. Goodchild, J. Kember, W. Solly, T. Ferrett, R. Stock and D. Kirkaldie.

Over the next five years there were more than seventy-five wreck incidents in the area. From these, cargo after cargo was auctioned off locally and their various inventories make interesting reading. From the steamship *Orion*, sugar, coffee, composite candles, hides and tobacco were sold off at the warehouse for wrecked goods, near St George's Church, Ramsgate, on 19th January 1870. Nine months later more tobacco came under the auctioneer's hammer when, on 15th October, some twenty tons of leaf from the German ship *Etha Rickmers* were sold at the Customs House, the average price paid being 1d per lb or, for the better leaves, 2½d. From this wreck there was not a single survivor from her crew of twenty-three. On a lighter note, a smile must have crossed the face of the Receiver of Wreck when, on 5th July 1871, in completing a deposition form for the master of the Ramsgate-owned collier *Aunt Sally*, he wrote: '…said vessel was involved in collison and suffered minor damage after striking a lamp post on the quay'! Five months earlier during the winter gales, when both the Kingsdown and Walmer lifeboats were out to the barque *Linda* (the former having been replaced by another *Sabrina* and the Walmer boat by the *Centurion*) the latter capsized twice, fortunately without loss of life. In the December of 1871 four ships were again found to be on the Goodwins at the same time, bringing the total number lost that year to twenty-two and 109 over a ten-year period.

The last six weeks of 1872 were to prove as eventful as any the Downs had known in its stormy history and it was towards the end of this period that the famous *Sorrento* rescue took place. The sequence of disasters began at 2.33 p.m. on 13th November when the Falmouth-owned barque *Hiawatha* went onto the Goodwins. Fourteen out of her fifteen crew were drowned, the only survivor being her helmsman, Charles Brown. He spent almost four hours in the sea and was almost insensible from cold and shock when picked up by the galley punt *Leander* and promptly transferred to the *Hertha Geng*, at anchor in the Downs. When informed that his ship had stranded on the sands, the *Hiawatha*'s master went below to his cabin, shut the door and was never seen again.

The next wreck was that of the *Genolind*, often miscalled the *Jenny Lind*, which occurred on 13th December. This Russian barque, bound from Hull to Genoa with coal, had been aground some twelve hours when discovered by the Ramsgate and Deal lifeboats and was already well down in the sand. Five of her crew of eleven were still alive in the rigging, including Capt Lingkell, but one seaman, Gustaf Karlsan, swung dead at the end of a rope lashing, his head wounds suggesting that he had died after repeatedly striking the bow of the ship. The following day four more vessels got on to the Goodwins including the *Abyssinian*, but all four managed to extricate themselves. Considering the time of year, it was considered nothing short of a miracle that the next victim, the brig *Wangerland* of Oldenburg, was saved on 15th December. She was carrying 163 emigrants, seven cabin-class passengers and a large crew when she struck the North Sand Head and a major disaster was narrowly averted when she was successfully refloated by the lugger *Buffalo Gal* and towed into Ramsgate by the tug *Restless*. Describing the event, the 'The Kent Coast News' wrote, 'The emigrants are of a very poor class and several of them are of advanced years. They were taken off the vessel at Ramsgate and put in a building at the back of the meat market. Much sympathy has been shown locally for these people and £8 for their benefit has been raised by public subscription.'

It was a dark and windy night on 17th December 1872 when, at 2.00 a.m. distress signals were heard from the direction of the South Sand Head. Both the Walmer and Kingsdown lifeboats were launched under their respective cox'ns, William Bushell and Jarvist Arnold. It was agreed that the *Sabrina* should go right through the surf zone and burn a red flare if there was any sign of a wreck. A steamship was spotted stranded on the South Caliper, so the second boat was summoned and both craft were laid alongside the wreck which proved to be the *Sorrento*, homeward bound from the Mediterranean to Newcastle. Half the crew of each lifeboat were detailed to go aboard to assist, after which both lifeboats with the rest of their crews and cox'ns dropped astern, and waited at anchor. Working side by side, the lifeboatmen and the *Sorrento*'s crew heaved cargo overboard to lighten ship, manned her pumps and attempted to get up steam again but on the flood tide it became obvious that the sea had already won. Then the 5-inch hawser of the Walmer lifeboat's anchor parted and she drifted almost a mile to leeward before she could be brought up again with the spare anchor. With half her crew still on board the steamship, it was impossible for her to get back alongside, so everything depended on the *Sabrina*. She too had a depleted crew numbering eight and the only hope for the fourteen lifeboat men and thirty-two crew, huddled on the tiny bridge of the *Sorrento* was for a line to be floated down to the Kingsdown boat. An eighty-fathom length of heavy rope was first tried but this sank and recourse was then made to an old cork fender secured to the end of a deep-sea sounding line. This succeeded and within minutes a heavier line had been passed and the stranded men were able to haul the lifeboat alongside. The captain of the *Sorrento* was the last to leave and as he stepped aboard the *Sabrina* the steamship's funnel and masts collapsed and she broke in two. The cork fender was kept in the village for many years afterwards and out of respect for the *Sabrina*'s coxswain, Jarvist Place, in Kingsdown, still bears his name.

The final incident of this period occurred on 19th January 1873 when the iron barque *Merle* rammed Deal pier and became firmly stuck. It took many days to extricate her as her masts and rigging had first to be cut away and then all her cargo and stores removed. However, the syndicate which purchased the wreck for £500 came out of it well for she was refloated, repaired and later sold back into service.

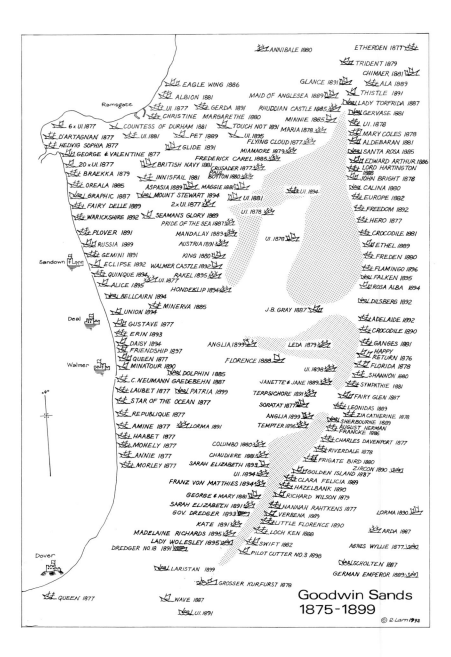

Goodwin Sands
1875-1899

© R. Larn 1992

116

Chapter Six

STEAM ON THE GOODWINS: 1875-1899

Although sail continued to predominate as the principal method of propulsion at sea throughout this twenty-five year period, steam was slowly but surely taking its place. Already in use on the majority of cross-Channel routes, as well as on the majority of regular packet services plying between London and Ireland, the presence of steamships was reflected in the increasing number of incidents and wrecks in which they were involved on the Goodwins. This applied particularly to collisions and more than a few of these involved the light-vessels which marked the outline of the sands.

The introduction of steam at sea was not simply a substitution of one type of vessel for another, and in the Downs particularly, the change was to have a dramatic effect on the way of life of every boatman and ultimately to bring about the decline of the area as an anchorage. Whereas sailing ships once used the Downs as a haven whilst awaiting a fair wind, steamships could proceed regardless of wind direction and, more often than not, in far worse sea conditions. They also had no need to anchor off Ramsgate or Deal to replenish their water supply or take on fresh provisions, nor did they seek the services of local pilots. Outward-bound ships would take on a Channel pilot at Gravesend who would be only too happy to go all the way to Falmouth. Similarly, Cornish pilots from the mainland or the Isles of Scilly would reciprocate if their services were required in the opposite direction. With few steamships in the Downs and an ever dwindling number of sailing vessels, the number of anchors lost locally was greatly reduced so that the centuries-old occupation of 'sweeping' and the salvage of lost ground tackle fell into disuse. With the reduced number of ships came an automatic fall in the number of customs officers and coastguards employed, and the number of beach boats dwindled dramatically as men looked elsewhere for a living. Eventually even the number of lifeboats stationed around the Downs was reduced, so that slowly a way of life for an entire community began to change.

But sail or steam, gales continued to take their toll of ships and men and those of November 1877 were probably the most persistent and severe to strike the Kent coast in modern times. For two weeks from 11th November the Downs were almost continually storm-bound and in that short time approximately forty-seven vessels went ashore with a heavy loss of life. Throughout the night of the 11th the wind howled in from off the sea with hurricane force and at first light six ships were seen to be stranded in Pegwell Bay. The masts and sails of a further two were to be seen protruding above the surface in the Gull Stream and at Dumpton, a mile north-east of Ramsgate, a large French brig lay on the rocks.

The two masts of the 592 gross tons British tug s.s. *Rumania* show above the surface after she stranded and sank off the North Foreland on 11th February 1956.

(Lt. Cdr. J. Mackay, RN)

The *Bradford* lifeboat had been so badly damaged in a minor service the previous week that a temporary replacement had been necessary, and as this had arrived only the day before the Ramsgate crew had had no opportunity to test her seaworthiness. Nor did her smaller size inspire the confidence of her crew, who considered her less stable than their normal boat and, when called out that night by distress signals from the Gull lightvessel, they refused to let slip the tug's tow rope for fear the lifeboat would be swamped. Consequently they returned to harbour empty handed but within the hour were again at sea, as was the North Deal lifeboat *Van Kook*, summoned this time to the French schooner *George & Valentine*, one of the vessels ashore in Pegwell Bay. Later that same night they also attended the *Soratat*, the *D'Artagnan*, a French brig, and the Swedish barque *Hedvig Sophia*. The Ramsgate boat was, in fact, kept so busy that the crew completely ignored a large Dutch barque stranded only a short distance from the harbour entrance, assuming that the local luggers would render assistance and, indeed, a number of passengers, including women and children, were so saved from her and lodged at the Royal Hotel. Seventeen men were saved from the *Hedvig Sophia* and the *D'Artagnan*, so that on her return the Deal lifeboat carried five Frenchmen and twelve Swedes in addition to her own crew of fifteen. Her cox'n received a silver medal for bravery that night and, the lifeboat having sustained extensive damage to her bows when striking the Swedish wreck several times, the citation accompanying the medal mentioned a hole in the boat, '...so large, a man could have crept through the rent.'

Although the wind decreased, the sea remained rough and the weather unsettled until 24th November when storm-force winds again arose, this time preceded by heavy and continuous rain. For a time the wind blew from the south-west and then backed through almost 270° to settle at north-west, throwing vessels at anchor in the Downs into great confusion. At midnight the French topsail schooner *Gustave*, Capt Crocq, drove down towards Deal pier and might well have collided with it had not John Lawrence, the toll keeper, screamed at the crew to luff-up. Missing the pier by only a few feet the schooner went ashore on the northern side opposite a Dr Mason's house and within a few yards of the esplanade. The break-up of the wreck must have been spectacular since an eye witness declared, '...there ensued a scene terrible to describe' as the vessel split longitudinally, the deck parting completely from the hull. After several unsuccessful attempts had been made to fire a rocket line across the wreck hand traversing lines were thrown and the entire crew were dragged through the breakers to safety.

As the night wore on another schooner, the *Queen* of Dartmouth, Capt Head, bound from Shields to Devon with coal, plunged straight into the pier, rebounded, and then struck a second time smashing four of the cast-iron pillars and their entablatures as well as ripping-up the wooden deck with her broken mast stumps. The toll keeper managed to pull the mate, James Callard, and a fourteen-year-old lad and his father, named Kinney, to safety before the vessel went right under the pier and out the other side. As the wreck emerged it struck the seawall near the Time Ball Tower, then capsized before going completely to pieces and drowning Capt Head and two seamen, Henry Gilbert and Robert Davison, whose bodies were later found on the beach between Deal Castle and Kingsdown. Weakened by the collision and a series of huge waves which struck the under decking, almost 200 feet of the pier had been demolished and the refreshment room completely destroyed by morning, damage which cost over £5,000 to repair. The pier was again badly damaged on 26th January 1884 when a Beaumaris schooner, the *Alliance*, smashed its way through from the southern side.

From opposite Lloyds' signal station, near the Time Ball Tower, to St Margaret's Bay, the coast was a mass of wreckage with five ships ashore in close proximity. The first to go ashore was the Norwegian barque *Haabet*, Kragero to Bristol with timber, whose twelve crew were saved by rocket apparatus. Close at hand was the *République*, a French brigantine also carrying coal, from which only two men were rescued; also the *Star of the Ocean*, the *Armine* (or *Annie*) and the *Mohely*. Forty-two lives in all were saved from these strandings while at sea the Margate lifeboat *Quiver* and her larger companion boat, *Friend of All Nations*, rescued 130 people, seventeen from the barque *Hero* and the remainder from wrecks actually on the Goodwins. The remains of the *Star of the Ocean* were sold by auction on 4th December to a Mr Pott; the hull of the *Gustave* was purchased by Morris Langley, who resold it to a Mr Ralph for £30, while the heap of timber which had once been the *Queen* fetched exactly £3 as firewood! The

Laden with telegraph poles and her upper deck partly awash, the coaster MV *Hunzeborg* holed herself on a wreck on the Goodwins and was brought into the Downs off North End, Deal, to be pumped out. (Skyphotos Ltd, Hythe, now Fotoflite)

The crew and Secretary (right) of the Walmer lifeboat c1900, on station on the beach.
(Deal Maritime Museum)

locals were not slow in picking up anything on the beaches that took their fancy and Robert Yeoman of Ramsgate was successfully prosecuted for being in unlawful possession of clothing belonging to Charles Lynd, the mate of the schooner *Jean Cameron* which had been wrecked near Margate. In subsequent but less violent storms that same year a ship of the Liverpool Line, the *Crusader*, became a total wreck on the Goodwins on 1st December, all three of the Downs lifeboats being launched to her assistance. Eleven days later the twelve-year-old German *Hannah Rathkens* became another victim. Named after her captain's wife, this timber-laden vessel quickly went to pieces after nine of her ten crew had been rescued by the tug *Aid*.

In January 1878 the Ramsgate lifeboat the *Bradford* was at sea six times in a seven-day period, and later, in May, was employed on the gruesome task of recovering a great many corpses strewn the length of the sands and in the Gull Stream. These were the bodies of German sailors drowned when the battleship *Grosser Kurfürst* sank offshore from Dover following a collision with the *König Wilhelm* during exercises. In all, over 500 lives were lost in this one disaster.

The year 1881 was memorable for three gales all sufficiently severe to be called hurricanes which wrought even more damage on land than at sea. On 18th January, with a south-east wind blowing directly into Dover harbour, three luggers were smashed to pieces against the quay, the wreckage being tossed into the road where it blocked all traffic for several days. So widespread was the effect of the gale that the capital was described as 'arctic London', 'waves as high as the clock tower' crashed down on the sea front at Dover, while at Deal the sea came right into the town, breaking at least 200 windows. During a four-day period following 14th October eighty vessels were brought into Ramsgate harbour for shelter, trees 3-4 feet in circumference were uprooted and the large window in the lounge of the Albion Hotel was blown in, injuring a visitor from Exeter. At sea, six local fishing smacks were lost and Queen Victoria contributed £50 to the widows and orphans fund which was subsequently opened. During those violent four days no less than forty-five survivors were handed over to the care of the Shipwreck Institution at Ramsgate whose resources soon became so depleted that an appeal was made for old clothing, hats, boots and comforters. Some of the survivors were from the *Countess of Durham*, two from a Deal boat lost in Pegwell Bay, but the majority came from the Liverpool ship *Ganges*, wrecked on the Goodwins. On passage from Middlesbrough to Calcutta with a cargo consisting of iron railway chairs weighing 85 lb each and wooden sleepers, the latter shifted in a rough sea and the vessel had been forced to put back to the Downs to restow her cargo. The tug *Hibernia* managed to get a line aboard but was unable to make any headway and the *Ganges* went ashore on the inner face of the sands opposite Deal. In response to signals from the Gull lightvessel, the *Bradford, Vulcan* and *Mary Somerville* went out and rescued all of her thirty-five crew, seventeen being saved by Deal boats but three were presumed to have been drowned. Two members of the *Ganges'* crew who were saved had been previously shipwrecked on the Goodwins, one of them twice

The Panamanian oil tanker s.s. *Sovac Radiant* ashore under the 200 ft high cliffs at the South Foreland, 14th January 1952. (Graphic Photo Union)

before, which must be something of a record. At the subsequent Board of Trade inquiry held at the Wreck Commissioner's Court in Westminster Mr Commissioner Rothery stated that the vessel was probably overloaded and that a combination of chairs and sleepers was an exceptionally dangerous cargo. The captain was cleared of all blame for the vessel's loss but sharply criticised for showing unnecessary haste in jumping into a lifeboat before ensuring that the rest of the ship's boats had been launched.

These gales reached a climax in late November, with Ramsgate taking the worst of the storms. In the town the hoardings enclosing the skating rink in the High Street were blown flat, thirty feet of the colonnade at the rear of the Royal Crescent came down, and all the small boats in the harbour sank. In Betteshanger Park, the residence of Sir Walter James, Bart, MP, situated four miles inland from Deal, at least 500 trees were blown down and at Dover a gun and carriage were washed clean out of an emplacement on the Admiralty pier. Called out to attend the Irish brig *Innisfall* stranded on the Brake Sand, the *Bradford* was unable to help the brigantine *Albion*, laden with coal, which went ashore at the back of the east pier at Ramsgate at 1.00 p.m. Capt Jones, the harbourmaster, wanted to launch the commissioners' small rowing boat but his boatmen refused to help, declaring that the sea was too rough. Both vessels became total wrecks and, of the *Albion*'s cargo, a local newspaper reported that, 'on the Sunday morning, the poorer class were seen on the sands with barrows and sacks, collecting coal.'

Perhaps the most unusual incident in the gale was the loss of the Liverpool ship *British Navy* on 26th November. Whilst at single anchor in the Downs she began to drag and instead of dropping her second and starboard anchor Capt Skelly ordered more chain to be veered out on the port anchor. With ninety fathoms out she struck the iron-hulled *Larnaca* and sank with the loss of her captain, pilot and eighteen crew. It was an altogether strange affair since neither vessel showed distress signals either before or after the incident, nor sought assistance from vessels close at hand. The 1,217-ton *British Navy* sank directly over what was then called the Cinder Bank because a cinder-laden vessel had been wrecked there in 1858 and with only six feet of water over her deck she was a serious navigational hazard. She was buoyed until salvage work could begin but, even so, at least two ships ran into the sunken vessel.

The first successful salvage of a steamer in the Downs was that of the paddler *Dolphin* which sank following a collision with the s.s. *Brenda* on 18th September 1885. Owned by the General Steam Navigation Co., the 641-tons gross *Dolphin* had left the Thames under Capt Elwood the previous day bound for Le Havre with passengers and a general cargo which included some 300 casks of sherry. At about 1.00 a.m. they passed the Gull lightvessel and Amos Sedden, the chief mate, wrote in the ship's log, 'All well, lights burning brightly, proceeding at full speed.' The masthead light of another vessel then appeared ahead and while the *Dolphin* was taking avoiding action the other vessel, the *Brenda*, turned the same way and struck the *Dolphin*'s starboard quarter, tearing a large hole in her hull about 30 feet from her stern. Distress rockets were fired and within a short time the tug *Granville* had the sinking ship in tow, making for shallow water off Walmer, while the Kingsdown lifeboat *Charles Hargrave* stood by. The steamer finally sank some three-quarters of a mile offshore, leaving four feet of mast above the surface. Besides her crew of twenty-four, the paddle steamer carried thirteen or fourteen passengers, and it was their cabins which took the main force of the collision. Five lives were lost, two male and two female passengers and the ship's donkeyman, John Churchill, and at an inquiry at the Zetland Arms in Kingsdown the master of the *Brenda* was severely reprimanded for not having kept a better lookout and for failing to stop to pick up survivors.

Another unfortunate collision involving steamships occurred between the *German Emperor* of Sunderland, which sank with the loss of fifteen passengers and crew, and the *Beresford* on 18th May 1889. The latter was at anchor at the time, close to the East Goodwin lightvessel, when the *German Emperor* appeared out of the fog and struck the other steamer a terrific blow in a head-on collision. Holed from the deck of the forecastle to below the waterline the *German Emperor* sank in less than three minutes, directly beneath the bows of the other vessel and for a time remained almost vertical with her stern well clear of the sea. Following the cry 'All hands on deck — the ship's sinking', most of

The French s.s. *Agen*, carrying a deck cargo of mahogany and hardwoods, wrecked on 'Calamity Corner', the south-eastern part of the Goodwin Sands, on 13th January 1952. She broke clean in two.
(Skyphotos Ltd, Hythe, now Fotoflite)

the crew and passengers ran aft but ten of them had the presence of mind to clamber through the hole in the bow and get aboard the *Beresford* before the ships drifted apart. The *Beresford* lowered two boats and after picking up Richard Gordon, a seaman, and two passengers, one of whom had a broken leg, took them to Dover, but on returning got lost in the fog and drifted around for three hours.

Three days later, with the fog still persisting, five of the crew of the London schooner *Aspasia* left their ship in a small boat to row across and read the name on a large navigational buoy and so establish their position. Having determined that it marked the Brake Sand they then found they could no longer see their own ship, and drifted about for hours until picked up by the ketch *Perseverance* of Cardiff, which brought them back to the Downs. Later, the Deal galley *Seaman's Glory* found the guano-laden *Aspasia* at anchor dangerously close to the Brake with only her master and a boy aboard and assisted them clear of danger to a safe anchorage. The same galley, owned by a Mr Porter of Deal, was at sea again on 22nd May and literally stumbled upon the steamship *Sherbourne* stranded on the Goodwins, of whose predicament no one else was aware. Between them, the two crews managed to get her afloat again and she continued on her voyage to London. Unfortunately the *Seaman's Glory* herself became a victim of the sea on 25th August when caught by a squall. The four-year-old one-ton sailing boat sank half a mile north-east of Deal Bank, drowning one of her crew along with three of four passengers.

Before the year was out three more sailing ships had gone on the sands: the *Clara Felicia* of Port Madoc and the *Mandalay* of Glasgow, both on 12th December, and the Truro schooner *Maid of Anglesey* on the 18th. The *Mandalay* was refloated and saved but only after some 200 tons of railway iron had been heaved overboard to lie on the Goodwins in a great heap until in time it slowly disappeared. In this service the North Deal lifeboat *Mary Somerville* almost came to grief when a steel towing hawser between the tug *Cambria* and the wreck got under her keel. As the two vessels rolled in heavy seas the wire suddenly went taut, lifting the heavy lifeboat into the air clear of the sea, then allowing it to fall back directly across the bulwarks of the wreck. Any less sturdy boat would almost certainly have broken its back and the crew were fortunate indeed that it did not at least capsize.

Unusually cold weather and rough seas heralded in 1891 a year full of incidents for the Goodwins, including the 'great blizzard' of March which caused widespread misery but few shipping losses locally, a collision between a sailing ship and one of the lightvessels, a great many more shipwrecks and the famous *Indian Chief* rescue. The latter incident occurred on the Longsand, a sandbank in the Thames estuary and hence outside the scope of this volume, but it is generally regarded as the most famous of the Ramsgate lifeboat rescues. On 3rd January the *Bradford* and the tug *Aid* went out in response to a report that Dover men had sighted the masts of a steamer sticking out of the sea near the South Caliper, but after searching for hours they found nothing. Next day, in answer to

A victim of collision, the Danish schooner *Fyn* was run down by HM Destroyer *Scorpion* off Dover on 15th November 1911, and had to be assisted into the Downs by the tug *Lady Vita*, where she was beached at Deal and broken up. (Deal Maritime Museum)

Wreck at Walmer. 12/1/11

The German schooner *Flores*, which dragged her anchors and went ashore so close to Deal pier that one of her booms carried away a gas lamp standard on the south-east corner. She then drifted on down the beach, ending up closer to Walmer on 12th January 1911. (Deal Maritime Museum) the Gull light, they launched again and for a second time returned empty handed after remaining at sea all night long. That same afternoon the crew were once again called out, this time to the brig *Kate* which had gone ashore on the sands. Twenty-four hours later the *Bradford* was at sea yet again, heading for the *Crocodile*, a barquentine carrying stone, which was already under water on the north-east spit by the time the lifeboat arrived. With the crew of the wreck in the rigging and half frozen, Cox'n Fish had no alternative if he was to save them but to take his boat in very close, and this he did in appalling conditions, with a full north-east gale blowing, the temperature well below freezing and in blinding snow squalls. Six men were rescued but the seventh, Capt Kimber, fell from the mizzenmast and drowned just as he was about to be rescued. The *Crocodile* had previously gone ashore at Deal in 1890 with the same captain in charge.

Shortly after the *Crocodile* went ashore the Broadstairs lifeboat was seen making for Ramsgate with survivors aboard. These were the crew of the 145-ton schooner *Glance* of Ramsgate, which had collided half a mile east of the North Foreland with a sister ship, the 197-ton *Glide* registered at the same port, and both vessels had sunk in ten fathoms. These schooners were employed on a regular coal run beween Sunderland and Ramsgate, the principal owner being a local coal merchant named Deveson. The master of the *Glide*, Capt Eastland, who was also part-owner of the vessel, appears to have been somewhat prone to shipwreck since this was the fourth vessel in which he had served that had been lost.

In March the full-rigged ship *Plover* of London was almost cut in two in the Downs before sinking, after being struck by the steamer *Benefactor*, and in another collision, this time off Dover, between the s.s. *Godmandun* and the Norwegian barque *Lorma*, the latter capsized and sank, taking eight of her nine crew with her. A few days later Trinity House raised the wreck and the tender *Warden* towed it, still upside down, to Pegwell Bay. There it was blown up using guncotton, and in a spectacular explosion wreckage was flung several hundred feet into the air. Other incidents involved the Russian barque *Gerda* which struck Ramsgate pier and sank on 14th October; the *Austria* of Riga, stranded and lost on the Goodwins on 26th October; the government dredger No. 18, sunk near the South Sand Head on 22nd October, and the *Touch Not*, the *Thistle* and the *Gemini*, all on 11th November.

The ketch *Touch Not* was lost just outside the east pier at Ramsgate. Loaded with china clay and bound from Charlestown, in Cornwall, for Aberdeen, her mizzenmast carried away in a squall off Deal, whereupon four local men boarded her and, despite the lack of any agreement with the master, took charge and anchored the vessel. Later, insisting that the ketch should enter Ramsgate harbour, whereas the master wanted to wait for high water, the Deal men slipped both anchors and cables, again without permission, headed in for the entrance and promptly ran the ketch aground.They then took to the ship's boat, rowed ashore and disappeared. Although not wrecked totally, the tragic loss of the Deal hovelling lugger *Walmer Castle* on 15th March 1892 deserves

Stranded in the Downs near Sandown Castle, the Rotterdam registered MV *Mercurius-H* was eventaully refloated and saved. (Skyphotos Ltd, Hythe, now Fotoflite)

A neutral steamship, the *Batjan* ran ashore off Deal on 2nd December 1914, remaining fast for a month until the next spring tide to refloat her. There was a rumour that her double bottoms were full of mines. (Deal Maritime Museum)

special mention as six local men and a fine boat then came to grief. On the lookout for pilot work, since changing circumstances had now forced the men to look further afield, the *Walmer Castle* was driven onto a lee shore on the Isle of Wight and sank in Horseshoe Bay, Bonchurch. Overwhelmed by huge seas she went to the bottom but the wreck was later washed ashore. The bodies of Henry and David Axon, James Arnold, William Cusney, James Hoile and William Gilchrist were conveyed by rail, free of charge, back to Deal for burial and a local relief fund for the dependants raised £514. This was not the first Deal lugger to be lost on the Isle of Wight. In October 1887 the *Pride of the Sea* went onto the rocks at Yellow Ridge, near Shanklin, causing the death of all eight of her crew.

At a time when the anchor lights of ships in the Downs were still so numerous that the spectacle was described as 'England afloat', it is not surprising that many collisions occurred, the worst offenders being steamships. The *Zircon* was one such victim, run down and sunk just clear of the East Goodwin on or about 23rd May 1895. Laden with sugar and salt for Preston, she was struck by the s.s. *Ahdeer* and sank almost immediately. A contemporary local report refers to the 500-ton *Jargoon* of Glasgow also said to have been sunk by collision, but this cannot be verified. Another incident concerned the s.s. *Laristan*, of 2,134 tons gross which hit the sailing vessel *Crimea* in fog on 22nd October 1899, but in this case it was the former that sank. One month later the Downs claimed one of its largest victims, the 5,000-ton American liner *Patria*, carrying fifty crew and 150 passengers as well as a general cargo. When found by the Russian *Ceres* about twelve miles from the North Hinder lightvessel the *Patria* was on fire. Using the liner's boats, everyone aboard was transferred to either the *Ceres* or the smack *Adieu* and the *Patria* was abandoned. Still blazing, it finally sank inside the Goodwins, between Deal and Kingsdown. Within two months the Swedish salvage steamer *Belos* had arrived and, after carrying out an underwater survey, was joined by the *Stradler* and the *Svare* but their combined attempt to raise the wreck appears to have been unsuccessful. In January 1902 an Admiralty notice to mariners stated: '...The wreck having been so far dispersed so that there is now thirty feet of water over the whole wreck at LWS, the wreck-marking light-vessel will be removed on or about 5th January and replaced by a conical gas-lit buoy painted green and marked "WRECK".'

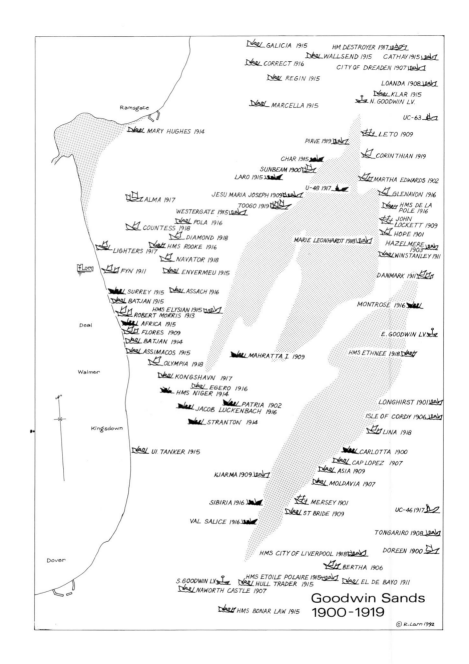

GALICIA 1915   HM.DESTROYER 1917
WALLSEND 1915   CATHAY 1915
CORRECT 1916   CITY OF DREADEN 1907

REGIN 1915   LOANDA 1908
KLAR 1915
MARCELLA 1915   N.GOODWIN LV.

Ramsgate   UC-63

MARY HUGHES 1914   LETO 1909
PIAVE 1919   CORINTHIAN 1919
CHAR 1915   MARTHA EDWARDS 1902
SUNBEAM 1900
LARO 1915
ALMA 1917   JESU MARIA JOSEPH 1909   U-48 1917   GLENAVON 1916
TOOGO 1919   HMS DE LA POLE 1916
WESTERGATE 1915   JOHN LOCKETT 1909
POLA 1916   HOPE 1901
COUNTESS 1918   MARIE LEONHARDT 1918   HAZELMERE 1903
DIAMOND 1918   WINSTANLEY 1911
LIGHTERS 1917   HMS ROOKE 1916
NAVATOR 1918   DANMARK 1911
FYN 1911   ENVERMEU 1915
SURREY 1915   ASSACH 1916
BATJAN 1915   MONTROSE 1916
HMS ELYSIAN 1915
ROBERT MORRIS 1913
Deal   AFRICA 1915
FLORES 1909   E.GOODWIN LV.
BATJAN 1914
ASSIMACOS 1915   MAHRATTA I 1909   HMS ETHNEE 1918
Walmer   OLYMPIA 1918
KONGSHAVN 1917
EGERO 1916
HMS NIGER 1914   LONGHIRST 1901
PATRIA 1902   ISLE OF CORDY 1906
Kingsdown   JACOB LUCKENBACH 1916
STRANTON 1914   LINA 1918
OIL TANKER 1915   CARLOTTA 1900
CAP LOPEZ 1907
KJARMA 1909   ASIA 1909
MOLDAVIA 1907
SIBIRIA 1916   MERSEY 1901
ST BRIDE 1909   UC-46 1917
VAL SALICE 1916   TONGARIRO 1908
DOREEN 1900
Dover   HMS CITY OF LIVERPOOL 1918
BERTHA 1906
S.GOODWIN LV.   HMS ETOILE POLAIRE 1915   EL DE BAYO 1911
HULL TRADER 1915
NAWORTH CASTLE 1907

Goodwin Sands
1900-1919

HMS BONAR LAW 1915   © R.Larn 1992

Chapter Seven

THE WRECK OF THE *MAHRATTA:* 1900-1919

In October 1885 the North Sand lightvessel parted from her cables and went adrift in a furious gale, the South Goodwin vessel following suit on 28th December 1899. The latter drifted right into the surf zone of the sands where she lay for three days before the Walmer lifeboat was able to get sufficiently close to save the crew, a service for which they received thirty shillings each. When eventually the weather moderated, a Trinity House tender got a line aboard the derelict lightvessel and towed her back into position, none the worse for having been aground for the best part of a week. Of the four lights, which were eventually reduced to three when the Gull vessel was no longer considered essential, it was always the East and South lights which suffered the most accidents. The East Goodwin light was again damaged by collision during the early hours of 1st December 1903 while on station one and a half miles east of the sands in twenty-nine fathoms. The one man on look-out had earlier sighted a steamer which appeared to be heading straight for them but even after a warning gun had been fired it did not alter course. Minutes later it slammed against the lightship's bow mooring chain, then glanced off to strike the port bow a terrific blow. The colliding vessel proved to be the Cardiff-registered *Hazelmere* of 722 tons, in ballast, and further damage was inflicted when the lightvessel rebounded from the initial blow. Temporary repairs were effected but in a gale two days later she leaked so badly that it was necessary to withdraw her from service to carry out repair work costing over £400. Yet another collision caused serious damage to the South Goodwin light in November 1904 and the same vessel broke from her moorings and went adrift in December 1914.

During the early years of the twentieth century one of the more notable shipwrecks on the sands was that of the four-masted iron barque *Mersey*. Although owned in Norway this 998 gross tons vessel, originally built as a steamer in 1859, was registered in London and hence carried an English crew. On passage to Grinstad from Santa Fe with 3,000 tons of dye wood she passed Dover on 29th December 1901, signalling Lloyds that all was well, but that night when close to the East Goodwin light the wind dropped and she was suddenly at the mercy of the tide. Though every stitch of canvas was set and then both anchors dropped, she was swept relentlessly onto the sands. The wind then chose to blow hard from the south, pushing the wreck further ashore where she began to break up. Her distress signals brought out a Kingsdown galley but before it could arrive the *Mersey* had broken in two. The Walmer lifeboat *Civil Service No. 4* and the *Charles Hargrave* from Kingsdown were launched and

Ashore near the South Foreland, the freighter s.s. *Germania* was later refloated and saved.
(Skyphotos Ltd, Hythe, now Fotoflite)

A winters gale put the Finland schooner *Kaleva* ashore at Deal, where she became a total loss. An auction of her timbers and fittings took place on the promenade, opposite where she was broken up on 11th November 1921. (Deal Maritime Museum)

went alongside the wreck, saving all thirteen crew just as the entire fore part of the barque collapsed. Another Scandinavian loss was that of the *Bertha* of Esbjerg, almost cut in two by the Dutch steamer *American* on 20th June 1906. This accident occurred close to the South Goodwin light, the three-masted barquentine sinking so quickly that the captain's son was the sole survivor. Along with the majority of the crew who were below decks, Peter Norholm was asleep in his bunk when disaster struck. Instinctively he dashed up on deck, heard someone shout 'Save yourself boy', and leapt overboard just as the ship sank. The *Bertha* took to the bottom six crew, two passengers and a valuable cargo of salted skins.

Although there had been previous signs of discontent between the various lifeboat stations in the Downs it was not considered to be serious, nor did it show publicly until 1904 when open accusations were made concerning improper launching of lifeboats. Had there been a central authority in control of all four boats, such situations as all of them appearing at one wreck and none at another would not have been possible, but with each station independent of the others there was open and sometimes hostile competition between them, a situation which continued until 1912 when the number of boats was reduced. This was, however, only the tip of an iceberg of discontent and there were many other related problems later to be made manifest. In the meantime an ever increasing number of steamships were either going ashore on the Goodwins or else foundering through collision. Typical of these was the *Carlotta* on 9th October 1900, from which the *Civil Service No. 4* lifeboat saved thirty-five lives. This was followed by the *Longhirst* of 2,048 tons on 21st June 1901, sunk near the East Goodwin light after striking the *Setubal*; the *Patria*, already mentioned; the *Isle of Caldy*, also near the East Goodwin in June 1906, and the *City of Dresden*, an Irish steamship, on 19th January 1907. By this time the North Deal lifeboat was no longer the *Mary Somerville*, which had been on station in the Downs since August 1888, but the new *Charles Dibdin* Civil Service boat, installed in 1905 and named after the most famous of all the Royal National Lifeboat Institution's secretaries. No less than four lifeboats purchased by the Civil Service Fund were named after this exceptional man, who had started off as a clerk in a savings bank. But for his untimely death in 1910 Charles Dibdin would have received the knighthood which King George V had intended to confer on him that year.

New Year's Eve 1906 was to be long remembered at Deal as on that day a public enquiry opened in the Town Hall to investigate a strike by the Walmer lifeboat crew, its attendant circumstances, and a host of grievances connected with the lifeboat service. It was presided over by Lord George Hamilton, with Capt Acton Blake of Trinity House as the nautical assessor, while other specialists included the Institution's chief inspector and Capt Foote, the lifeboat inspector for East Kent. The Walmer lifeboat crew had taken the precaution of engaging a Dr Hardman to represent them and the enquiry was concerned with a difference of opinion that had arisen between the central and local

The British schooner *Robert Morris*, which went ashore near Deal on New Years Eve 1913, later successfully refloated and saved. (Deal Maritime Museum)

The liner s.s. *Mahratta* wrecked near Bunt Head, Trinity Bay, on the Goodwin Sands, 9th April 1909. Over 100 men worked to jettison her cargo of tea, rubber, jute and rice, but she broke her back. (A.J. Langridge, Deal)

The British steamship *Winstanley*, stranded on the Goodwin Sands 1st April 1911, refloated and saved.   (Deal Maritime Museum)

committees of the institution regarding the launching of the Walmer boat the previous April. As a result, friction between the two authorities had culminated in the refusal of the Walmer men to man the lifeboat.

Cox'n Harry Parker of the *Civil Service No. 4* boat described the conditions of the service in which his crew had participated on 23rd April, when all four of the Goodwins' lightvessels had fired distress rockets at 2.30 a.m. He explained that it was not uncommon for several vessels to go onto the Goodwins at the same time and had assumed this to be the case on the night in question. Conditions at the time were bad, being very dark with thick haze, so he had exercised his discretion as coxswain, launched the boat and found a vessel that had been in collision with the East Goodwin light. Continuing, he confirmed that the Walmer boat was the first afloat and the first to reach the East Goodwin area, and this was substantiated by telephone messages recorded on official report sheets. As was the custom on the return of a lifeboat, the local secretary — in

The American Liberty ship *James Harrod* caught fire after collision with the anchored Liberty ship *Raymond B. Stevens* in the Downs, off Deal on 16th January 1945. Beached in Pegwell Bay, whilst the fire was extinguished, she broke in two. Her bow section was later towed to Bremerhaven, filled with chemical ammunition and scuttled at sea.

(Deal Maritime Museum)

this case the Rev. Stanley Treanor — recommended that the crew be paid but this was rejected by the London Central Committee on the grounds that the Walmer boat should never have been launched. On hearing this, the Walmer crew refused to 'go in the boat again' until their claim had been met and the 'weather rule' done away with. They also told the Lifeboat Institution that they might as well remove the boat since no one would use her again. In the meantime the boatmen who had constituted the crew used their own craft to attend wrecks and had been out several times that month already.

It was the 'weather rule' that was the root of the trouble, that and the fact there were too many lifeboats on a short stretch of coast. The rule stated that, '...in really bad weather, the action of the Goodwins lifeboats will not be scrutinised too closely, *but as a rule*, only the weather boat is to be launched'. Cox'n Parker contended that the Walmer boat, stationed as it was between two others and only three miles apart, could never be right in launching. It was also his opinion that no lifeboat should ever go out to the Goodwin Sands alone since they often required assistance themselves, and he proceeded to prove his point by quoting several recent examples. He pointed out that when they launched to the ship *Mersey*, the Walmer boat was first out, and had rescued some of the crew before the Kingsdown boat had even found the wreck, yet on return he had been told that the *Civil Service No. 4* should never have been launched. Called to give evidence, Capt Nepean stated that the rule was necessary to prevent lifeboats being launched in flat calm weather, when 'even a Serpentine skiff could float with safety'. At present the Goodwins lifeboats were going out to anything, anywhere, and the service was being brought to ridicule as a result. A local pilot who had himself been shipwrecked four times already, commenting on the incident twelve months earlier when the cox'n had not been paid, reminded the assembly that there had been 200 persons aboard that particular stranding. 'What use would one lifeboat have been then, had she broken up?', he asked, a question which met with loud applause. After a heated discussion following a suggestion by the central committee that the unnecessary launches were only being made for the money, it was finally accepted that the Walmer lifeboat had acted for the best in the circumstances and that the crew should be paid, but relations between the crews continued to be strained until one of the three Downs boats was subsequently withdrawn. Disturbing new evidence also came to light when the official weather reports of the various lightvessels and lifeboats were compared. These showed complete agreement between the ships, but the wind direction was heavily biased towards the locality of each respective lifeboat station! As a result, the wording of the weather rule was altered to read, 'In fine weather the boat in the most advantageous position having regard to the wind, tide and distance from the casualty is the only one to be launched.'

Lifeboat politics notwithstanding, there was no reduction in the demands on the service. Two steamships were in trouble on 19th January 1907 when the Ramsgate boat was called out to the *Moldavia*, stranded on Bunt Head just inside the Goodwin Fork light buoy; and all three boats were put on stand-by for the *Naworth Castle*, sunk by collision with the Red Star Line's *Vaderland*, though only one boat went out to her. When the Belgian steamship *Cap Lopez* was wrecked on the sands on 21st December 1907 two lifeboats were there, the Kingsdown crew landing Capt Schmidt and his crew of thirteen. In the course of this rescue the Walmer boat was badly damaged and had to be towed ashore by the Kingsdown men, a situation which did nothing to ease relations between the two towns. In succession, a string of steamships were in trouble over the next five years. On 27th November 1908 the *Drumlanrig* and the *Tongariro* were in collision; the coal-laden *St Bride* went onto the south-east part of the Goodwins on 6th February 1909; another collier, the *Kjarma*, stranded on the south-west side of the sands on 10th March 1909, followed by the *Mahratta* exactly a month later. As a direct result of a collision between the New Zealand steamer *Tongariro* and the *Drumlanrig*, after which both vessels were run ashore near Dover, the Deal town council appointed 'A committee to enquire into the new methods of signalling casualties on the Goodwins, in the interests of life and property, and of the boatmen of Deal'. The council were looking in particular at wireless equipment, and felt that a Marconi station at Deal, 'which was the centre of the wreck area,' would solve many problems.

A Belgian steamship, the 5,182 gross tons *Kabinda*, wrecked in Trinity Bay, 8th December 1939. The break in her hull can clearly be seen level with her funnel. In the lower photograph, she has broken into three sections. (Will Honey, Deal)

Although at the time of her loss the *Mahratta* was almost certainly the largest vessel ever claimed by the 'ship swallower', she is best remembered in history for a most remarkable coincidence. The *Mahratta* was wrecked on the Goodwins on 9th April 1909 whilst on passage from Calcutta to London and Dundee with passengers and a general cargo. A little over thirty years later, on 6th October 1939, a second *Mahratta*, also owned by the Brocklebank Line, on the same voyage and carrying passengers and a general cargo, was wrecked less than a mile from her predecessor. The original *Mahratta* had left Calcutta on 6th March 1909 with ninety crew, seventeen passengers and 10,000 tons of cargo, mostly tea, jute, rubber and rice, and was in charge of a Trinity House pilot when she went aground in Trinity Bay, close to the Fork Spit. Every effort was made to refloat the ship using her engine, but when Capt Ellery learnt that she was leaking badly, her propeller shaft was bent and that rivet heads had sheared off in their hundreds, the assistance of tugs was sought. About one hundred local boatmen and labourers appeared on the scene offering to save the cargo and were engaged en masse to work on the basis of a 33 per cent net award on everything they landed. By the time the first of the tugs had arrived all 621 cases of tea aboard had been landed, in addition to 280 bales of jute and eighteen cases of rubber. Seven tugs engaged to pull her off failed to move the huge vessel, so the number was increased to eight, but even at high water on 10th April the *Mahratta* remained fast aground. In desperation, since the vessel was by now leaking badly, the number of tugs was increased to nine and these literally pulled the ship in two at 9.00 a.m. on 11th April. With a noise like gunfire she parted right across the line of her bunkers and saloon. There followed a mad rush for the boats and sixty Lascar seamen were so convinced the *Mahratta* was sinking that they leapt straight off the upper deck into lighters alongside. The few remaining passengers, crew and local men were all saved, the only casualty being Samuel Gibson, the chief engineer, who was found dead on the floor of his cabin with self-inflicted throat wounds, the reason for which was never established. In the hope that at least the after section of the wreck could be saved, the Liverpool Salvage Co. sent the salvage steamer *Enterprise*, but within three days both halves were well down in the sand and by 20th April were completely submerged at high water.

Most of the wreck incidents in this area over the previous ten years had occurred either on the Goodwins or else to the east, in deeper water, with very few strandings at Deal or Walmer. Then, as if in prelude to the dozens that were to run ashore here during the First World War, three sailing vessels were stranded, two of which became total wrecks. The first was the 60-ton German schooner *Flores* which dragged so close to the pier at Deal on 12th January 1911 that one of her booms carried away a gas lamp on the south-east corner. She went ashore opposite the premises of Hinds & Sons, estate agents, and when a distress rocket was fired to summon assistance the projectile roared so low over the deck that it very nearly decapitated two of the crew! The *Flores* quickly went to pieces, after which several hundred chamber pots, part of her cargo, graced

For a short period in June 1973, the Goodwins revealed one of its countless victims, the German submarine *U-48*, sunk on 24th November 1917. It had previously made another brief appearance in 1921. (Peter Powell, Broadstairs)

the promenade while awaiting sale by auction. On 15th November 1911 the Danish schooner *Fyn* was struck by HM Destroyer *Scorpion* at sea off Dover, so crippling the sailing vessel that the tug *Lady Vita* was summoned to get her into the Downs before she sank. They managed to reach Deal where the schooner was beached in the hope of saving her, but even after her masts had been cut away she was completely submerged by the rising tide.

In 1912 a special meeting of all concerned was held at Deal to consider the lifeboat service in the area in general and, in particular, the advisability of reducing the number of boats from four to three. Statistics relating to the total number of services and lives saved by each boat were considered, Ramsgate excepted, and these showed that the three Goodwins boats between them had up to December 1901 saved 760 lives, of which North Deal was credited with 428, Walmer 171 and Kingsdown 161. A motion that the Walmer station be closed and its lifeboat withdrawn from service was defeated by a narrow margin in a free vote, but nonetheless the central committee of the RNLI in London ordered the lifeboat removed and the station was closed in July of that year. Less than fifteen years later it was to be re-opened and is today the sole survivor of the original three stations.

The censorship of all newspapers and similar sources of information during the latter half of the First World War has unfortunately left little or no record of shipping losses associated with the Goodwins between 1916 and 1918, whereas for the earlier part of the war there are detailed reports of shipping incidents, whether by accident or enemy action. During this war the Downs assumed a great deal of its earlier importance as a protected anchorage and became a base from which a vast fleet of minesweepers and patrol boats operated against the enemy. Merchant vessels of all nationalities were brought in for inspection to ensure they were not carrying contraband and allied ships torpedoed in the Channel were beached so regularly at Deal that this part of the Downs became known as 'the hospital'. A foretaste of what lay ahead came in the form of a single German torpedo fired from a submerged submarine in the vicinity of the South Sand Head. This first crossed the stern of a Dutch vessel, then a Spaniard, and either by luck or very accurate sighting struck the torpedo-gunboat HMS *Niger* which was lying at anchor. At about noon on 11th November 1914 there was a tremendous explosion, black smoke poured from the forepart of the warship and she began to sink by the bow. The *Niger*, of 810 tons and built in 1892, was a familiar sight in the area, having been stationed there on patrol duties since the outbreak of war in August, and was lying about one and a half miles out from Deal pier when she was hit. Although both the Deal and Kingsdown lifeboats were launched, it was the Deal galley punt *Hope*, master John Budd, that reached the area first. They found all ninety-five of the warship's crew struggling in the sea and the *Hope* herself came very close to sinking as man after man clambered over her gunwhale, until there were forty-eight men aboard. Within twenty minutes of being hit the *Niger* was standing almost vertical, her bows touching the bottom in fifty feet of water. Then with a great rush of steam her boilers burst and she went under.

The great number of casualties amongst merchant steamships on the outbreak of war precludes mention of every incident but amongst the better known ones were vessels such as the *Batjan*, which was run ashore at Deal on 2nd December 1914 and remained there for a month. Later it was alleged that her double bottom was full of mines, since after her re-floating and departure from the Downs three ships sank in her wake, and it is reputed that she was later intercepted down Channel and taken into Portsmouth. The steamship *Montrose*, famous for having carried Dr Crippen and his mistress to the United States, was selected to be sunk as a blockship to Dover but, in fact, ended her days on the Goodwins. After being filled with cement and made ready for scuttling she was blown out of Dover harbour by a gale on 28th December 1914 and stranded one and a half miles north-west of the East Goodwin lightvessel, where she broke in two. A victim of collision, the *Stranton* of Dundee was struck by the s.s. *Ben Vorlich* at night on 3rd January 1915 and sank close to the South Sand Head without loss of life, but a similar accident cost the lives of all seventeen crew of the *Char*. This was a small government patrol and inspection tug which failed to

Already partially engulfed, the South Goodwin lightship lies on her starboard side, with rescuers searching for possible survivors, 29th November 1954.   (Skyphotos, Hythe)

answer radio signals from 16th January 1915. Her wreck was eventually found off Deal, with only the tops of her two masts showing above the surface. It was later established that she had been run down and sunk at night by the steamer *Erivan*, which suffered severe damage to her bows.

A victim of enemy action, the Cardiff-registered *Westergate* came in short of her sternpost and rudder on 2nd January 1915 to sink at her moorings, whilst the *Hull Trader* foundered near the South Goodwin light on 13th February after her cargo had shifted in rough weather. The Norwegian steamship *Regin* simply vanished in one great explosion near the North Sand Head eleven days later, and within less than forty-eight hours the Federal Steam Navigation Co. ship *Surrey* was towed in and beached at Deal. Laden with food and coal she remained high and dry for three months and was joined in September by a large oil tanker whose cargo, mixed with rotten meat from the *Surrey*, polluted the beaches for weeks. Perhaps the best remembered of the steamers run ashore near Deal was the *Africa*, which was brought in after being torpedoed on 16th September 1915. Beached opposite the coastguard station the huge wreck, with four hospital railway carriages on deck, caused the local boatmen and lifeboat crew a great deal of trouble and was eventually demolished by explosives. In June 1972 a sport diver found a 13-inch Roman amphora among the remains of the wreck and this led to much speculation as to whether it had been aboard the *Africa* when she sank or had been uncovered by the sea and become trapped in the wreckage.The Elder Dempster Line's *Ilaro*, with a cargo of palm oil and nuts, came into the Downs on fire after striking a mine on 24th October 1915. She, too, had to be beached, offshore from Sandown Castle, and became a total wreck.

With a great many requisitioned trawlers working for the Admiralty as mine-sweepers and patrol vessels, losses amongst them ran high. HM trawler *Bonar Law* was lost following a collision on 27th October 1915, as was the *Klar* after being mined on 26th November. Another trawler, HMS *Etoile Polaire*, also fell victim to a mine in December and the thirty-four-year-old steamship *Envermeu* sank off Deal following a collision with the Greek ship *Nefeli* the same month. The *De la Pole*, another armed trawler, was lost on the Goodwins in February 1916, the *Correct*, a steamship, was lost by enemy action one and a half miles from the North Goodwin lightvessel, whilst the *Egero* sank in the Gull Stream following a collision on 4th March. The *Jacob Luckenback*, an American steamer loaded with barley, was lost one mile north of the Downs light after striking the Glasgow-owned *Eddystone* on 5th July 1916, and was followed by the *Polta*, the *Val Salice* and the *Sibiria*, all within twenty-four hours of each other between 18th and 20th November of the same year. In rescuing survivors from the last three incidents the No. 2 Deal lifeboat, *Frances Forbes Barton*, was damaged and put out of service and her crew had barely returned to the beach from attending the *Val Salice* when the *Sibiria* went ashore at almost exactly the same place at the height of a severe gale. The No. 1 Deal boat, *Charles Dibdin*, which had already been out and rescued thirty survivors from the *Val Salice* — a rescue which brought 'Bonnie' Adams, her cox'n, his second silver medal — then went out in company with the Ramsgate boat and found the *Sibiria*, which still had fifty-two men aboard. In attempting to get alongside the Deal boat was caught by a huge wave which tore her sails to shreds and caused the anchor rope to rip a thwart clean out of the boat. Full of water, with several crew injured and the boat crippled, they turned back to Deal and had hardly left the vicinity of the wreck when a similar accident befell the Ramsgate boat, whose crew suffered several broken limbs. Only the Ramsgate reserve boat and the *Charles Hargrave* of Kingsdown were left intact and it was the latter that finally managed to reach the *Sibiria* and bring back all fifty-two survivors on 20th November.

During 1917 three German submarines were sunk by British warships close to the Goodwins. The first of these was the *UC-46*, which was rammed and sunk by the destroyer HMS *Liberty* on 8th February. On 1st November the British submarine *E-52* torpedoed and sank the *UC-63* from which there was only one survivor, Capt von Heydebreck; three weeks later HM destroyer *Gipsy* and four armed drifters shelled the *U-48*. Caught on the surface whilst re-charging her batteries, the *Majesty*, *Paramount* and *Present Help* gave chase and in a short surface engagement a lucky shot from the former, fired from 1,200 yards, ripped open the submarine's pressure hull. Other warships now joined in the hunt, driving the crippled *U-48* over the northern part of the Goodwins, where she stranded. During the summer of 1973 changes in the outline and depth of sand on the Goodwins caused the almost intact wreck of the submarine to emerge. She became a target for local sport divers and in the brief period before she was again covered the *U-48* was stripped of a great many souvenirs and valuable non-ferrous fittings. Following press publicity about the reappearance of the wreck, a letter appeared in a London newspaper of 28th June, written from West Germany by the son of the submarine's captain. In this, besides recalling details of the sinking, he dispelled the myth that Capt Edling had cut his throat with a razor in the conning-tower rather than be taken prisoner.

Following the armistice, a rescue without parallel was the saving of ninety-eight men from the wreck of the American steamship *Piave* on 29th January 1919. On her maiden voyage from New York to Rotterdam carrying a valuable and much needed cargo of foodstuffs, the 6,000-ton *Piave* stranded at night on the north-west edge of the Goodwins. With all her deck lights switched on neither the Gull lightvessel nor Cox'n Adams of the *Charles Dibdin* lifeboat had any difficulty in locating her but the weather was bitterly cold, with frequent and heavy snow squalls, so that it was midnight before the Deal boat arrived alongside. Three of her crew clambered aboard to offer assistance in refloating the steamer, only to be politely informed that the captain was still asleep in his bunk, ignorant of the situation, and had left orders that he was not to be disturbed until 7.30 a.m.! A tug from Dover with Capt Irons, the harbourmaster, aboard appeared on the scene and agreement was finally reached concerning salvage. The first attempt to refloat the *Piave* proved unsuccessful, so some 1,000 bags of flour and hundreds of cases of lard and bacon were thrown overboard. A second attempt using six tugs also failed, so more cargo was jettisoned and 1,500 tons of fuel oil pumped overboard, causing the death of thousands of sea birds around the Downs. During the evening of 31st January, prior to another attempt by tugs to refloat her, the *Piave* suddenly parted amidships and the vessel was plunged into darkness as the generators failed. There was a mad scramble for the boats and in the confusion the ship's lifeboats were let slip and left hanging vertically, men leapt overboard or into the Deal lifeboat while others slid down ropes to end up in the sea. It was a miracle that not a single life was lost. Tugs and patrol boats rescued most of the crew and, following a continuous period of forty-eight hours at sea without rest and in terrible weather conditions, the *Charles Dibdin* returned with twenty-nine survivors to a hero's welcome. Five days later the wreck was so deep in the sand that her deck and hatches were completely covered and only her masts and funnels indicated her position. For this service, Cox'n Adams received a gold watch from the President of the United States, a gold medal was presented to every member of his crew, together with an award of £250 to be shared between them.

Before the year was out 'Bonnie' Adams was to receive yet another silver medal, his third, for saving two men from the three-masted schooner *Toogo* on

144

1st November. The weather was so bad when they launched that it took the lifeboat three hours to reach the wreck, stranded on the Goodwins, where they found two men clinging to an upturned boat. On returning to Deal 'Cobbler' Stanton and a fresh crew took the *Charles Dibdin* to sea again in search of two other vessels in distress, one of which, the ketch *Corinthian*, had been aground for sixteen hours. Three men could be seen in her rigging and it was not until all had been taken aboard the lifeboat that one was found to be already dead. The reserve lifeboat was also launched that night with William Hoile in command but found no further survivors from the *Corinthian*'s crew of eight, nor any from the other vessel, the barge *Glenavon*, which had already sunk. It was not until the following day that the remarkable bravery of William Stanton, which earned him a bronze medal, was made public. Confined to his bed and very ill with cancer of the throat, this indomitable man had got up, dressed and taken the lifeboat to sea for several hours, so that when his doctor called he was told his patient was out on the Goodwins! One of the men who went out to the *Toogo* in the *Charles Dibdin*, Frederick Brown, in still alive today.

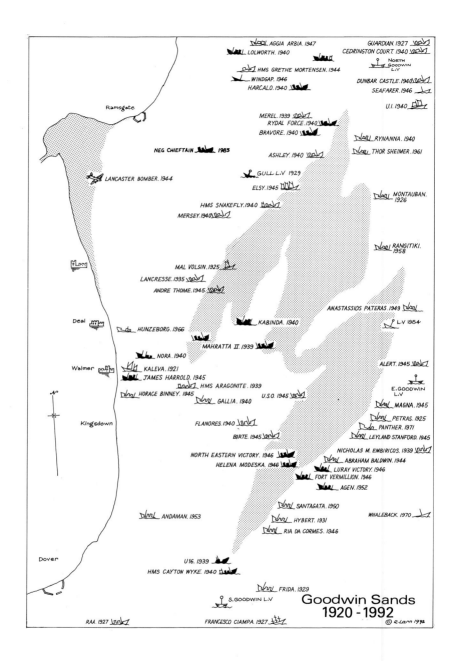

AGGIA ARBIA. 1947
LOLWORTH. 1940
GUARDIAN. 1927
CEDRINGTON COURT. 1940

North
GOODWIN
L.V

HMS GRETHE MORTENSEN. 1944
WINDGAP. 1946
HARCALO. 1940

DUNBAR CASTLE. 1940
SEAFARER. 1946

U.I. 1940

Ramsgate

MEREL. 1939
RYDAL FORCE. 1940
BRAVORE. 1940

RYNANNA. 1940
THOR SHEIMER. 1961

NEG CHIEFTAIN. 1985

ASHLEY. 1940

GULL L.V 1929

LANCASTER BOMBER. 1944

ELSY. 1945

MONTAUBAN.
1926

HMS SNAKEFLY. 1940
MERSEY. 1940

RANGITIKI.
1958

MAL VOLSIN. 1925
LANCRESSE. 1935
ANDRE THOME. 1945

ANASTASSIOS PATERAS. 1949

Deal

HUNZEBORG. 1966

KABINDA. 1940

L.V 1954

MAHRATTA II. 1939

Walmer

NORA. 1940

ALERT. 1945

KALEVA. 1921
JAMES HARROLD. 1945
HMS ARAGONITE. 1939
HORACE BINNEY. 1945

E. GOODWIN
L.V

GALLIA. 1940

U.S.O. 1945

MAGNA. 1945

Kingsdown

FLANORES. 1940

PETRAS. 1925
PANTHER. 1971
LEYLAND STANFORD. 1945

BIRTE. 1945

NORTH EASTERN VICTORY. 1946
HELENA MODESKA. 1946

NICHOLAS M. EMBIRICOS. 1939
ABRAHAM BALDWIN. 1944
LURAY VICTORY. 1946
FORT VERMILLION. 1946
AGEN. 1952

SANTAGATA. 1950

ANDAMAN. 1953

HYBERT. 1931

WHALEBACK. 1970

RIA DA CORMES. 1946

Dover

U16. 1939
HMS CAYTON WYKE. 1940

FRIDA. 1929

S. GOODWIN L.V

**Goodwin Sands
1920 - 1992**

© R. Lamm 1992

RAA. 1927

FRANCESCO CIAMPA. 1927

146

Chapter Eight

VICTIMS OF PEACE AND WAR: 1920-1975

William Stanton, who had so deservedly earned the nickname of 'storm-king', died in the autumn of 1920. Aggravated by the *Corinthian* rescue in 1919, his illness became worse and he never went to sea again. William Hoile was appointed in his place but served for only three months, as in January 1921 the boat was borrowed for Ramsgate and in May the post of reserve cox'n ceased when the second Deal lifeboat was permanently withdrawn.

By now, the proportion of sailing vessels to steamships was the order of 1:10 and this, coupled with the introduction of wireless and electric lighting aboard ships, resulted in a sharp decline in the annual total of shipwrecks, not only around the Goodwins but worldwide. Possibly the most dramatic effect locally was the impending closure of both the North Deal and Kingsdown lifeboat stations and the reinstatement of the once controversial Walmer boat. Hence the thirteen year period 1920/33 was eventful to say the least, and began when a wintry gale on 11th November 1921 put the Finnish schooner *Kaleva* ashore at the top of Exchange Street at Deal. At the auction of her remains, held on the promenade, the timbers and fittings were sold to a Tommy Upton for only £50. In 1925 the ketch *Mal Volsin* and the steamer *Petras* were both wrecked on the sands; in 1926 another steamship, the *Montauban*, was stranded but later refloated and saved.

After sixty-two years in service the Kingsdown lifeboat station finally closed in 1927 and its boat, the *Barbara Fleming*, which had already saved 241 lives, was handed over to the re-formed Walmer crew. Although there were three wreck incidents that year all involving steamships, only one required the services of a lifeboat and for this the Ramsgate boat was summoned. Of these the *Francesco Ciampa*, an Italian vessel of 3,611 tons register, carrying iron ore from Benisaf to Rotterdam, sank within fifteen minutes of collision with the coal-carrying *Signe* of Denmark on 11th February. This incident occurred one and a half miles south-east of the South Goodwin lightvessel and it was fortunate for the thirty-man crew of the Italian ship that though in great danger of foundering, with her bows stove in and her forepeak flooded, the *Signe* stood by to rescue them. Two days later, in fog so dense that a local shipmaster described it as 'quite the worst I have seen in a lifetime', the Norwegian *Raa* of 816 tons was almost cut in two by the Spanish-owned *Gordejvelda* and finally sank about four miles offshore, near Folkestone. When the 318-ton *Guardian*, laden with scrap iron in the form of railway lines, sank six miles north-east of the North Goodwin lightvessel on 29th November, the first intimation that anything was amiss came from the chief engineer. At 2.00 p.m. he rushed up from the engine room to announce that the

The crew of the 30ft motor yacht *Tarhund III* wait for the flood to refloat their vessel after stranding on the Goodwins on 27th August 1973.　　　　　(Peter Powell, Broadstairs)

Some sixty-seven years later, the pier was again in trouble when the Dutch motor vessel *Nora*, badly damaged by a mine, crashed through it on 29th January 1940.　　　(Daily Mirror)

bottom of the ship was giving way and the cargo literally dropping through! Her crew snatched up a few belongings and stepped into their only boat as the *Guardian* sank beneath their feet. Guided by the North Sand Head foghorn they reached the lightvessel in such an exhausted state, after rowing against the tide, that a buoy had to be floated down to them on a line as they drifted past.

During February and March 1929 fog was so dense and persistent that the noise of ships' sirens, foghorns and maroons made it difficult for the people of Deal to sleep. At the same time it brought disaster to two of the four lightvessels that guarded the Goodwins. Shortly before noon on 24th March the German steamship *Oliva* of 7,885 tons, Bilbao to Hamburg with ore, crashed head-on into the South Goodwin vessel. The Deal-owned motor boat *Lady Beatty* went out in answer to distress signals and found the lightvessel extensively damaged but still afloat. It was 18th April before repairs were completed at Ramsgate and she was back in her original position. In the meantime and still in the grip of fog the Gull lightvessel was rammed and sunk during the early hours of 18th March. This was not the usual lightvessel but relief No. 38 carrying the normal crew, the original having been removed for overhaul the previous week. The Ellerman liner *City of York*, 7,834 tons gross, was proceeding up Channel to London when she charged into the moored light, cutting it in two so that it sank like a stone. The watchman and five of the six crew asleep below all found themselves in the sea and were rescued, but the body of Capt Williams had to be recovered from the wreck by divers. Since the location could not remain unmarked for long, especially as the masthead daymark of the Gull light showed just above the surface, the *Lady Betty* motor boat, crewed by Harry Meakins, the brothers Pritchard, Edward Grigg, Thomas Baker and Richard Brown, was employed as a temporary mark. Their only method of signalling was a small red flag on a stick and a muffin hand bell, which they took it in turns to ring with an unusual urgency. Within three days a conical light buoy was in position close to the wreck and a day later a new lightvessel, named *Brake* instead of *Gull*, was on station. It took until June of that year to raise the sunken vessel.

It was inevitable that the North Deal lifeboat station would one day also close and in 1932, having rescued a total of 859 (RNLI Service Boards state 880), the crew and station were disbanded and the era of the Goodwin Sands' lifeboats came to an end. The boat itself, the *Charles Dibdin* which saved 395 lives, sold for £87 10s and, surprisingly, is still in use although hardly recognisable in her present role of cabin cruiser. For a time she cruised between the Helford river in Cornwall and France, then in 1973 her Penryn owner sold her for £1,675 and she is now moored near Exeter, having forsaken the hazards of the open sea for less adventurous activities.

In the few years remaining before the Downs were once more in the forefront of a war, with shipwrecks almost non-existent for a time, the only flurry of excitement amongst the boatmen concerned treasure. In 1932 the Deal lugger *Tiger* was chartered by a wealthy London party who set themselves up in the Royal Hotel and announced they were there to dig up the treasure that lay under

The 3-masted schooner *Elsy* of Vastervic, a Swedish auxiliary vessel stranded on the Goodwin Sands on 26th August 1945, but refloated and saved.   (Deal Maritime Museum)

The Walmer lifeboat *Charles Dibdin, Civil Service No. 2*, leaving the scene of the wreck of the 2,327 gross tons s.s. *Silvia Onorato* carrying lead ore between Rijeka and Rotterdam, wrecked on the East Goodwin, 2nd January 1948.   (G. Goldsmith-Carter)

the Goodwins for the asking. Mention was made of an Armada ship sunk in 1588, various holes were dug in the sands between tides but, despite their claim that 'dozens of chests have been recovered', it is certain that they left wiser and certainly empty-handed.

The first major shipping disaster on the Goodwins following the outbreak of the Second World War was not a spectacular torpedoing but the stranding of the *Mahratta II* on 6th October 1939. She broke convoy to pick up a pilot in the Downs and went ashore on the Fork Spit so quietly that at first her master suspected there was something wrong with her engine. Like her namesake of 1909 she also broke her back, adding another 6,690 tons to the countless weight of metal already buried beneath the sand. A total of three German submarines were sunk in the area betwen 1939 and 1945 and the remains of one of these, the *U-16*, sunk on 24th October 1939, lie little more than half a mile to the north-west of the South West Goodwins light buoy. The exact location is given as Lat 50°09′03″N, Long 01°28′13″E. It is worth noting that the armed trawler HMS *Caton Wyke* which sank the *U-16* by depth charge after finding her stranded on a sandbank, herself lies on the bottom close at hand in 51°08′58″N, 01°28′16″E, having been torpedoed by an E-Boat on 8th July 1940. A local newspaper report

One that got away — the Danish steamship *Magna*, stranded on the Goodwin Sands on 19th October 1945, later refloated without damage. (Deal Maritime Museum)

The Swedish steamship *Birte* stranded on the Goodwin Sands, 4th October 1945, whilst carrying a full cargo of timber, including a full deck cargo. She was later refloated and saved. Note the lifeboat alongside and the neutral Swedish flags painted on her hull.
(Deal Maritime Museum)

dated 17th November 1939 states that a number of bodies of German sailors had been washed ashore between Hythe and Rye, all wearing Drager submarine escape apparatus.

War losses were extensive in the Straits of Dover and around the Goodwins and once again the Downs became a useful 'hospital' for damaged ships. On 4th November 1939 the Greek-owned *Nicolaos M. Embricos* (ex-*War Pansy*, ex-*Seguard*, ex-*Langton Grange*) struck a mine and sank near the East Goodwin lightvessel; HM Trawler *Aragonite* suffered the same fate off Deal on 22nd November; *Merel*, a General Steam Navigation Co. steamship of 1,088 tons was mined and sunk on 8th December, the *Kabinda* on 10th December, all forty-four of whose crew were saved by the Walmer lifeboat and the *Cedrington Court* (ex-*War Viper*) sank two miles north-east of the North Goodwin light on 7th January 1940. A magnetic mine which exploded directly beneath the bridge of the 10,000-ton liner *Dunbar Castle* put her on the bottom on 9th January, close to the same light, and the loss of life might well have been high but for HMS *Calvi* which was minesweeping off the North Foreland. She dashed to the rescue and picked up two lifeboats holding seventy-three survivors, crew and passengers, some of whom were women and children. The captain was found dead in the bilge of one of the boats, while a fireman, too shocked to leave, died later in a coma.

In 1940 yet another vessel went through Deal pier, causing extensive damage. This was Dutch motor coaster *Nora* of 298 tons gross which set off a magnetic mine about a mile to the east of Deal and drifted ashore, smashing down most of the inshore section of the pier. In 1974 a sport diver found a ship's bell marked *Berent* in the vicinity and this was thought to have come from some old wreck until it was realised that the *Nora* was the ex-*Berent*, having changed her name. Losses due to enemy action continued to mount in alarming proportions. The 9,974-ton Norwegian motorship *Gallia* sank in the Downs on 10th February 1940; the Italian *Tima Primo* on 18th March and the *Mersey*, a passenger vessel owned by the London, Midland & Scottish Railway, sank on 20th April. The *Lulworth* was sunk on 23rd April and both the *Bravore* and the *Rydal Force* on the following day. An unusual enemy loss on 9th July 1940 was that of a Heinkel HE59 floatplane, number D-ASUO, serving as an air ambulance to pick aircrew out of the sea after they had ditched. Two sections of Spitfires from No. 54 Squadron forced the enemy seaplane to land on the Goodwins, where the crew were taken prisoner. It was later towed off by the Walmer lifeboat and beached at Deal where it attracted a great deal of attention.

The American Liberty ship *James Harrod* will long be remembered by anyone who lived in Deal during the war. Carrying a vast quantity of war stores destined for Antwerp, she came into the Downs in convoy and accidentally hit the steamer *Ramon Stern*. There was a violent explosion, the *James Harrod* burst into flames and but for the bravery of Capt Heida of the Dutch coaster *Tromp* in laying his ship alongside, the entire crew might have perished. After the wreck had been beached off Kingsdown a gale caused her to float away to the north until she

Although not directly connected with the Goodwins, the loss of the Panamanian tanker *Texaco Caribbean* off Dover on 11th January 1971, which led to the collision and sinking of the *Brandenburg* and the *Niki*, the twentieth century's most tragic disaster in the English Channel to date. (Skyphotos, Hythe)

grounded on the Malm rocks opposite Deal Castle, where she broke in two. Besides a deck cargo of vehicles the *James Harrod* carried many thousands of cans of high octane petrol and troops of the US Labour Corps stationed at Oxney Bottom were employed in their salvage. Many of the burnt-out vehicles were dumped overboard but the rest were landed and stored, along with the petrol cans, in the goods yard of Walmer railway station. Several soldiers were killed when, at a later date, part of this dump exploded. The wreck itself, lying parallel with the coast and only a quarter mile offshore, proved a serious hazard and eventually had to be demolished by Trinity House. Following the *James Harrod*, the last of the war victims included the *Henry B. Plant* sunk on 6th February 1945; the British cable ship *Alert* on 25th February; the *Filleigh* on 18th April and the *Horace Binney*, beached at Deal on 8th May but later refloated.

With all navigational lights and beacons around the Goodwins extinguished for the duration of the war and for some months after, there then followed short periods when a remarkable number of large steamships, mostly American, came to grief on the sands through their reluctance to use pilots. The first of these was the United States troopship *Leyland Stanford* with over 500 servicemen aboard. She stranded on 25th November 1945 but was fortunate in being refloated, as was the *Ria da Cormes*, although the latter reached Dover only to sink in the harbour. At seven o'clock on 30th January 1946, as the dawn broke, a large ship was seen to be ashore near the West Goodwin buoy. This proved to be the *Luray Victory*, of some 9,000 tons, which quickly became a total wreck despite efforts to save her. With cox'n Fred Upton at the helm, the *Charles Dibdin* (Civil Service No. 32) lifeboat went alongside the steamship no less than forty-eight times and not one of the American crew was lost. In the September the remains of the *Luray Victory* were joined by the *Helena Modjeska*, 7,000 tons, carrying trucks, tractors and general machinery for Germany valued at £¾m in addition to 3,000 tons of foodstuffs and thirty-five tons of high-explosive. Eight tugs were employed to pull her off after she grounded on the 13th but she, too, was finished. After she broke her back her crew were taken off and it was only at the last minute that two stowaways, German prisoners-of-war, emerged from a crate in which they had been hiding. Special gunsights and radio equipment were removed when a gale was forecast and that night the vessel parted in the middle, the two halves drifting away from each other. Two weeks later, on 30th September, the *Fort Vermillion* stranded less than half a mile from the wreck of the *Helena Modjeska* but was eventually saved after some 2,000 tons of iron ore had been dumped overboard. On Christmas Eve of the same year the *North Eastern Victory* went onto the Goodwins four and a half miles north-east of the South Goodwin light and also broke in two. Other ships in trouble here included the Liberty ship *Ira* (ex-*Harry Percy*), carrying 8,000 tons of coal, which drove ashore in March 1947 in a very dangerous position midway between the two sections of the *Luray Victory* and was lost. The reason for so many accidents here cannot be attributed to any single cause but was in part at least brought about by the wording of a letter from G.H. Hembold, Assistant Deputy

Naval ratings and officers of the Royal Navy Inshore Survey Fleet playing a cricket match on the Goodwin Sands, July 1973.   (Author's photograph)

Administrator for Ship Operations, which read: 'Numerous cases have been observed where pilots have been employed by shipmasters at great expense and without prior authority for waters such as the English Channel, North Sea and Baltic Sea. Employment of pilots for such waters is considered unnecessary; the navigational requirements are regarded as lying well within the professional capacity of competent shipmasters.' The same letter then concludes, '...the subject waters are of wide expanse and relatively free of dangers...therefore the employment of pilots for those waters is disapproved.'

Despite the publicity given to these wrecks, ships continued to fall victim to the sands; on 2nd January 1948 the *Silva Onorato*; the *Anastassios Pateras*, a Greek-owned steamer, on 29th December; the *Santagata* on 24th December 1950, and the mahogany-laden *Agen* (Plate 29). She stranded on the eastern edge of the Goodwins on 13th January 1952 close to the *Luray Victory* at the height of a full gale and after she had broken in two the remains of three large wrecks could be seen within a radius of a few hundred yards in what became known as 'Calamity Corner'. From these three vessels alone the Walmer lifeboat saved 115 lives. In the case of the *Agen*, cox'n Upton took the lifeboat through the 30-feet gap separating the two parts of the ship no less than three times in order to save the *Agen*'s master but he refused to abandon his command and only after he had spent a night aboard alone did he consent to be taken off. This rescue brought Fred Upton another silver medal, Percy Cavell another bronze, and vellum certificates for all seven crew of the Walmer lifeboat. Surprisingly, one wreck which is known to contain bullion and does not date back to some earlier century, but only to 25th May 1953, is the 4,765-ton Swedish-owned *Andaman*. She was carrying eight ingots of silver, each of 30 lb weight, and although one of the ship's officers came ashore with one of the ingots in his hands the remainder are still in the wreck which lies between Deal and Dover.

Of the many accidents to befall the various lightvessels stationed around the Goodwins none compares with the total loss of the South Sand light on 28th November 1954. During one of the worst gales to be remembered on the coast the vessel was driven from her moorings up the eastern side of the sands where she capsized, drowning all seven of her crew. Three lifeboats, from Walmer, Dover and Ramsgate, were in attendance as well as the Trinity House tenders *Vestal* and *Patricia*, HMS *Romola* and a team of naval divers. At first light a helicopter hovered over the wreck as it lay on its side, partly buried in sand, but there was only one survivor, twenty-two-year-old Ronald Murton, a Ministry of Agriculture scientist engaged in bird watching. A memorial service was held at sea on 3rd December at which the Ramsgate and Walmer lifeboats tied up alongside each other close to the wreck while wreaths were cast upon the water. Seven years later on 12th November 1961 the East Goodwin light also broke adrift and drove southwards, following the edge of the sands, which necessitated a seventeen-hour vigil by the Walmer lifeboat in sea conditions so rough that the boat almost capsized. Despite modern navigational aids such as radar and echo sounders, position finders and beacons, lightships and buoys, ships still continued to strike the Goodwins. The great liner *Rangitiki* stranded here on 26th September 1958 at a point where there was supposed to be ninety feet of water, whereas an immediate re-survey showed severe shoaling of the eastern edge. The *Thorsheimer*, a Norwegian motor vessel, went aground in December 1961 while the *Hunzeborg* was involved in a collision with the *Diamandis* on 13th August 1966 and had to be beached at Sandown to prevent her sinking.

Although not directly associated with the Goodwins the events of 11th/12th January and 28th February 1971 represent one of the worst wreck incidents in the Channel in recent times. On 11th January at 3.10 a.m. the huge Panamanian tanker *Texaco Caribbean* sank after collision with the *Paracas*. The following day the West German motorship *Brandenburg* hit the stern of the wrecked tanker and sank, while on 28th February another motor vessel, the 2,371-ton *Niki*, fouled them both and went to the bottom. There was little excuse for either of the latter to have struck the *Texaco Caribbean* since the wreck was well buoyed and lit; as it was, several other ships missed disaster only by yards as they steamed at full speed through the danger area apparently oblivious of the situation. in 1971 tugs averted a potential disaster by refloating the Liberian tanker *Panther* which had stranded on the sands on 30th March. Had she broken her back, as is usual with Goodwin wrecks, some 25,000 tons of crude oil would have been released into the Downs.

Members of a BBC TV camera crew and Royal Marines from Deal toast each other in champagne. Tide stopped play during a cricket match played on the South Goodwin Sands, July 1978, in which the author and his wife took part.   (Author's collection)

The story of the Goodwin Sands and Downs is one without end, since ships will come to grief here for as long as men sail them, the last example to date of any note being the Panamanian tug *Neg Chieftain*, 199 tons gross, built in 1971, which foundered south of the Ramsgate channel on 10th August 1983 whilst towing stone-carrying barges for the Ramsgate ferry terminal. Of necessity, countless aspects of the sands have had to be only touched upon or omitted simply because it would take several volumes to embrace them all. This includes the various funerals which have taken place, the many cricket matches and races, firework displays and parties, and such curious finds as a horse-drawn hackney carriage. In recent years reclamation has again been suggested in order to create an international port, or an airport: it has even been suggested that a nuclear device should be buried and detonated to remove the Goodwins once and for all. In time — perhaps a thousand or ten thousand years hence — siltation will inevitably cause the Goodwin Sands and the mainland to merge and the age-old hazard will then disappear for ever. When this begins to occur and the sands drain and become stable, it will be possible for the first time to excavate the area and this could well prove to be one of the most exciting and rewarding archaeological projects the world has ever known.

BIBLIOGRAPHY

Bayley, G.B. *Seamen of the Downs* (1929)

Burchett, J. *Complete History of the most remarkable Transactions at Sea* (1720)

Bush, E.W. *The Flowers of the Sea* (1962)

Campbell, G. *My Mystery Ships* (1928)

Carter, G.G. The Goodwin Sands (1953)

Chamberlain, D. *Forgotten Ships of the Downs* (1993)

Chowen, G. *A Voice from the Goodwins, or a plan for the Prevention of Further Casualties on the Goodwin Sands* (1857)

Clowes, L.W. *A History of the Royal Navy*

Colledge, J.J. *Ships of the Royal Navy,* vols 1 & 2, Newton Abbot (1969)

Curzon, M. *Walmer Castle and its Lord Wardens*

Dawson, A.J. *Britain's Lifeboats* (1923)

Defoe, D. *The Storm, or a Collection of the Most Casualties and Disasters* (1704)

Dibdin, J.C. & Ayling, J. *The Book of the Lifeboat* (1894)

Duncan, A. *The Mariner's Chronicle, or Authentic and Complete History of Popular Shipwrecks,* 6 vols

Freeman, E.A. *History of the Norman Conquest of England* (1868)

Furley, R. *History of the Weald of Kent,* vol 1 (1871)

Gattie, G.B. *Memorials of the Goodwin Sands* (1890)

Gilly, W. *Narrative of Shipwrecks of the Royal Navy between 1793 and 1849* (1850)

Gilmore, J. *Storm Warriors or Life-Boat Work* (1879)

Gosset, W.P. *The Lost Ships of the Royal Navy 1793-1900* (1986)

Grant, R.M. *U-Boats Destroyed* (1964)

Greenhill, B. *The Merchant Schooners,* vols 1 & 2, Newton Abbot (1968)

Harris, J. *History of Kent* (1719)

Hasted, E. *History of Kent,* 8 vols

Haydon, A.L. *The Book of the Lifeboat*

Hillier, C. *The Bulwark Shore* (1980) Granada Publishing

HMSO *British Vessels Lost at Sea 1914-18* (1977) Patrick Stephens

HMSO *British Vessels Lost at Sea 1939-45* (1976) Patrick Stephens

Hocking, C.A. *A Dictionary of Disasters at Sea, in the Age of Steam, 1824-1962,* vols 1 & 2 (1969)

Holland, C. *From the North Foreland to Penzance* (1908)

Hooke, N. *Modern Shipping Disasters* (1989) Lloyd's of London Press

Jameson, W. *The Most Formidable Thing* (1965)

Laker, J. *History of Deal,* Deal (1917)

Larn, R.J. *Shipwrecks of Great Britain & Ireland* (1981)

Le Fleming, H.M. *Warships of World War I* (1965)

Lund, P. & Ludlam, H. *Trawlers go to War* (1971)

Magalotti, L. *Travels of Cosmo, the 3rd Grand Duke of Tuscany, Through England & Wales, in the Reign of Charles II* (1821)

Mason, F.K. *Battle over Britain* (1969)

Maxwell, D. *Uknown Kent* (1921)

Mitchell, W. & Sawyer, L. *British Standard Ships of World War 1* (1968)

Mitchell, W. & Sawyer, L. *The Oceans, the Forts & the Parks* (1966)

Mitchell, W. & Sawyer, L. *Empire Ships of World War II* (1965)

Pritchard, S. *History of Deal,* Deal (1864)

Redding, C. A History of Shipwrecks and Disasters at Sea, 4 vols (1835)

Roskill, S.W. *The War at Sea,* vols 1 & 2 (1954)

Sawyer, L. & Mitchell, W. *The Liberty Ships* (1970, '73 & '85)

Sawyer, L. & Mitchell, W. *Victory Ships & Tankers* (1974)

Stanton, W.J. *The Journal of a Deal Pilot,* Portsmouth (1929)

Stevenson, D.A. *The World's Lighthouses before 1820,* Oxford (1959)

Tennent, A.J. *British Merchant Ships sunk by U-Boats 1914-18* (1990)

Treanor, T.S. *The Cry from the Sea*

Treanor, T.S. *Log of a Sky Pilot* (1894)

Treanor, T.S. *Heroes of the Goodwin Sands* (1904)

Ward, L. *Deal and Walmer,* County Guide, 5th edition

Ward, E.M. *English Coastal Evolution* (1922)

Whymper, F. *The Sea, its Stirring Story of Adventure, Peril and Heroism*

Young, J.M. *Britain's Sea War, a Diary of Ship Losses* (1989)

Newspapers, Journals, etc

Annual Register, from 1774

Burney Newspaper Collection, various 1603-1800

Calendar of Fine Rolls, State Papers

Calendar of Pipe Rolls, State Papers

Calendar of Domestic State Papers

Calendar of Treasury State Papers

Catalogue of the Archives of the Confederate of the Cinque Ports & Right of Wrecks (1656)

Channel Pilot, vol 1, 14th edition (1957)

Daily Telegraph, various issues

Deal Mercury, various issues

Deal Telegram, various issues

Deposition Books for Ramsgate, 1891/4 & 1892/4

East Kent Mercury, various issues
Gentleman's Magazine, various issues
Instructions re wreck at Ramsgate, 1601/2
Keble's Margate and Ramsgate Gazette, from 1870
Kent Coast Times, various issues
Kent Herald, various issues
Kent Mercantile Gazette, 1894-1970
Kent News and Advertiser, various issues from 1857
Kent Weekly News, from 1877
Kentish Chronicle, various issues
Kentish Gazette, from 1768
Kentish Mercury, 1838-1964
Kentish Observer, various issues
Kentish Weekly Post and Canterbury Journal, from 1768
Lifeboat, Journal of the Royal National Lifeboat Institution
Lloyds Casualty Returns
Lloyds List, from 1743
Lloyds War Losses, The First World War (1990)
Lloyds War Losses, The Second World War (1989)
Lloyds Universal Register, various issues 1764-1975
Lord Warden's Court of Registers, 1615-1916
Margate and Ramsgate News, 1877/8
Naval Chronicles, various issues
Perry's Margate and Ramsgate News, from 1871
Sea Breezes, various issues 1932-1975
Sherborne and Yeovil Mercury, various issues
State Papers, Board of Trade inquiry into wreck of the *North*
State Papers, Board of Trade report on Shipwrecks, 1865/74
Thanet Advertiser, from 1871
The Advertiser and Trades Journal, 1892
The East Kent Times, from 1896
The Kent Coast Times and Ramsgate and Margate Observer, 1866/96
The Morning Post, various issues
The Naval and Military Record
The Shipwrecked Mariner, from 1880
The Times, various issues

INDEX OF SHIPWRECKS

Page references in italic denote illustrations. Ships without a page reference are known to have taken place, but are unmentioned in the text. (R) indicates the date of the wreck as *reported* by Lloyds or in newspapers, and is used only where the actual date of the incident is uncertain. This index is broken down into the respective areas of the Downs, i.e. Kingsdown, Walmer, Deal, Sandwich etc. with the North & South Goodwin Sands a separate index, which includes all known unidentified shipwrecks. Whilst every reasonable attempt has been made to ensure accuracy in placing wreck incidents in their correct locations, in a great many instances the location is recorded only vaguely, i.e. 'on the Goodwin Sands', or, 'in the Downs', and hence some licence has been necessary.

Abbreviations used to denote ship types

Bg	barge	Kt	ketch
Bq	barque	Mv	motor vessel
Bqn	barquentine	Mfv	motor fishing vessel
Br	brig	Pl	polacca
Brn	brigantine	Pt	privateer
Dr	dredger	Sk	smack
El	East Indiaman	Sl	sloop
Frs	full-rigged ship	Sc	schooner
Fv	fishing vessel	SS	steamship
Gl	galleass/galliot	S	sailing vessel
HM/2	2nd rate man o'war	Sn	snow
HM/3	3rd rate man o'war	Tg	tug
HM/4	4th rate man o'war	Tr	transport vessel
HM/5	5th rate man o'war	Ub	German submarine
HM/6	6th rate man o'war	Yt	yacht
HM/T	HM trawler/drifter	X	other, propelled
Lg	lugger	Z	other, non-propelled
Ls	lightship		

Name	Type	Date	Page
South Foreland — St Margaret's Bay			
Agnes	S	25.04.1895(R)	
Batavia	SS	31.10.1889	
Bengal	S	10.02.1810(R)	
Jane E. Foster	Brn	31.08.1891	
Jean Baptiste	Sl	29.12.1860	
John P. Doe	SS	25.03.1946(R)	
Jollanda	SS	18.12.1920	
Junona	S	31.05.1908	
Loanda	SS	31.05.1908	
Maine	SS	02.04.1914	
Myrtle	Kt	21.06.1913	
Providence	S	13.01.1748(R)	
Sedgmore	HM/4	02.01.1689	
Strathclyde	SS	17.02.1876	
Texaco Caribbean	SS	11.01.1971	
Vigilante	Pt	30.10.1798(R)	
Wave	S	19.09.1887	
Unidentified	S	18.02.1807(R)	
Unidentified	Sc	27.12.1852	
Kingsdown			
Adventure	S	25.01.1765	
Annie	Br	29.11.1877(R)	119
Basseterre	S	14.04.1770	
Bellcairn	SS	13.10.1894	
Brisk	Br	13.01.1811	67
Devonshire	SS	07.11.1857	
Haabet	Bq	25.11.1877	64, 119
Jackson	Br	19.11.1860	
Jersey	Sc	01.04.1853	
Jolland	SS	18.12.1920	
Laubet	Bq	25.11.1877(R)	
Mohely	Bq	25.11.1877	119
Napoleon	SS	14.10.1881	
Olympia	Kt	13.03.1918	
Racine	Brn	11.02.1870	
Republique	Brn	25.11.1877	119
St Andre	S	24.05.1853	
Sophia Magadelema	S	01.12.1801	
Star of the Ocean	Br	25.11.1877	119
Stranton	SS	30.12.1914	
Unidentified	Bq	18.02.1807	67
Walmer			
Amine	Br	25.11.1877	64
Anemone	Br	23.04.1854	
Anna Chararina	S	23.01.1773	
Conqueror	S	30.09.1889	
De Stadt Goes	S	21.01.1772	

Dolphin	SS	18.09.1885	
Elizabeth	S	02.02.1812	
Flores	Sc	12.01.1911	
George	S	00.00.1807	
Georgia	S	30.03.1861	103
John	S	02.04.1765(R)	
Laura	S	17.01.1748	
Lord Wellington	S	21.11.1809(R)	
Mountaineer	Br	24.11.1829	
Norah	Tr	31.01.1748	
Polly	S	07.12.1744(R)	
Reliance	S	00.00.1856	94-5
Selskar	Mv	01.04.1949	
Unidentified (2)	S	11.10.1639	
Unidentified	Br	00.10.1805(R)	67

Deal

AC.1067	Z	30.11.1917(R)	
AC.1108	Z	30.11.1917(R)	
Ada	Z	30.04.1867	
Africa	SS	16.09.1915	142
Alice	Lg	08.12.1911	
Alliance	Sc	26.01.1884	119
Andorinha	Sc	26.04.1849	
Ann	S	17.06.1812	
Anna Lena	Br	12.02.1870	
Aragonite	HM/T	22.11.1939	153
Ardoe	SS	31.01.1898	
Assimacos	SS	11.09.1916	
Bellcairn	SS	00.10.1894(R)	
British Navy	S	26.11.1881	
British Queen	Lg	26.04.1849	
Brothers	Tr	04.11.1811	67
Caesar	S	09.12.1760	
Char	Tg	16.01.1915	141
C. Neumann Gaedebehn	Br	03.11.1887	
Constant Betty	S	15.03.1763	
Countess	Kt	02.03.1918	
Cruiser	S	10.12.1902	
Daisy	Lg	13.07.1895	
Dasher	S	25.09.1811	67
Dinard	SS	08.12.1939	
Dolphine	S	00.10.1624	
Dorothy	X	23.08.1904	
Duke of Clarence	S	01.12.1801	
Eliza & Alice	Kt	02.03.1918	
Elizabeth	Br	01.01.1803	
Envermeu	SS	24.12.1915	143
Eskburn	HM/T	30.11.1916	
Euclid	Sc	10.12.1841	
Euphau	S	13.02.1763	
Europa	SS	21.01.1888	
Felice Rosso	Br	22.10.1842	

Flores	Sc	12.01.1911	139
Friendship	S	01.04.1897	
Frithiof	S	11.11.1852	
Greyhound	HM/6	00.00.1781	
Gustave	Sc	24.11.1877	*108*, 119
Henry	S	16.11.1810(R)	
Horace Binney	SS	08.05.1945	
Highland Lass	S	02.01.1801	
Hope	Sc	06.10.1854	
Ilaro	SS	24.10.1915	143
Industry	Brn	15.12.1777	
Iris	S	00.00.1807	
James Harrod	SS	16.01.1945	*136*
Kaleva	Sc	11.11.1921	*132*, 147
Lancresse	SS	22.11.1935	
Lethe	S	18.10.1909	
London	Br	11.01.1852	
Mandingo	Br	22.10.1842	
Merchant	S	15.01.1771	
Merle	Bq	24.01.1873	*110*, 115
Minerva	Br	29.10.1885	
Minotaur	Lg	04.04.1890	
Mountaineer	S	24.11.1829	73
Nancy	S	00.08.1842(R)	
Nelson	S	00.00.1828(R)	
Novator	Z	02.03.1918	
Niger	HMS	11.11.1914	141
Nora	Mv	29.01.1940	*184*, 153
Patria	SS	19.12.1899	129, 133
Polly	S	13.02.1763	
Providence	S	09.12.1760(R)	
Quatre Frères	Sl	27.12.1852	
Queen	Sc	25.11.1877	119
Rachael	Tr	20.02.1795	
Racine	S	11.02.1870	
Reform	Lg	16.12.1871	107-8
Resolution	Sc	00.05.1841(R)	
Rooke	HM/T	03.08.1916	
Royal Escape	HM/6	08.01.1760	
St Joseph	Br	23.02.1762	
Sir Walter Scott	S	22.10.1842	
Star of the Ocean	S	00.11.1877	*50*
Success	Sl	20.11.1770	
Surrey	SS	26.02.1915	
Squib	HM/6	00.10.1805	
The Diamond	X	02.03.1918	
Thomas	S	05.12.1758(R)	
Victory	Lg	06.01.1857	
Williams Adventure	S	13.10.1860(R)	
Unidentified	S	20.12.1757	57
Unidentified	Sn	15.03.1763	
Unidentified	S	20.02.1770	
William & John	Frs	24.01.1800	61
Windsor Castle	HM/2	28.04.1693	

Downs

Adjutant	SS	22.10.1914	
Alice	S	11.08.1895	
Alpha	Gi	05.03.1853	
American Hero	S	11.11.1800(R)	
Amiable Society	S	11.11.1763(R)	
Amine	Br	25.11.1877	
Anastasie	Sc	12.11.1877	
Anne	S	12.01.1753	
Assach	SS	05.10.1916	
Aurora	S	19.12.1854	
Bellcairn	SS	13.10.1894	
Betsey	S	04.04.1788	
Betsey	S	10.11.1795(R)	
Betty	S	23.02.1747	
Bikubon	Br	02.12.1869	
Bravore	SS	24.04.1940	153
Bredonia	Mv	11.09.1939	
Brighton Belle	SS	28.05.1940	
British Navy	S	27.11.1881	123
British Queen	Sc	29.11.1869	
Campbell	Br	16.11.1859	99
Carlisle	HM/4	19.09.1700	47-9
Carolina	Gl	24.02.1743	55
Catherine	S	21.01.1682(R)	
Cathrina Augusta	S	11.12.1801(R)	
Champion	Sc	21.10.1878	
Cicero	S	25.10.1808(R)	
Copy	Sc	27.01.1860	
Courier	Br	04.02.1867	111
Crookendon	S	24.02.1743	55
Daisy	S	13.07.1894	
Dasher	S	27.09.1811(R)	
Delphin	Brn	12.09.1866	
Dolphin	S	24.02.1743	
Dolphin	SS	18.09.1885	123
Drie Kienden	Gl	19.12.1814	
Dromo	Sc	29.11.1869	
Duchess	Pt	16.02.1781(R)	
Duke of Clarence	Frs	27.11.1801	
Eclipse	S	18.11.1893	
Edith	S	10.01.1852	
Eglantine	Bq	13.02.1870	
Egero	SS	04.03.1916	143
Elizabeth	S	18.12.1744(R)	
Emily Eliza	Lg	30.01.1860	
Emma	SS	02.06.1940	
Empress	Br	00.01.1863(R)	
Endeavour	Sl	11.03.1783	
Erin	S	11.09.1893	
Esther	HM/6	12.02.1781	
Europa	HM/6	06.10.1794	
Experiment	Pt	16.02.1781(R)	

Faith	Lg	08.12.1860	
Ferdinand	S	11.11.1762	
Filleigh	SS	18.04.1945	155
Fyn	Sc	16.11.1911	*126*, 140
Galicia	SS	31.07.1915	
Gallia	Mv	10.02.1940	153
Gemini	S	11.11.1891	127
Genoa	Gl	24.02.1743	55
George	S	27.11.1763	
Gerda	Bq	14.10.1891	
Giraroin	Sc	05.03.1871	
Globe	S	24.02.1743	55
Golden Rose	S	23.02.1625	
Gottenberg	S	22.12.1758	
Graphic	SS	03.11.1887	
Hawk	S	11.11.1762	
Hippolyte	Br	03.01.1865	
Hopewell	HM/6	03.06.1690	
Hunzeborg	Mv	13.08.1966	
Idris	Sc	05.01.1891	
Ilaro	SS	24.10.1915	
Industry	S	24.02.1743	55
Jacob Luckenback	SS	05.07.1916	143
Jennett	S	24.02.1743	
Jeune Arthur	S	07.04.1863	103
Jeune Louisa	S	05.10.1852	
Kaleva	Sc	11.11.1921	
Kongshavn	SS	01.02.1917	
Lady Ann	S	19.12.1809	
Lady Neville	S	09.09.1835	
Larnaca	S	26.11.1881	
Lea	Bq	06.01.1871	
Leader	Lg	27.02.1878	
London Merchant	S	30.01.1764	
Lucent Aurora	S	12.01.1781(R)	
Mary	S	24.02.1743	
Mary	S	02.12.1794	
Mount Pleasant	S	13.01.1764(R)	
Nancy	S	01.12.1795	
Newbiggin	S	00.00.1833(R)	
Naworth Castle	SS	19.01.1907	
Newport Trader	S	16.05.1850(R)	82
New Success	S	15.08.1766	
N.S. Senora de Rosario	S	20.12.1757(R)	
Ocean Queen	X	28.08.1917	
Orange	S	09.01.1764	
Ousel	SS	14.09.1917	
Oxford	S	24.02.1743	55
Pereira	S	27.07.1588	
Peterhead Packet	Sc	13.12.1819	
Phoenix	S	10.11.1795	
Plover	Frs	14.03.1891	127
Pola	SS	18.11.1916	
Poll	X	15.11.1842	

Providence	X	28.10.1642(R)	
Queen of Portugal	S	11.11.1762	
Quinque	S	13.11.1894	
Rakel	Brn	19.10.1895	
Recovery	S	24.02.1743	
Reform	Lg	16.01.1871	
Renard	Sl	26.11.1901	
Report	S	29.03.1654	
Remembrance	Br	03.01.1874	
Resolution	S	10.01.176	
Resolution	Sc	00.05.1841(R)	
Royal George	S	27.11.1763	
Russia	Sc	14.12.1889	
San Genaro	HM/6	00.01.1763(R)	57
Sarah	S	23.02.1850	
Seamans Glory	X	25.08.1889	125
Seamans Pride	Lg	22.01.1866	
Shelburn	S	16.11.1773	
Simopoulos	SS	21.11.1908	
Sisters	S	05.01.1873	
Snipe	HM/6	00.12.1872(R)	
St Dominic	S	13.03.1743	
Success	S	24.02.1868	
Superior	Bq	15.02.1868	
Tempter	Kt	27.03.1896	
Thistle	S	11.11.1891	127
Triton	S	16.11.1773	
Twilight	X	11.02.1908	
Union	S	30.12.1894	
Venus	S	13.10.1758(R)	
Wallsend	SS	09.09.1915	
Warwickshire	S	09.12.1892	
Westergate	SS	02.01.1915	142
William's Adventure	Sc	28.09.1860	
William Harper	Bq	13.02.1870	
William & Mary	Brn	02.09.1883	
William & Sarah	S	24.02.1743	55
William Skinner	Br	12.02.1869	
Unidentified (12 vessels)	S	00.12.1532	
Unidentified (2 vessels)	S	04.01.1616	
Unidentified	S	25.11.1616	
Unidentified	S	05.10.1624	
Unidentified (up to 20 vessels)	S	03.10.1624	
Unidentified	S	08.11.1624	
Unidentifeid	S	22.11.1624	
Unidentified (3 vessels)	S	15.02.1625	
Unidentified	S	04.03.1625	
Unidentified	S	30.01.1637	
Unidentified (6 vessels)	S	11.10.1639	
Unidentified	S	00.09.1640(R)	
Unidentified	S	20.12.1642	
Unidentified (2 vessels)	S	23.11.1657	
Unidentified	S	19.12.1657	
Unidentified (several vessels)	S	22.03.1660	

Unidentified	S	14.05.1660	
Unidentified	S	19.11.1666	
Unidentified	S	09.03.1743	
Unidentified (2 vessels)	S	15.09.1752	
Unidentified	S	29.12.1775	
Unidentified (4 vessels)	S	14.01.1764	
Unidentified	Br	28.11.1801	
Unidentified (6 vessels)	S	06.12.1815	
Unidentified	S	00.00.1858	123
Unidentified	Brn	03.12.1867	
Unidentified (2 vessels)	S	12.11.1877	
Unidentified	Z	22.10.1891	
Unidentified	S	00.00.1895	
Unidentified	S	28.03.1905	
Victoria	Lg	29.03.1853	85
X.L.	Sc	02.06.1860	

Sandwich

Alarm	Sc	*31.03.1883(R)*	
Ann	S	02.10.1789(R)	
Ann Lyon	S	28.11.1623	37
Atlantic	S	14.09.1798(R)	
Basnet	S	20.12.1748(R)	
Bell	S	24.01.1800	
Bellcairn	SS	00.10.1894	
Biscay Merchant	S	30.12.1682(R)	
Blessing	S	16.11.1773(R)	
Bravore	SS	24.04.1940	
D'Artagnan	Br	11.11.1877	118
Earl of Holdness	Frs	11.01.1764	57
Eclipse	Bq	12.01.1858	
Fame	S	06.10.1794(R)	
Industry	S	20.12.1748(R)	
John & James	S	20.12.1748	
John & Philip	S	18.11.1755(R)	
Jonge Bornazca	S	25.11.1783	
Juno	Br	00.10.1812(R)	
Livetanto	S	19.12.1814	
Marquis of Granby	S	16.11.1773(R)	
Mary	S	25.11.1755(R)	
Montague	Tr	06.04.1753(R)	
Platoff	S	30.08.1833	
Rakel	Bn	22.10.1895	
Ranger	Sl	07.12.1788	
Robert Morris	Sc	31.12.1913	
St Dominic	S	13.03.1743	
Sandwich	S	04.03.1757(R)	
Sandwich	S	11.12.1764(R)	
Stubbs Galley	S	20.12.1748(R)	
Success	S	24.02.1743	
Susannah Carmichael	Sn	20.11.1770(R)	
Tillicherry	S	02.02.1798(R)	
William & John	S	24.01.1800	

Worcester	S	21.11.1797(R)	
Young Hero	S	06.10.1794(R)	
Unidentified	S	07.06.1215(R)	32
Unidentified, 'a great ship'	S	00.00.1483(R)	32
Unidentified	El	06.06.1653(R)	
Unidentified	S	01.09.1752	
Unidentified	S	16.11.1755	
Unidentified (several vessels)	S	06.10.1794(R)	
Unidentified	S	18.02.1807	
Unidentified	S	24.11.1877	
Unidentified (20 vessels)	S	24.12.1877	

Brake Sand

Abeona	S	23.05.1834	
Antelope	S	19.01.1875	
Aspasia	Sc	21.05.1889	
Beaver	S	13.03.1810(R)	
Cornwall	Frs	08.05.1817	70
Eu	Frs	27.12.1852	
Harriet	*Sc*	*12.02.1869*	
Hope	Br	12.02.1869	
Industry	Sl	30.01.1842	
Innisfall	Br	26.11.1881	122
Jane White	S	10.02.1853	85
Lady Torfrida	SS	08.05.1887	
Little Emma	S	13.07.1903	
Matilda	Bq	20.10.1842	
Olive Branch	S	15.12.1809(R)	
Princess Maria	S	09.02.1658	43
Sadak	Sc	27.12.1852	
Soratat	S	11.11.1877	
Speranza	X	27.07.1877	
Thistle	Kt	11.11.1891	
Voyager	Sc	07.11.1852	
Unidentified	Br	27.12.1852	
Unidentified	Sc	00.01.1869(R)	112
Braekka	Bq	16.2.1879	
Emma	Br	12.02.1854	
George & Valentine	Sc	15.09.1873	118
Hedvig Sophia	Bq	11.11.1877	118
Lorma	Sc	31.07.1891	127
Navarino	Sc	16.01.1867	111
Oreala	S	14.12.1885	
Princess of Wales	S	16.02.1781(R)	
St Michael	S	04.11.1777(R)	
Union	Sc	30.12.1894	
Victory	Sc	26.01.1852	83
Unidentified	S	01.09.1752(R)	
Unidentified (10 fishing boats)	S	01.09.1752	
Unidentified (6 vessels)	S	12.11.1877	
Unidentified	Br	27.11.1881	

171

Ramsgate

Aid	Tg	24.04.1872	
Albion	Brn	26.11.1881	122-3
American Hero	S	11.11.1800(R)	
Anne	S	02.01.1753(R)	
Antwerp	S	07.01.1772(R)	
Apollo	S	22.12.1790(R)	
Argo	Sc	06.03.1859	
Avona	X	15.07.1901	
Belinda	Br	08.12.1852	
Benn	S	23.01.1776	
Bethel	Sk	15.02.1870	
Betsey	S	07.03.1818	
Britannia	S	06.11.1753	
Britannia	S	24.02.1812	
Castor	S	02.02.1798(R)	
Cassandra	Br	05.09.1861	
Cesira	Br	03.05.1853	
Charles Kerr	S	06.10.1794	
Charlotree	S	29.09.1772(R)	
Christine Margrethe	Bq	02.11.1880	
Cornelia	S	04.03.1818	
Daring	Sk	25.04.1867	111
Dawn	X	02.11.1918	
Eagle	Tr	19.12.1797(R)	
Eagle Wing	Sc	08.12.1886	
Elizabeth	S	20.12.1748(R)	
Elizabeth	S	25.09.1772(R)	
Elizabeth	S	11.03.1783	
Elizabeth	S	00.01.1790(R)	
Elizabeth	S	17.02.1797(R)	
Elizabeth		04.03.1818	
Elizabeth & Rebecca	S	11.12.1770	
Enterkin	Frs	12.12.1891	
Ergo	SS	00.07.1915	
Fauvette	SS	09.03.1916	
Favourite	S	13.01.1789	
Fawn	Sk	06.12.1868	
Fee	Bq	22.11.1854	
Forest Belle	Sc	16.03.1912	
Funtingdon	S	04.03.1794	
Gazelle	Br	25.11.1850	
General Murray	S	27.10.1852	
Gerda	Bq	14.10.1891	127
Hannah	S	04.03.1818	
Hazard	S	17.12.1790(R)	
Hazard	S	23.11.1820	
Henrietta	S	26.04.1799(R)	
Henry	S	14.01.1833	
Ida	Kt	22.10.1914	
Jane	S	07.03.1818	
Jane & Eleanor	S	08.04.1788	
Josephine	X	10.10.1857	

J. Quatro Fratelli	Brn	14.02.1850	
Judith	S	22.10.1812	
Lady Cockburne	S	29.12.1821	
La Farne	S	28.11.1755(R)	
La Pierre de Brevedent	S	03.11.1790(R)	
Leda	X	15.12.1809(R)	
Lee Lea	S	06.11.1801(R)	
Liberty	S	17.12.1793(R)	
Liberty	Sk	00.03.1841(R)	
Linda	Bq	11.02.1871	
Maria Ann	Sk	20.10.1855	91
Mary	S	02.12.1794(R)	
Maryann	S	06.04.1810(R)	
Mary Ann	Bqn	30.09.1899	
Mary Hughes	Tg	18.11.1914(R)	
Master Mason	S	02.04.1813(R)	
Mispah	S	06.01.1867	
Neg Chieftain	Tg	10.08.1983	158
New Flora	Sk	31.01.1895	
Norfolk	S	01.10.1799(R)	59
Olive Branch	S	05.02.1799(R)	
Orion	S	13.12.1814	69
Palm Balm	S	25.12.1801(R)	
Pet	Sk	13.02.1889	
Perseverence	S	23.09.1794(R)	
Petrel	Sk	10.01.1895	
Polly	S	05.08.1753	
Rosine & Aglae	Br	13.12.1814	69
Samarang	S	13.01.1843	
Samuel & Elizabeth	S	31.12.1816(R)	
San Genaro	HM/4	02.03.1763	
Sorata	S	11.11.1877	
Speranza	S	27.07.1877	
Spring	S	09.02.1813	
St Michael	S	04.11.1777(R)	
Swift	S	00.00.1834(R)	
Thomas	S	20.11.1795(R)	
Touch Not	Kt	11.11.1891	127
Two Arthurs	S	22.02.1760(R)	
Union	S	19.10.1775	
Unity	S	30.12.1818	
Venyowa	S	30.08.1757(R)	
Vrow Catharina	S	04.03.1796(R)	
Young Jacob	S	26.09.1758(R)	
Whiff	Sk	24.03.1870	
Wildman	S	02.12.1794(R)	
William & Mary	S	19.02.1771	
Wilhemina	S	26.02.1750(R)	
Winnean	S	00.08.1757(R)	
Worcester	S	21.11.1797(R)	
Young Jacob	S	26.09.1758(R)	
Unidentified	S	12.07.1623	
Unidentified	Bq	30.11.1624	

Unidentified (2 vessels)	S	16.01.1631(R)	
Unidentified (3 vessels)	Br	24.10.1775(R)	
Unidentified	S	12.12.1777(R)	
Unidentified	X	07.06.1870	
Unidentified	Br	11.03.1783	

Ramsgate to North Foreland

Ben Venue	S	00.11.1891(R)	
Blengfell	S	17.10.1898	
Challenge	Bg	12.04.1913	
Dover	S	12.01.1753(R)	
George Cadman	S	00.07.1842(R)	
Glance	Sc	06.01.1891	
Glide	Brn	06.01.1891	
Iona Feliciana	S	12.01.1870	
Jane	S	21.09.1818	
Kitty	S	00.00.1833(R)	
Lord Dufferin	Kt	28.03.1916	
Lulworth	SS	23.04.1940	
Marie Rose	S	28.08.1853	
Marchant	S	01.09.1833	
Northern Belle	S	06.01.1867	
Nottingham	S	24.02.1743	
Puritan	Kt	08.12.1913	
Rumania	Tg	11.01.1956	*118*
St Michael	S	04.11.1777(R)	
Star of the Ocean	Brn	12.10.1893	
Success	S	25.10.1834	
Theory	Ss	18.12.1919	
Unity	Sc	02.03.1842	
Unidentified	S	23.12.1748(R)	

Goodwin Sands

Abraham	S	04.01.1616	35
Abraham Baldwin	SS	00.00.1944(R)	
Abyssinian	S	14.12.1872	114
Active	S	21.03.1776	
Adelaide	Sc	02.11.1892	
Admiral Gardner	EI	25.01.1809	10, 67-9
Adventure	S	21.12.1739	
Adventure	S	16.12.1761	
Adventure	S	30.10.1772	
Agen	SS	14.01.1952	*124, 156*
Agnes Wyllie	S	01.01.1877	
Aggia Arbia	SS	11.03.1947	
Aimwell	S	13.01.1818	
Ala	Bq	05.03.1889	
Albert	S	24.02.1854	
Aldebaran	Sc	03.05.1881	
Alert	SS	25.02.1945	155
Alida	Bq	10.09.1872	
Alexandra	Lg	26.03.1870	

Alpha	Gl	05.03.1853	
Alyda	S	30.10.1773	
Amazon	Bq	15.09.1873	
American Hero	S	11.11.1800	61
Amor	Br	12.01.1869	113
Amorette	Br	26.07.1891	
Amour	Brn	00.12.1867	
Amphion	Br	19.12.1800	61
Amplegarth	SS	10.05.1918	
Anastassios Pateras	SS	29.12.1930	156
Andaman	Mv	24.05.1953	157
Andre Thome	SS	00.11.1945	
Anglia	Brn	08.07.1899	
Ann	S	23.08.1776	
Ann	Br	13.01.1853	85
Ann Elizabeth	S	04.11.1844	
Anna	S	04.04.1796	
Anna	Br	16.01.1844	
Anna Catherine	S	19.07.1803	
Anna Jacobee	S	17.09.1765	
Anne	S	04.11.1844	
Anne Longton	Frs	29.08.1869	
Anne Maria	S	12.05.1741	
Annette	Br	31.12.1853	
Annette Gilbert	Br	07.06.1852	
Annibale	Br	07.05.1880	
Antelope	S	04.11.1844	
Antwerp	S	07.01.1772	
Apollo	Br	26.01.1809	
Arctic Trapper	SS	10.02.1941	
Arda	Bq	27.03.1887	
Argo	Sc	06.03.1859	
Ariel	Sn	02.11.1872(R)	
Ariel	S	16.11.1793	
Ariel	Bq	24.09.1860	99
Ariel	Br	26.12.1872	
Ark Noah	S	00.00.1621	37
Ashley	SS	09.03.1940	*70*
Asia	SS	20.04.1909	
Atlantic	S	15.11.1848	81
Auguste Herman Francke	Br	20.04.1886	
Aurora	Tr	16.12.1805(R)	66
Aurora	Br	19.12.1814	70
Aurora Borealis	Bq	05.01.1867	109
Austria	Bqn	26.10.1891	127
Bacchus	S	15.10.1771	
Barbara	S	00.00.1834	
Bartley	Br	24.09.1856	91
Beacon Light	SS	07.02.1895	
Belina	Wl	23.11.1824	*36, 70-1*
Bertha	Br	23.09.1853	
Bertha	S	20.06.1906	133
Bessie	Br	15.03.1852	

Bessie	Sc	10.01.1872	
Betsy	S	24.02.1789(R)	
Betsy & Jane	Tr	11.05.1784	
Birtie	SS	04.10.1945	
Blervie Castle	Frs	21.12.1859	
Blind Fortune	Bq	00.01.1618(R)	37
Bonar Law	HM/T	27.10.1915	143
Brali	Mv	14.04.1949	
Brandore	SS	24.04.1940	
Brendonia	SS	11.09.1939	
Bretagne	Lg	22.06.1859	97
Brighton Belle	SS	28.05.1940	
Britannia	EI	25.01.1809	10, 67-9
British Queen	S	17.12.1814	69
British Queen	Sc	29.11.1869	
Briton	Sc	24.01.1853	85
Brothers	S	06.01.1761(R)	
Brothers	S	11.03.1796	
Browns	Sc	11.11.1868	
Buona Sarte	S	15.12.1795(R)	
Cadiz	S	08.07.1825	
Calina	SS	17.01.1880	
Calypso	S	17.01.1853	85
Cap Lopez	SS	21.12.1907	137
Carl	Br	26.01.1869	
Carlotta	SS	09.10.1900	133
Carl Robert	Br	10.10.1841	81
Cas	Br	24.09.1876	
Catharine	S	23.08.1771	
Cathay	SS	05.05.1915	
Catherine	S	06.01.1761	
Cayton Wyke	HM/T	08.07.1940	151
Cedrington Court	SS	07.01.1940	153
Celestina	Sc	01.10.1911	
Charles Carter	S	13.04.1811	67
Charles Davenport	S	11.11.1977	
Charlotte	Frs	09.05.1815	
Charlotte	S	01.09.1833	
Charming Sally	Tr	17.11.1775(R)	
Childe Harold	S	08.11.1853	
Chilham Castle	S	13.04.1811	67
Chimaer	Sc	26.11.1881	
Christina	Bq	04.01.1894	
Christoph Frederic	S	28.11.1851	
Cicerone	Sc	13.06.1906	
City of Dresden	SS	19.01.1907	133
City of Liverpool	HM/T	31.07.1918	
Clara Felicia	S	12.12.1889	125
Clarinda	S	16.06.1873	
Colin Campbell	Br	29.12.1866	
Colinie Van Surinam	S	00.01.1744(R)	55
Colombo	Br	24.03.1853	85
Conceiao Mario	Mv	06.04.1949	
Concord	S	12.02.1796	

Concordia	S	27.12.1771	
Concordia	S	19.12.1809(R)	
Corinthian	Kt	01.11.1919	145, 147
Cornelius	Br	14.01.1824	
Cornelius & Maria	S	07.03.1788	
Correct	SS	00.02.1916(R)	143
Countess of Durham	S	16.10.1881	
Cranbrook	HM/3	17.11.1775(R)	
Crocodile	Bqn	06.01.1891	
Crusader	Frs	01.12.1877	121
Cuvier	SS	09.03.1900	
Danmark	Sc	31.01.1911	
David	S	16.04.1765(R)	
De la Pole	HM/1	04.02.1916	143
Delfina	Br	02.02.1819	
Der Wanderer	Bq	09.10.1867	111
De Rudder	Bq	01.08.1859	97
Devonia	Bq	25.12.1854	88
Diamond	S	10.05.1812	
Diligence	S	00.01.1670(R)	
Diligence	Sk	17.05.1803	
Dilsberg	SS	12.12.1892	
Dolphin	S	27.10.1624	39
Doreen	S	09.08.1899	
Doric	Kt	02.06.1895	
Doris	S	04.01.1822	
Dove	S	09.12.1816	
Dreadnought	HM/4	00.00.1803(R)	
Dredger No. 18	Dr	22.10.1891	127
Dronthein	S	09.07.1776	
Druid	S	29.11.1793	
Drumlanrig	SS	27.11.1908	137
Dublin Lass	Brn	10.05.1870	
Duguay Trouin	Bq	01.01.1861	
Duke	S	21.08.1744	
Dunbar Castle	SS	09.01.1940	153
Duo Fratres	Br	07.11.1857	
Durham	Br	15.12.1847	
Eagle	S	16.06.1775	
Eaglet	Kt	08.12.1900	
Ebbwvale	SS	09.01.1891	
Edenbridge	S	3.02.1798	
Edith Banfield	Bq	16.06.1869	
Edith Maria	Sc	12.09.1869	
Edward Arthur	Sc	12.05.1886	
Edward & Sophia	Kt	31.10.1851	
Effort	S	21.12.1818	
Egremont	S	15.12.1797	
Eileen	S	22.07.1914	
E.L. de Bayo	SS	12.05.1911	
Elenore	Sc	08.11.1853	86
Elenora	Mv	30.05.1979	
Elizabeth	S	24.11.1775	
Elizabeth	S	17.02.1797	

Elizabeth Angela	HM/T	14.08.1940	
Elizabeth Antoinette	S	23.07.1844	
Ellison	S	25.05.1841	
Elsy	Sc	26.08.1945	
Emblem	S	00.09.1870(R)	
Endeavour	S	28.07.1766	
Endeavour	WI	08.02.1805	
Enigheid	S	01.11.1791	
Envermeu	SS	24.12.1915	
Ertha Rickmers	Frs	19.09.1870	113
Espion	HM/4	17.11.1799	59-60
Ethel	Sc,	08.02.1889	
Ethel	HM/6	28.10.1889	
Ethnee	HM/T	15.01.1918	
Etoile Polaire	HM/T	03.12.1915	143
Euthemia	S	15.12.1820	
Europe	Bq	03.04.1882	
Fair Lady	S	26.11.1793	
Fairy	S	25.12.1798	
Fairy Glen	Sc	24.03.1887	
Fairy Queen	Br	10.11.1877	9
Falken	SS	03.05.1895	
Fanny	Sc	19.01.1855	89
Febro	Br	31.03.1853	85
Fiesten	Mv	18.10.1954	
Flamingo	S	07.05.1896	
Flandres	SS	12.02.1940	
Flora	Sc	16.02.1850	
Florence	Sk	07.12.1888	
Florentine	S	24.08.1675	44
Florida	Brn	23.02.1878(R)	
Floridan	Bq	06.03.1841	
Flying Cloud	Brn	26.07.1877	
Forest Queen	Bq	11.11.1868	
Fort Frederica	SS	23.02.1949	
Fortschritt	S	15.12.1848	82
Fortune	S	31.01.1764	
Fortune	S	17.06.1766	
Fortune	Br	09.04.1819	
Foxhound	S	25.05.1841	
Francesco Ciampa	SS	11.02.1927	147
Frank Shaw	Frs	19.10.1869	
Franz Von Matthies	Brn	11.02.1894	
Freden	Bq	20.11.1880	
Frederick	S	21.11.1797	
Frederick	S	29.10.1811	67
Frederick Carel	S	31.10.1885	
Frederike Carolina	S	12.02.1886	
Freedom	S	17.02.1892	
Frida	S	09.12.1929	
Friendship	S	16.01.1767	
Friendship	S	28.12.1817	
Friendship	S	25.09.1818	
Frigate Bird	Bq	15.12.1880	

Friheten	S	00.12.1758(R)	
Fyn	Sc	15.11.1911	
Ganges	Frs	14.10.1881	121
Garibaldi	Sc	04.12.1870	
Garland	Sc	06.01.1867	
Gazelle	Br	24.11.1850	82
Gelinconied	Brn	24.03.1870	
Genimar	Mv	01.10.1872	
Genolind	Bq	13.12.1872	114
Georg	SS	14.04.1895	
George Forster	Br	30.11.1856	91
George & Elizabeth	S	01.09.1833	
George & Mary	Sc	11.02.1881	
George William	Br	27.10.1852	84
German Emperor	SS	21.05.1889	123
Germania	Brn	24.03.1870	
Glance	Sc	06.01.1891	
Glenavon	Bg	01.11.1919	145
Gold Coin	Mv	04.12.1872	
Golden Island	Sc	15.05.1887	
Golden Lion	S	17.12.1592	34-5
Golden Rose	S	00.00.1624(R)	39
Golden Wagon	S	21.08.1618	37
Good Friends	S	28.06.1774	
Good Intent	S	09.03.1792	
Grasston Bothmer	S	08.04.1880(R)	61
Gretha	Sc	30.11.1939	
Grethe Mortensen	X	07.11.1944	
Greyhound	HM/6	00.00.1781	
Guardian	SS	29.11.1927	147-9
Guttenburg	Frs	01.01.1861	99, 102
Guy	S	01.11.1765	
Hammonica	S	25.11.1783	
Hannah Rahtkens	Bq	12.12.1877	121
Happy Return	Sc	30.04.1876	
Harcalo	SS	06.06.1940	
Harmony	S	10.02.1786	
Harriet	Br	26.04.1853	
Harriet	Sl	12.02.1869	113
Harschundal	S	00.12.1734(R)	55
Hazard	S	11.01.1763	
Hazard	S	07.12.1843	
Hazelbank	Frs	28.10.1890	
Hazelmere	SS	01.12.1903	
Hedessa	Sc	03.06.1891	
Helena Modeska	SS	13.09.1946	98,100,155
Henderina Jacoba	S	10.10.1764	57
Henrick & Jacob	S	28.10.1786	
Henry B. Plant	SS	06.02.1945	155
Henry Taylor	Br	04.10.1849	
Hermann	SSX	29.10.1906	
Hero	S	23.10.1872	
Hero	Bq	25.11.1877	119
Hiawatha	Bq	13.11.1872	113

Hibernia	S	31.01.1809	
Highland Chief	Bq	12.02.1869	112
Hirundo	Sc	16.03.1891	
Hit or Miss	Bq	31.01.1809	
Hoeffnang	S	13.06.1799	59
Hoffanding	Br	16.11.1821	
Holly	S	24.12.1773	
Hondeklip	Br	18.02.1894	
Hony Sverne	Bq	10.10.1870	
Hope	S	14.03.1697	
Hope	S	12.10.1764	
Hope	S	10.12.1790	
Hope	S	17.10.1792	
Hope	S	03.07.1798	
Hope	S	00.00.1827(R)	
Hope	Bq	21.10.1842	
Hope	Br	12.02.1869	113
Horatio	Br	31.08.1853	85
Horatio	Sn	02.11.1861	
Hull Trader	SS	13.02.1915	142
Hursley	SS	16.11.1930	
Ida	Br	08.08.1824	
Ilos	Bq	24.08.1859	99
Inaver Sophia Elizabeth	Sn	11.03.1783	
India	Frs	18.12.1871	
Indiana	S	14.04.1800	61
Industry	S	18.03.1750	
Industry	Brn	15.12.1777	
Iona	Kt	06.10.1909	
Ionia	Brn	13.11.1854	
Ira	SS	00.03.1947(R)	155
Iron Crown	S	07.02.1865	
Island	Sc	07.11.1906	
Isle of Caldy	SS	15.06.1906	133
James	S	24.01.1656	
Jan Hendric	Frs	28.06.1852	
Janette & Jane	S	27.01.1889	
Jenny	S	15.12.1772	
Jenny	S	01.10.1776	
Jessie	Sc	20.03.1877	
Jessie Annie	Br	22.09.1856	91
Johan	Brn	01.11.1912	
Johanna Maria	Bq	07.03.1850	
Johanne	Bq	10.01.1617	37
Johanne & Frederick	S	16.02.1788	
Johannes Specht	S	00.12.1739(R)	
John	S	25.01.1669	43
John Bright	Sc	27.01.1878	
John & Margaret	S	18.08	1789
John & Margaret	S	28.01.1813	
John & Mary	S	28.10.1796	
Jonah	Tr	01.02.1814	
Jonas	S	04.01.1616	35
Jongepas Carolina	S	07.02.1748	

180

Jonge Gefina	S	01.04.1785	
Jonge Peters	S	04.08.1780	
Juffrow Jacoba	S	10.11.1803	
Julia	S	15.06.1834	
Julia	S	17.11.1857	
Jussrow Lucia	S	10.04.1764	
Kabinda	SS	10.12.1939	*138*, 153
Katherina	Sn	23.05.1755	
Katindaki	SS	15.01.1972	
Kentish Bell	Fc	18.02.1923	
King	Sc	29.12.1880	
Klar	HM/T	26.11.1915	143
Kristina	Bq	04.01.1894	
La Baleine	Pt	19.12.1707	
La Barone de la Houze	S	11.01.1793	
La Brevedent	S	02.11.1790	
Lady Luvibund	S	13.02.1748	
Lady Taylor	S	02.09.1796	
Laristan	SS	22.10.1899	129
Lavre	Lg	01.02.1866	
Lavantse	S	07.02.1748	
Lavater	S	20.01.1790	
Leda	S	28.12.1879	
Leevart	S	01.04.1780	
Lekat	S	00.11.1750(R)	
Lelean	Sc	19.12.1855	91
Le Marin	Brn	11.11.1852	
Lena	Br	30.11.1867	
Leonidas	S	14.01.1833	
Leonidas	Bq	11.02.1889	
L'espion	HM/5	16.11.1799	
Liberal	Sl	15.04.1859	96-7
Liberty	S	00.00.1834(R)	
Lightship, (Gull Stream)	Z	18.03.1929	149
Lightship, (South Goodwin)	Z	28.11.1954	*142*
Lina	Sc	23.09.1918	
Linda	Bq	24.09.1860	99
Lindholmen	SS	18.12.1908	
Lisa	Sc	23.09.1918	
Little Florence	Lg	17.11.1890	
Little John	Sc	24.10.1800	61
Little Teaser	Lg	16.12.1910	
Lizzie Fern	Kt	13.05.1872	
Loanda	SS	31.05.1908	
Lolworth	SS	23.04.1940	
Longhirst	SS	21.06.1901	133
Loosdrecht	El	19.02.1736	57
Lord Donoughmore	S	20.05.1800	61
Lord Hartington	Bq	30.11.1888	
Lorma	Sc	30.07.1890	
Louisa Ulrica	S	29.04.1766	
Lulworth	SS	23.04.1940	153
Luray Victory	SS	30.01.1946	29, 155-6
Madelaine Richards	Bq	20.04.1895	

Madona	El	09.11.1793	59
Madre Dios	S	05.03.1697	
Mahratta I	SS	09.04.1909	*134*, 137
Mahratta II	SS	06.10.1939	139, 151
Maid of Anglesea	Sc	18.12.1889	
Mal Volsin	Kt	00.00.1925(R)	147
Manitobah	Bq	03.02.1872	
Maren	Brn	11.12.1870	
Margaret	S	00.09.1678(R)	
Margaretta Dorothea	Sl	11.08.1784	
Margot	SS	17.12.1919	
Margreth Dorthe	S	04.05.1764	
Maria	S	07.02.1786	
Maria	Sc	25.05.1841	
Maria	Sc	17.11.1865	
Maria	Kt	30.01.1878	
Maria	Bq	17.09.1901	
Maria Ann	S	09.03.1859	
Maria Antoinette	S	16.03.1871	
Maria Catharina	S	15.03.1796	
Maria Charlotta	S	28.12.1797	
Maria Cheeseman	Kt	11.11.1910	
Mariana Henriette	Br	30.01.1824	
Marie	Bq	17.09.1901	
Marie-Leonhardt	SS	16.01.1912	
Marie Roche-Bernard	Br	26.11.1855	91
Marion	S	12.11.1852	
Margot	SS	17.12.1919	
Martha Edmonds	Bqn	22.11.1902	
Mary	HM/3	27.11.1703	9, 51
Mary	Sc	21.12.1862	
Mary Coles	Brn	24.08.1878(R)	
Mayflower	S	28.04.1853	
Meermond	El	19.02.1736	57
Mercurian	S	31.10.1815	
Merel	SS	08.12.1939	153
Mersey	Bq	29.12.1901	131
Mersey	SS	20.04.1940	153
Mia Madre	Bq	25.08.1879	
Mill	S	30.07.1681	
Minni	Kt	14.03.1885	
Mizpah	Sc	08.01.1867	109
Modeste	Lg	00.11.1892(R)	
Montrose	SS	28.12.1916	141
Morant	S	22.02.1760	
Mount Park	SS	16.02.1911	
Mount Stewart	SS	24.07.1894	
Nagro	Mv	01.12.1972	
Nancy	S	15.11.1748	
Nancy	Bq	15.10.1842	78
Nancy Moran	Tg	30.05.1946	
Naworth Castle	SS	19.01.1907	137
Nelly	S	25.09.1761	
Neptumus	S	05.04.1799	

New York	Bq	11.09.1870	
Niagra	S	19.12.1800	61
Nicolaos M. Embiricos	SS	04.11.1939	153
Nieuv Roep	S	11.08.1784	
Niger	HMS	11.11.1914	
Nightingale	HM/5	18.01.1672	44
Nile	S	15.12.1825	
No.2 Pilot boat	Sc	11.12.1908	
Norna	Sc	07.02.1854	
Norra Fizland	S	28.08.1772	
North	S	30.08.1866	105-6
North Eastern Victory	SS	24.12.1946	29, *102*, 155
Northumberland	HM/3	27.11.1703	9, 51
Nostra Senora de Gariead	S	18.01.1757	
Nostra Senora del Carmem	;s	15.10.1790	
Oaste Emes	S	22.01.1783	
Occanus	Bq	02.08.1854	
Ocean	S	01.08.1844	
Ocean Hound	Mfv	10.08.1991	
Ocean Queen	S	07.12.1871	
Oceanus	Bq	02.08.1854	
Ogle Castle	El	01.11.1825	71-3
Onon	Gl.	14.02.1818	
Oostereem	S	21.01.1783	
Orange Tree	S	26.10.1692	
Orielton	Sc	20.04.1852	
Orion	S	13.02.1818	
Orion	SS	19.01.1870(R)	113
Orlando	SS	17.12.1872	
Osta Junis	S	12.07.1783	
Otter	S	15.11.1774	
Oxielton	Sc	20.04.1852	
Paquebot No.5	Sc	13.08.1899	
Paul Boynton	Frs	19.09.1880	
Pearl	S	16.11.1764	
Peerless	Sc	23.03.1866	
Pegasus	Pr	00.00.1598(R)	
Perseverance	S	00.00.1829(R)	
Pet	Sc	06.01.1843	
Petras	SS	00.00.1925(R)	147
Phoenix	S	00.00.1616	
Piave	SS	29.01.1919	144
Pilot Cutter No.3	S	04.09.1898	
Polly	S	21.02.1776	
Portland	S	18.11.1791	
Poseidon	Br	25.09.1860	99
Pretty Polly	S	02.10.1772	
Pride of the Sea	S	00.10.1887	
Prince	S	16.11.1790	
Prophet Jonah	S	29.04.1748	
Prosper Adele	Br	17.02.1854	
Providence	S	11.10.1677	
Providence	Frs	23.12.1869	
Purcell	S	02.12.1755	

Raa	SS	13.02.1927	147
Rannee	S	06.04.1868	
Red Lion	S	17.12.1592	
Regia	Bq	26.12.1906	
Regin	SS	23.02.1915	142
Ross Revenge	Mv	20.11.1991	
Sea Gull	Tg	30.11.1918	
Resolutie	Brn	07.11.1894	
Restoration	HM/3	26.11.1703	51
Rhine	S	07.04.1863	103
Richard & Harriet	S	11.01.1871	*54*
Richard Wilson	Kt	14.02.1879	
Robert & John	S	00.10.1701(R)	
Robin & Ann	S	01.04.1785	
Rochester	S	00.12.1657	
Rooswyck	El	30.12.1739	55, 57
Rosa	Bq	01.11.1873	
Ross Tariffa	Mfv	00.00.1948(R)	*92*
Roxburgh Castle	Frs	05.01.1872	
Rydal Force	SS	24.04.1940	153
Rynanna	SS	21.01.1940	
St Antonio	S	20.01.1768	
St Joseph	S	08.07.1796	
St Joseph	S	07.12.1871	
St Tobys	S	31.03.1675	
St Peter	S	15.11.1592	33-4
Sadak	S	10.02.1853	85
Saint Roman	Mv	11.07.1959	
Salina	SS	23.09.1921	
Sampson	S	00.01.1618(R)	37
Sandwich	S	31.05.1803	
San Hara Lambo	Br	26.10.1849	
Santagata	Mv	24.12.1950	*106*, 156
Sapsburg	Bq	02.02.1873	
Sarah Elizabeth	Sc	14.01.1893	
Scholten	SS	00.11.1887	
Scottish Lass	S	04.11.1867	111
Sea	S	07.12.1871	
Sea Flower	Br	23.04.1853	
Sea Gull	Tg	30.11.1918	
Sedgmore	HM/4	02.01.1688	
Shannon	Br	05.02.1880	
Shepherdess	Br	16.01.1844	
Sibiria	SS	20.11.1916	143
Silva Onorato	SS	02.01.1948	*151*,156
Sorrento	SS	18.12.1872	*348*, 113-5
Start	S	12.02.1869	113
Stirling Castle	HM/3	26.11.1703	9, 51
Stralsund	S	06.091875	
Stranton	SS	30.12.1914	141
Sun	S	19.02.1788	
Sunbeam	Kt	10.02.1900	
Swanlight	Frs	00.00.1852(R)	
Teniers	Sc	07.05.1850	

Terpsichore	S	24.11.1890	
Terra Nova	Brn	14.11.1861	
Thomas	S	11.03.1818	
Thomas & Ada	S	20.03.1856	
Thomas & Anne	Br	20.03.1855	
Thomas & Wilson	Sl	12.02.1869	113
Tima Primo	SS	18.03.1940	153
Toogo	Sc	01.12.1919	144-5
Trident	Sc	08.12.1879	
Trojan	Kt	14.07.1911	
Tryphina	Sc	11.12.1827	
Union	S	25.11.1794(R)	
Unity	S	30.07.1681(R)	
Unity	S	19.02.1796(R)	
Urienden	S	27.08.1771(R)	
U-16	Sm	24.10.1939	151
U-48	Sm	24.11.1917	9, 29, *140*, 143-4
UC-46	Sm	08.02.1917	143
UC-63	Sm	01.11.1917	143
Val-Salice	SS	20.11.1916	143
Verbena	Fv	21.02.1889	
Vertland	WS	30.05.1867	111
Victory	Br	17.08.1859	99
Victory	Sc	23.12.1869	
Vigilant	Br	18.12.1819	
Violet	Ps	05.01.1857	93
Virchild	S	13.12.1757	
Volkass Volkhause	S	24.09.1793(R)	
Volunteer	Sc	11.01.1905	
Vreede	S	12.01.1750	
Vroune Cornelia	S	03.03.1773	
Vrow Maria	S	10.01.1775(R)	
Vrow Neeltje	Gl	04.01.1854	
Wackender Boeye	S	26.09.1744	55
Wallsend	SS	09.09.1915	
Walmer Castle	S	15.03.1892	
Wangerland	Br	15.12.1872	114
Wapen Van Vlissingen	S	26.11.1670	43
Welsh Girl	Sc	03.05.1901	
Wesley	Kt	08.03.1905	
Westmorland	Pt	17.06.1803	
Whaleback	Yt	12.05.1970	
White Swan	S	15.07.1624	39
William & Henry	S	16.05.1850(R)	
Windgap	Yt	07.08.1946	
Windsor Castle	HM/2	29.04.1693	45
Yulan	Kt	30.01.1911	
Zeldenrost	S	15.05.1765	58
Zia Caterine	Br	21.12.1878	
Zingra	Sc	09.03.1891	
Zircon	SS	23.05.1895(R)	129

Unidentified Shipwrecks

'12 ships lost this winter'	S	00.01.1533(R)	32
'Carrying wheat and iron'	Bq	18.02.1542	33
'A Portuguese vessel lost'	S	00.00.1543(R)	33
'Three ships all at once'	S	00.00.1544(R)	33
'Several wrecks'	S	00.00.1555(R)	33
'Several wrecks'	S	00.00.1567(R)	33
'Several wrecks'	S	00.00.1577(R)	33
'Three great ships wrecked'	S	00.12.1592(R)	33
'Unidentified great ships'	S	04.01.1616(R)	35
Unidentified	S	16.12.1616(R)	
Dutch ship, 'with deals'	S	22.05.1617	37
'Another Dutch wreck'	S	00.12.1619(R)	
'A rich vessel, with money'	S	00.02.1622(R)	
Unidentified, 'A king's ship'	S	00.10.1624(R)	39
Several ships wrecked	S	17.02.1625	
Many wrecks, Dutch & English	S	31.01.1635	
3 or 4 Hollanders 'cast away'	S	13.01.1636	
'A great Spanish ship'	S	12.04.1650	
Four Dutch men o'war lost	Ws	28.09.1652(R)	43
Unidentified	S	21.10.1657(R)	
'A hoy and a great ship'	S	06.12.1657	
Two Ostenders 'cast away'	S	05.12.1666	
French man o'war, & another	S	15.12.1666	
Danish vessel, carrying deals	Sl	21.08.1668	
A Hamburger, with 24 guns	S	22.12.1668	
Several wrecks on the Sands	S	00.01.1669(R)	
A Guinea ship, on S. Goodwins	S	25.01.1669	
A Belgian ship, with linen	S	26.02.1669(R)	43
Two ships on the Goodwins	S	02.01.1670	
An English ship, with wines	S	00.01.1670(R)	
A Calais ship, from Newcastle	Sl	02.08.1670	
A Flemish East Indiaman	EI	16.11.1670	43
Small vessel, fast ashore	S	00.04.1671(R)	
A prize to HM *Nightingale*	S	16.01.1672	
'A Dutch caper of 12 guns'	S	18.01.1674	44
An unidentified Virginian	S	00.11.1674(R)	
A merchantman of 300 tuns	S	10.12.1674(R)	
A 'small Dutch ship'	S	10.01.1686	
Unidentified Dutch fireship	HM/6	13.06.1689(R)	
A Swedish ship carrying salt	S	00.07.1691	
A small French privateer	Pt	22.4.1697	
'A Dutchman lost in the storm'	S	25.11.1703	50
'Two merchantmen, lost'	S	27.11.1703	51
A Dunkirk privateer, 61 crew	Pt	00.12.1707(R)	53
A Swedish ship, with tobacco	S	24.02.1743	
A large Dutch ship	S	13.03.1743(R)	
A Dutch dogger	S	26.10.1744	55
French privateer, 34 guns	Pt	00.06.1747(R)	55
A large unidentified collier	S	03.08.1749	
An unidentified Dutch hoy	S	26.01.1750	
Unidentified	S	12.03.1750(R)	
Unidentified	S	25.08.1752(R)	

Two ships on the E. Goodwin	S	15.09.1752(R)	
A Bristol ship with staves	Sn	00.12.1753(R)	
A Hamburg merchant with iron	S	29.12.1753	
An unidentified large ship	S	30.11.1755	
Unidentified, from Yarmouth	Sc	09.12.1757(R)	
Unidentified Spanish polacca	S	17.11.1758(R)	
Unidentified Dutchman	Gl	15.01.1760(R)	
Unidentified merchantman	S	30.01.1761	
Unidentified Stockholm ship	S	31.10.1762	
Swedish ship with stockfish	S	07.09.1763	
Unidentified	S	20.11.1763	
Two unidentified Dutch ships	S	20.12.1763(R)	57
'Two Dutchmen "lost"'	S	21.11.1764	57-8
A Dutchman with brandy & wine	Sn	10.09.1765(R)	
A Frenchman in ballast	Brn	15.09.1765	
Unidentified large Dutchman	S	10.12.1765(R)	
Unidentified Yarmouth ship	S	26.02.1766(R)	
A Frenchman, carrying corn	S	06.09.1767	
A Swede, with tar in casks	S	15.08.1768	
Unidentified	S	01.11.1771(R)	
A Dutch man o'war	Ws	11.01.1773	
Unidentified	S	18.09.1775	
Unidentified; hemp & iron	Sn	17.11.1775	
Unidentified	S	07.03.1786(R)	
Three masted Dutchman	S	04.03.1788	
Unidentified, with wheat	Gl	03.06.1794(R)	
An unidentified Venetian	Br	16.02.1796(R)	
Unidentified, N. Sand Head	S	30.08.1796(R)	
Large vessel, with staves	S	06.12.1796(R)	
'Flying Prussian colours'	Br	26.12.1797(R)	
'Carrying wheat & canvas'	S	15.07.1803	
'Carrying Hanovian troops'	Tr	02.11.1803	
Prussian West Indiaman	Wl	11.11.1803	
Dutch man o'war 'cast away'	Ws	00.00.1803(R)	
Unidentified Danish ship	Br	26.09.1804	
Unidentified	S	18.02.1807	
Unidentified, N. Sand Head	S	16.11.1810	
Two unidentified ships	S	13.04.1811	
Five vessels, all lost	S	23.12.1825	
French vessels, in ballast	Br	16.07.1829(R)	
Unidentified	Sc	25.05.1841	
Two unidentified wrecks	S	29.10.1842(R)	
Unidentified, carrying timber	S	05.12.1847	
Unidentified	S	13.02.1848	
Unidentified	S	27.12.1848	
Vessel carrying sulphur	Br	26.04.1849	
Unidentified, '4 men lost'	Br	04.01.1850	
Unidentified, '8 men lost'	Sc	28.01.1850	
Unidentified, '6 men lost'	Sc	07.05.1850	
Unidentified, '5 men lost'	Lu	27.06.1850	
Two small unidentified, lost	S	14.11.1850	
Two ships, with 'all hands'	S	05.12.1850	
Unidentified, '3 crew lost'	Br	05.03.1851	
Unidentified	Br	03.11.1852	

Unidentified, 300 ton ship	S	26.04.1853	85
Unidentified	S	07.05.1853	
Unidentified collier	S	06.09.1853	
Unidentified, Norwegian ship	Bq	00.01.1854(R)	
Unidentified, '3 crew lost'	Gl	03.01.1854	
Unidentified Dutchman	Sc	04.02.1855	89
Unidentified American ship	Frs	10.10.1857	95
Unidentified	Br	26.11.1857	95
Unidentified, '13 crew saved'	Br	05.12.1857(R)	
Unidentified	S	06.03.1858	
Unidentified	Brn	26.12.1860	
Unidentified American ship	Frs	10.09.1870	
Unidentified, Norwegian ship	S	20.11.1872	
Unidentified	Sc	28.01.1878	
Unidentified on N. Sands Head	S	30.01.1878	
'Two masts above the surface'	SS	03.01.1891	
French fishing vessel	Sm	05.01.1894	
Unidentified	S	00.00.1896(R)	52
Unidentified	S	13.02.1898	
Unidentified Dutchman	Sc	30.05.1940	

GENERAL INDEX

Admiralty – 12, 28, 65, 78-9, 82
Armada, Spanish – 151
Beacons – 39, 41, 59, 76-7, 80, 86
Beaumont, Rear Admiral – 25, 51
Beeching, James – 13
Board of Trade – 12, 28, 87, 101, 107, 111, 122
Brake Sand – 23, 25, 27, 59, 70-1, 76, 85, 112, 125
Broadstairs – 7, 13, 43, 69, 83, 89, 91, 94, 96, 103
Buckingham, Duke of – 9, 39
Bullock, Captain/Admiral – 21, 77, 80
Burlingate – 36
Bush, William – 76, 78-9
Caesar, Julius – 19, 25
Cannibalism – 35
Cannon, ship's – 29, 39, 43-4, 76, 89
Castles, various – 37, 57, 65-6, 73, 99, 103, 119, 143, 155
Cinque ports – 9, 31-2, 36, 39, 71, 82
Cricket matches – 87, *156, 158*
Crippen, Dr – 141
Deal – 7, 9, 11-2, 34-5, 37, 44, 48, 55-6, 58, 61, 65, 67, 73, 75, 77-8, 83-6, 88, 99, 101, 103-5, 117,
    119, 121, 125, 127, 129, 132-3, 136, 139, 143, 147, 155
Deal Maritime Museum – 55
Deal, piers – 75, 107, 115, 119
Defoe, Daniel – 28, 49, 56
Divers & diving – 39, 41
Dover – 13, 27, 31-2, 59, 89, 101, 107, 111, 121, 137, 141, 144, 153, 157
Exchange Street, Deal – 147
Foreland, North – 23, 82, 153
Foreland, South – 23, 85
Gattie, Byng. G. – 17, 33, 77, 83, 91, 99
Gentleman's Magazine – 63
Godwine, Earl – 19, 21
Gull Stream – 25, 27, 75, 85, 89, 91, 99, 101, 109, 121, 149
Horseshoe Bay, IOW – 129
Hotels, Deal; Royal – 12; Star & Garter – 78
Hovelling – 11, 15, 66, 83, 85, 102, 127
Indiamen, East – 10, 35-7, 41, 43, 55, 57, 67-8, 73, 75
Indiamen, West – 36, 70
Iggulden, Mr Agent – 65
Ingots, lead – 35, 44; tin – 39; silver – 157
Inns, at Deal – 65, 70-1, 84, 104; Kingsdown – 123
Institution, Lifeboat, RNLI – 11-3, 17, 83, 91, 94, 103, 133, 140
Johnson, Jacob – 9, 39, 41
Kellett Gut – 7, 9, 24-6, 80
Kingsdown – 11, 67, 95, 113-5, 119, 131, 137, 140, 147, 153
Kingsgate – 89
Leyland – 32
Lifeboats, general – 7, 81, 83-4, 86, 89, 105, 108-9, 131, 133-7, 140
Lifeboats, *Barbara Flemming* – 147
    Bradford – 103, 112-3, 118, 121-2, 125

Centurion – 17, *38*, 113
Charles Dibdin's – various, *80, 84*, 133, 143-5, 149
Charles Hargrave – 123, 131, 143
Civil Service No.2 – *151*
Civil Service No.4 – *14*, 71, *120*, 131, 133, 135, 137
Civil Service No.32 – *84*, 155
Frances Forbes Barton (Deal No.2) – 143
Friend of all Nations – 95, 119
Little Friend – 103
Mary Somerville – 121, 125, 133
Northumberland – 13, 83, 86, 89, 91-2, 96, 99, 101-3
Onzio – 104
Quiver – 119
Royal Thames Yacht Club – 13, 17, 194, 96, 103
Sabrina – 104, 113-5
Van Kook – 103-4, 118
Vulcan – 121
Lifeboat coxswains, Adams, 'Bonnie' – 143-4
   Bushell, William – 114
   Parker, Harold – 135-6
   Stanton, Williams – 145, 147
   Upton, Frederick – 155-6
   Jarman, Isaac – 102, 111, 113
   Jarvist, Arnold – 114-5
   Hoile, William – 145, 147
   Hogben, James – 89, 102
   Fish, Charles – 102, 113
   Wilds, R. – 104
Light of All Nations – 78-9, 80
Lighthouses – 74, 77-9
Lightships/vessels – 11, 13, *72*, 75-6, 85, 89, 91, *94*, 99, 101, 105, 123, 125, 131, 133, 135, 149, 157
Lloyd's Signal Station – 119, 131
Lomeo – 17, 21
Mamby, life-saving apparatus – 73
Margate – 13, 15, 23, 43, 59, 69, 89, 95
Martin, K.B., Captain – 23, 25
North Sand Head – 21, 35, 41, 48, 59, 75, 77, 81, 83, 86, 89, 93, 99, 101, 109, 114, 142, 149
Oxney Bottom – 155
Pegwell Bay – 9, 28, *98-7*, 111, 127, 136
Pelly, J.A. Sir – 21, 79
Ramsgate – 7, 11, 13, 15, 23, 34, 55, 59, 82-3, 85-6, 89, 91-5, 101, 111, 113, 117, 119, 122, 125, 143, 157
Richborough – 17
St George's, church – 56-7, 113
St Leonard's, church – 108
St Peter's, church – 34
Sailors Home, Ramsgate – 111
Salvage Company, Liverpool – 139
Sandwich – 9, 11, 18, 28, 31-3, 35-7. 70
Ships, HM men o'war, *Association* – 53; *Assistance* – 52; *Boxer* – 77; *Calvi* – 153; *Canterbury* – 52; *Chatham* – 52; *Content* – 52; *Cygnet* – 66; *Dreadnought* – 63; *Dunwich* – 53; *E-52* – 143; *Eagle* – 52; *Essex* – 52; *Gipsy* – 143; *Grosser Kurfurst* – 121; *Guardland* – 53; *Hampshire* – 47; *Hunter* – 53; *Hussar* – 63; *Kellett* – 25; *Konig Wilhelm* – 121; *Liberty* – 143;

Majesty – 143; Mary – 52; Mortar – 52; Nassau – 53; Newcastle – 52; Paramount – 143; Portsmouth – 52; Postillian – 53; Present Help – 143; Prince George – 52; Ralleir – 67; Resolution – 52; Reserve – 52; Roebuck – 59; Romola – 157; Scorpion – 140; Shrewsbury – 52; Swiftsure – 59; Vanguard – 52; Vigo – 52.

Merchant vessels/boats – Aera – 73; Adieu – 129; Ahdeer – 129; American – 133; Anna – 81; Aspasia – 125; Aunt Sally – 113; Bartley – 91; Batjan – 128; Belos – 129; Beresford – 123-4; Benefactor – 127; Berend – 110; Berent – 153; Betsy – 73; Birte – 152; **Bordeaux** – 84; Brandenburg – 154, 157; Britons Pride – 87; Buffalo Gal – 83, 114; Buis – 57; Burgundy – 82; Cambria – 125; Canton – 99; Ceres – 129; Charity – 39; Charlotte Ann – 84, 86; City of York – 149; Corinthian – 75; Cosmopolite – 101; Crimea – 129; Devastation – 67; Devonshire – 95; Diamond – 82; Diana – 85; Diana – 99; Earl Grey – 81; Eddystone – 143; Elsy – 150; England's Glory – 104; Enterprise – 139; Faith – 109; Fame – 91; Fanny – 55; Flores – 66; Fort Vermillion – 155; Garland – 85, 111; Germania – 132; Gladiator – 75; Godmandun – 127; Gordejvelda – 147; Granville – 123; Hazelmere – 131; Hertha Gent – 113; Hibernia – 81; Hope – 81, 108, 141; Horace Binney – 155; Hunzeborg – 157; Indian Chief – 125; Jargoon – 129; Johannishus – 112; Lady Betty – 149; Lark – 73; Leander – 133; Leyland Stanford – 155; Lord Warden – 88; Magna – 152; Mandalay – 125; Mercurious-H – 128; Monkey – 78; Nefili – 143; Neptune – 97; Niki – 154, 157; Noble – 65; Oliva – 149; Ondine – 87; Overyssel – 60; Panner – 157; Paracas – 157; Patricia – 157; Perserverance – 125; Poll – 81; Pride of the Sea – 129; Princess Helen – 88; Ramon Stern – 153; Reform – 105, 107; Ria de Comes – 155; Robert Morris – 134; St Barbe – 91; Sadak – 85; Saleby – 67; Seaman's Glory – 125; Seaman's Hope – 87; Shearwater – 78; Sherbourne – 125; Signe – 147; Sovac Radiant – 122; Sparrow – 70-1, 81; Spartan – 88; Star of the West – 11; Setubal – 133; Stradler – 129; Surrey – 142; Svare – 129; Tarhund – 111-148; Texaco Caribbean – 154, 157; Thorshieimer – 157; Tiger – 149; Tongariro – 137; Tromp – 153; Vaaderland – 107; William & Henry – 82; Winstanley – 135

Shipwreck Association – 89
Shipwreck Committee – 74-5, 76
Shipwreck Institution, Ramsgate – 121
Shovell, Clowdisley, Sir – 50, 57
Smeaton, John – 21
Smuggling – 11, 56
South Sand Head – 8, 21, 35, 45, 59, 75, 84-5, 86, 99, 101, 114, 141, 157
Specie – 8, 33, 35, 36, 37, 43, 45, 55, 57
Storm, the Great, 1703 – 28, 49-53
Thanet – 17, 19, 25
Time Ball, Tower – 107, 119
Treanor, S. Rev. – 136
Treasure – 149-50
Trinity Bay – 8, 20, 26-7, 63, 134, 139
Trinity House – 11, 13, 21, 23, 48, 59, 76-7, 79-80, 127, 131, 133, 139, 155, 157
Tugs, Aid – 8, 91, 95, 101, 109, 113, 121, 125; Cambria – 125; Granville – 123; Hibernia – 121; Lady Vita – 126, 140; Restless – 114; Samson – 84, 86, 91, 103; Vulcan – 99
Walker, James – 23, 80
Walmer – 8, 11, 12, 15, 17, 64-5, 81, 83-4, 85, 89, 94-5, 99, 101, 103-5, 113-4, 123, 131, 133, 135-7, 139-40, 147, 153, 155-6
Wantsum – 19, 28
Wellington, Duke of – 78-9
'Wrack Fishers' – 9
Wreckers/wrecking – 11
Wreck Commissioners Court – 122
Zouch, Lord – 35-7, 39